Community Care
Asking the user

Edited by

Gail Wilson

Lecturer in Social Policy and Ageing
The London School of Economics

CHAPMAN & HALL

London · Glasgow · Weinheim · New York · Tokyo · Melbourne · Madras

Published by Chapman & Hall, 2–6 Boundary Row, London SE1 8HN, UK

Chapman & Hall, 2–6 Boundary Row, London SE1 8HN, UK

Blackie Academic & Professional, Wester Cleddens Road, Bishopbriggs, Glasgow G64 2NZ, UK

Chapman & Hall GmbH, Pappelallee 3, 69469 Weinheim, Germany

Chapman & Hall USA, 115 Fifth Avenue, New York NY 10003, USA

Chapman & Hall Japan, ITP-Japan, Kyowa Building, 3F, 2-2-1 Hirakawacho, Chiyoda-ku, Tokyo 102, Japan

Chapman & Hall Australia, 102 Dodds Street, South Melbourne, Victoria 3205, Australia

Chapman & Hall India, R. Seshadri, 32 Second Main Road, CIT East, Madras 600 035, India

Distributed in the USA and Canada by Singular Publishing Group Inc., 4284 41st Street, San Diego, California 92105

First edition 1995

© 1995 Chapman and Hall

Typeset in Times 10/12pt by Saxon Graphics Ltd, Derby
Printed in Great Britain by Clays Ltd, St Ives plc

ISBN 0 412 59890 6   1 56593 419 9 (USA)

A catalogue record for this book is available from the British Library

Library of Congress Catalog Card Number: 95-74630

∞ Printed on permanent acid-free text paper, manufactured in accordance with ANSI/NISO Z39. 48-1992 and ANSI/NISO Z39.48-1984 (Permanence of Paper).

Contents

Contributors

Marion Barnes
Department of Sociological Studies
Sheffield University

Professor Roy Carr-Hill
DICE
Institute of Education
London

Martin Cattermole
Mencap Homes Foundation
Oxfordshire

Dr Julie Dockrell
Department of Child Development
Institute of Education
London

Dr Michael Donnelly
Health & Health Care Research Unit
Institute of Clinical Science
The Queen's University of Belfast
Belfast

Shah Ebrahim
Department of Public Health
Royal Free Hospital School of Medicine
London

Dr Rosalind Edwards
Social Science Research Centre
South Bank University
London

George Giacinto Giarchi
Community Research Centre
University of Plymouth

Chris Gilleard
St George's Hospital Medical School
Department of Geriatric Medicine
London

Patrick Gompertz
Department of Public Health
Royal Free Hospital School of Medicine
London

Dr Andrew Jahoda
Department of Psychology
Strathmartine Hospital
Dundee

Dee Jones
Department of Geriatric Medicine
University of Wales College of Medicine
Cardiff

Gloria Lankshear
Community Research Centre
University of Plymouth

Carolyn Lester
Department of Geriatric Medicine
University of Wales College of Medicine
Cardiff

Dr Nick Mays
King's Fund Institute
London

David Pilgrim
Health and Community Care Research Unit
University of Liverpool

Pandora Pound
Department of Public Health
Royal Free Hospital School of Medicine
London

Rachel Reed
South Downs Health NHS Trust
Brighton

Anne Rogers
Public Health Research and Resource Centre
University of Salford

Richard Shaw
London Borough of Southwark
London

Emmanuelle Tulle-Winton
Social Work Research Centre
Stirling University

Gail Wilson
Department of Social Policy and Administration
London School of Economics

PART ONE

Methods and Issues

Introduction

1

Gail Wilson

The most positive aspect of the health and social service reforms which are radically changing the British welfare state in the 1990s is the new emphasis on user views. For the first time legislation and central government guidance emphasize that service users must be consulted over a wide range of issues. User acceptability is now a recognized aspect of service quality: professionals are no longer assumed to be the sole arbiters. The old stereotype of a standardized service, which took no account of individual needs or wants and expected clients or patients to be grateful for what they got, is slowly disappearing.

SHIFTING THE BALANCE – A LONG-RUN TREND

However, the transition from new legislation to new methods of service delivery and service planning is not simple. Changes in the law do not guarantee changes in front-line professional practice. Entrenched values die hard and there is no reason to believe that users are suddenly finding themselves empowered by a new breed of consumer-conscious service provider. It will need hard work to get the best out of the new community care policies. Therefore, one aim of this book is to support managers and professionals who want to give patients, clients and carers a voice in their services.

It has to be acknowledged that the legislation has been accompanied by demands for efficiency savings, which usually translate into cuts, and this has raised many problems of staff resistance. First, however, it is worth looking at the forces which helped to initiate the legislation and which support the change. A range of trends, both material and intellectual, can be summed up by saying that service users are becoming part of a consumer society. They increasingly expect social services to approach them in the same spirit as other service industries – via market research, rather than on the old take it or leave it basis. The trends outlined below, some global and some more local, offer settings where new professional practice can develop.

In all Western countries ways of thinking about established hierarchies have altered to a greater or lesser degree. Leaders, whether they are politicians or professionals, have become less respected. Even doctors have become less godlike over the years and now find themselves being managed by people they used to call administrators (Strong and Robinson, 1990; Harrison *et al.*, 1992). At the same time post-war democracies have produced better educated and more prosperous populations where social status is determined as much by patterns of consumption as by the old hierarchies based on paid work (Phillips, 1993)

The rise of mass consumer cultures has given ordinary people the chance to express their own preferences and their own, as opposed to a class, identity. The traditional certainties of elite cultures have been undermined and to some extent replaced by a new emphasis on the way individuals understand the world around them (the post-modern or post-structural approach). According to this way of looking at the world, knowledge is no longer limited to a rational system defining laws and certainties and constructing overarching ideologies and inter-pretations of history or culture. Instead knowledge is seen as highly relative, more democratic, local and individualized (Rosenau, 1992). Professionals, as part of elite culture and as guardians of the types of knowledge which are now being revalued, may either feel threatened or they may welcome a more equal partnership with users. Indeed real professionalism, with its long tradition of service, may be seen as the ability to work in partnership with users, with all the opportunities for better care that are implied. Of course, few, if any, users are paid-up post-modernists, but the issue is more a matter of the changing climate of opinion than any particular set of beliefs or a conscious campaign.

The major problem with the new model, as readers of this book will be well aware, is that most ordinary users of community care lack consumer power. They are usually, though not always, less educated than the average, and nearly all are either unable to earn (pensioners, most people with learning difficulties or a severe physical handicap) or find themselves in low-paid work. Frail elders are predominantly women and include a rapidly growing number of people from minority ethnic groups. However, all should be able to benefit from a more consumer-oriented service and related changes in the welfare climate. The real problem is to make sure the benefits are not overwhelmed by negative effects that occur at the same time.

Markets and professionals

Faith in the market as a way of ordering economic and social life grew in the 1980s and, with the fall of communism, has swept all before it in the 1990s.

This, as outlined above, has made services more responsive to consumers but it also has major and complex implications for professionals.

The professions find themselves in an uneasy relationship with free-market ideologies. They have traditionally engaged in a range of antimarket or restrictive practices in order to maintain their prestige and earnings. Most have strict controls over entry. Knowledge bases are guarded by jargon and/or a long and costly training. At work, job demarcation lines (for example between housing and social services or between medical and nursing tasks) have been laid down and are maintained, although their original rationale is long passed.

The relationship between professionals and the market is further ambivalent because some professionals are well placed to benefit from the new freedom to charge for their services. Work as private consultants or in private hospitals or homes can be lucrative for the better off. But getting customers depends on selling acceptable services. Consumer choice may mean that services change. Professionals can find that they have to alter the way they work in order to keep their private customers. In other words they may lose some of their former power to determine the quality of their product. Often the customer is right and change is progress, but in some circumstances professional standards are endangered by the need to add selling points, such as deep-pile carpets or new paint work, at the expense of basic services or staff training. Also of course, the customer is not always right when a service is coercive and designed to be so. Even here services can be delivered more or less sensitively.

A shift away from collective service provision by the state in favour of marketization does not, in itself, end professional restrictive practices (if it did the American health system would be very different from what it is). On the other hand, marketization does offer ammunition to those who oppose professional power, whether they are neo-liberal politicians, pressure groups for disadvantaged service users (such as MIND) or managers trying to substitute lower-paid workers for costly professionals. As a result the old order finds itself under attack from a confusing number of directions and it is not surprising if morale is sometimes low.

Changing position of women

Government ideology, as expressed in community care policy, is out of step with long-run trends in terms of women's position in society. Government policy aims explicitly to encourage family and neighbourhood care and reduce paid care. There is little evidence that this will be possible unless much more attention is paid to women's needs. Exceptions exist, but policy makers can no longer assume that women feel an automatic duty to care for older relatives or adult children with mental health problems (Finch and Mason, 1992). Women's expectations have changed and so have the demands made upon them. Access to paid work reduces the time available for unpaid or informal caring. Family breakup, with the strains of single parenthood and the loosening of ties with elderly in-laws, further reduces the number of younger carers who are available. It is the steadily increasing numbers of older women, either caring for themselves or their husbands, or for the increasing number of children with disabilities who survive into later life, who are the new carers of the future. They will be joined by young carers of people with HIV/AIDS, and a growing number of older husbands caring for disabled wives. These people, mainly but not exclusively women, will only be able to carry on if much more attention is paid to their needs and services are designed to give them individual support. Women's claims will therefore be important in the future.

Local movements

These global tendencies to shift power away from professionals towards users are increasingly backed up by new organizations and movements which give more concrete form to vague social changes (Beresford and Croft, 1993). Pressure groups such as MIND (Chapter 14) and Mencap (Chapter 11) have taken a radical stance in campaigning for users. Some feed directly into the political process at national level, lobbying ministers and MPs. Others, particularly self-help groups, operate at local level and have a more variable impact on services (Chapters 15 and 16).

The combination of user campaigns and government belief in the benefits of enabling individuals to act as consumers in a free market has yet to be fully felt. Even so, it has already produced a range of policy innovations which involve radical change for service providers. In the National Health Service a steady stream of changes has been imposed from above. General management from 1983 onwards was intended to make the service more consumer-conscious as well as more efficient. The NHS and Community Care Act 1990 introduced an internal market into the health service and recommended a similar change for social services. While the rhetoric accompanying the changes was that of patient choice, the new customers of hospitals and community health services were the purchasers of care – not the patients, but other branches of the health service acting on behalf of patients. The *Citizen's Charter* (Harden, 1992), and subsequent documents such as the *Patient's Charter*, attempted to substitute service standards for market power, but according to Pollitt (1994) the effects have not so far been very great.

As pointed out in Chapters 6 and 10, the hotel services such as food, cleanliness and routine nursing that figure so largely in patients' charters do not cover the aspects of treatment that most concern patients. Their value lies more in the change in culture that they represent. It is now official that patients have a say in **something**, where they never had before. Another problem is that hotel services are not relevant to care in the community and the provisions of the various charters do not adapt well to community health services. Users still face serious problems after discharge from hospital.

In social services the big changes introduced by the 1990 Act proceeded more slowly. The policy of assessing the needs of carers extended the possibility of assessment to a whole new client group who had only been considered in passing before but carers still had no right to be assessed. Users and carers were also given the statutory right to complain and to be informed of formal complaints procedures. They were to be consulted at service delivery level by the professionals who drew up their care plans and at the local planning level when the overall community care plan was being produced (Chapter 15 describes one method of consultation).

Following the same trend, the Housing Corporation introduced guidelines for tenant participation and consultation (Chapter 13). Housing associations, like other agencies which are often run by traditionally minded voluntary organizations, were required to change their practice, at least on paper.

Not surprisingly in view of the fundamental nature of the changes needed, the legislation and early examples of departmental guidance from the Social Services Inspectorate ran way ahead of the ability to deliver (DoH/SSI, 1991). Civil servants, local authority personnel, health authorities and front-line professionals were often left groping in the dark. The culture was new to all, and no methods of implementation had been tried and tested before the legislation was passed. Enlightenment was not assisted by the contradictory nature of the policies being implemented. Choice for the user was apparently meant to be an outcome of service rationing – a virtual impossibility. Many otherwise willing professionals were converted into opponents of any changes coming from central government by the timing and packaging of the proposals. They were inescapably linked to health service funding that fell behind the needs of an ageing population and failed to keep up with the demands of new technology, to attacks on professional status, and to the long battle to control and reduce local authority spending.

RESISTANCE

As stated above, legislation alone, particularly ill-thought-out legislation that introduces new procedures without knowing how they are to be implemented in detail, is not enough to change professional cultures. To some extent the model was wrong to start with. It is a myth that ordinary individual consumers rule in the private sector. Firms and businesses spend large amounts of time, energy and money trying to make sure their customers do not have a free choice, but buy their own products or services rather than anyone else's. There is no reason to believe welfare services will behave any differently if they have to compete with each other for a share of a limited market.

More important, as far as individual users are concerned, the services they receive are provided by agencies operating in managed markets – not free markets (Saltman and von Otter, 1992). Individual users of community care services in Britain are not allowed to choose where to take their custom. The main exceptions are still residential and nursing care where choice may be offered to users or to their relatives.

Two schemes which did give individuals a measure of market power have both been cut off. The Disabled Living Foundation grant gave individuals cash to spend on their care as they wished, and the automatic access to Income Support for people on low incomes allowed them to choose to go into private residential or nursing care rather than staying at home. Small voucher schemes exist but it is largely true to say that users very rarely buy services themselves. Instead they have services bought for them by professionals and purchasing managers. This is true even when users or their families contribute to the cost. Hence service users have much less market power than the average private sector customer. Some hospitals and many providers of community care at the 'heavy end', where users are most stigmatized and most difficult to care for, still have local monopolies. They have no financial need to introduce new practices which will attract their customers.

There are therefore strong structural and organizational elements working against user choice and user input to service specification and service planning. There are also constraints at the level of professional practice or service delivery. Professionals have traditionally held a great deal of power based on special expertise in their fields. Now they are being asked to share their knowledge with unqualified users and to join with these users in reaching care decisions. There is a real danger that some less secure professionals will feel that their training (lasting over several years and often involving personal sacrifice) is being devalued.

The threat to professionals is magnified by the fact that some satisfaction surveys place users in the position of judging professional activities. The purchaser–provider split encourages purchasers to survey service recipients as one way of monitoring quality. When this happens it is easy for service providers to see users as just another aspect of surveillance, along with other new management practices such as performance indicators and computerized monitoring of devolved budgets.

The fact that users are almost wholly appreciative of professional practice (as shown by the studies reported in this book) is not the point. Appreciative or not, the traditional role for users has been to be 'grateful', or to vote with their feet and refuse the service. Either way they were no trouble and, if troublesome, could be categorized as manipulative or lacking insight (Parry *et al.*, 1979) and so neutralized. The new system transforms the provider–receiver relationship, either potentially or in reality. Users are now **potentially** the arbiters of continued employment for service providers. A bad report could conceivably mean the loss of a contract. This is a new threat, added to all the others, such as job dilution, service reorganization and budget cuts which have been, and continue to be, the experience of welfare employees. It can be hard to think positively about new developments when exposed to so many sources of stress.

OPPOSITION OR PARTNERSHIP?

Whatever the problems which are currently being experienced, most professionals want to provide a user-sensitive, user-friendly service. They also know a great deal about the quality of the services they provide and could contribute more to user surveys than they usually do at present (Flynn, 1993). Most users indicate respect for professionals and certainly do not wish to take over their powers and functions (Chapters 13 and 15). There is no doubt, however, that services could be provided more sensitively (as indicated, for example, by some of the experiences recounted in Chapter 5). Often, professionals do not realize the effect of their actions or words on users – a clear case where all could benefit from better communication. At other times, service providers who are over-stressed react in ways which put their own needs before those of vulnerable users, who are not in a position to assert themselves. The work of Lipsky (1980) showed how professionals could, often without knowing it, respond to day-to-day pressures in a range of ways which made their service less acceptable. As he asked, 'How is the job to be accomplished with inadequate resources, few controls, indeterminate objectives and discouraging circumstances?' In these circumstances, which apply to some extent to virtually all community care services, good management of front-line staff is essential. Even the best management, however, needs to be reinforced by pressure from users, either individually or as members of user groups. Maintaining and improving service standards depends on user input.

WHO ARE THE USERS?

Defining a service user is never simple. The users referred to by most authors in the book are the people who used to be known as clients, patients or carers. They are individual service recipients and make up a diverse group or groups. The interests of carers may coincide with those they look after, but they may also conflict. Furthermore, the delivery of community care is not a matter of one service providing for its users and their carers. Services overlap and one user will often receive care from two or more services. In other words services use each other in order to deliver acceptable packages of care. In health care it is quite possible for a district nurse and a community psychiatric nurse to be involved with a user on a long-term basis, while a hospital consultant may have more intermittent input. All three services are each other's internal customers. Possibly they are customers of social services as well. The managers of any one service will have to go some way to satisfying these internal users. Tension is inevitable when their interests conflict with each other or with individual users.

A further problem for managers and front-line staff in state services is that they are also accountable to local or central politicians and ultimately to voters in society as a whole. Community services are used by politicians to show that society cares, and that the state is enabling or providing an acceptable level of community care. Scandals therefore have to be avoided. It is hardly surprising that staff do not welcome user complaints when traditionally they have led to scandals and disciplinary action. Changing the culture to one where complaints are seen as constructive is likely to be difficult but is essential for real user sensitivity (Flynn, 1988).

Users, customers or consumers?

There is considerable confusion over these three terms (Chapter 2). Even though the exact labels, themselves, are perhaps not very important, the concepts involved matter because they relate to the relative power of service providers and individual service users. In the first place **customers** are free to buy or not to buy a product or a service. However, many users of community care are not free to buy. Either they do not have enough money or they would rather not receive the service if they felt they had any choice. They can be classified, following Harrow and Shaw (1992), as coerced or semicoerced customers. Patients who are compulsorily admitted to mental hospital are an example of the coerced user. Some people with learning difficulties and some victims of elder abuse who are moved into residential care may also fall into the same category. Most other service users would rather maintain their independence if they were able, but find that they are forced, by frailty of some kind, to accept services. They are semicoerced or reluctant customers.

The term **consumer** can also indicate a more collective approach to consumption than the individual term **customer**. When groups of customers identify a common interest and band together to fight the power of big business or of professional monopolies, they can form a consumer movement. Strong consumer movements pose a considerable threat to existing power structures and appear to be rare in health and social care. The stigmatizing nature of the services, and even of membership of user groups, has so far prevented users from developing high-profile consumer movements at national level in Britain. Voluntary pressure groups have had more effect, but often they are composed of interested advocates rather than groups of consumers themselves.

At local level there can be wide variations in the strength of consumer groups, from wholly absent to highly influential. Whereas service providers can welcome consumer groups which campaign for more resources and better funding, service planners may see problems if consumer power distorts equity and diverts funds from one group to another. In such cases the less stigmatized, such as young people with physical disabilities, are likely to benefit at the expense of people who command less popular sympathy or political support.

The term **user** is perhaps a more accurate description of relations between recipients and providers of community care than either **customer** or **consumer**. Payment in full for services is still rare, though growing, and the term **customer** is hardly accurate for reluctant users who are not exerting market control over their services. Equally, consumer power is relatively underdeveloped and unless or until it is, the term **consumer** can also be misleading.

A weakness of any collective labelling by client group is that it obscures issues of gender, class and ethnicity. Differences in power relations and issues related to service-specific needs can be more easily lost when consumer orientation becomes a matter of finding the lowest common denominator of acceptability. This is one danger of the new market research approach. Minorities and their needs can conveniently be lost under the larger heading of users or customers. Resources will not be allocated and services will not be planned to meet their needs.

WHY ASK THE USERS?

Asking about user opinions is part of the managerial portfolio carried by the new breed of health and social care manager. It goes along with customer consciousness, market research and the attempt to increase market share in a fixed-size market. (When health and social care budgets are capped, increasing market share becomes the service manager's substitute for aggressive sales expansion.) As shown in Chapter 2, much of this activity is mechanistic rather than productive, as far as users are concerned. This can be true even when the focus is on **quality**, another buzz-word for the new managers (Pollitt, 1993), which ought to benefit users but need not.

The same is true of evaluation. Services as well as projects are now routinely evaluated. User views should be a key factor in any evaluation (Chapters 7 and 12), since ultimately the service only exists because it has users. However, in both the cases mentioned, the authority ordering the evaluation had no special interest in user views and was more interested in other measures of outcome.

Individual users are more likely to benefit from studies which focus on processes of service delivery, such as assessment, user–professional interactions or ways of identifying service needs. The latter merges into the planning process which can benefit from user input at all levels – from simple surveys to high-level decisions on the allocation of resources.

As with other forms of participation, asking users for their views can be simply a way of defusing protest – locating the sources of opposition or manipulating opinion so that it does not get out of control; Skelcher (1993) classifies degrees of empowerment.

RESEARCH METHODS

Whatever the reason, or mix of reasons, that motivate staff and managers of community care services, it is clear that user views are needed and that asking for them is here to stay for the moment. Equally, as the contributors to the book show, there is no agreement on how to do it, and no certain best method of proceeding. Careful attention to the purpose of the study and a willingness to consider mixed methods is essential if users are to benefit.

Quantitative methods

Quantitative and qualitative methods have often been placed in an artificial opposition, but most contributors to this book see both as having an important place in any serious attempt to understand user views. The great strengths of quantitative methods are not only that they belong to a widely accepted 'scientific' paradigm, but also that they allow replication and comparison, over time and between services. As shown in Chapter 2, some of this apparent comparability is spurious, but in terms of research which aims to give a good enough approximation to reality (to allow useful conclusions on changes in quality, for example), quantitative methods, carefully used, are an essential tool. They can also be quicker and cheaper than qualitative methods. However, their advantages usually depend on using qualitative research as a first stage in understanding the research question.

Qualitative methods

A qualitative approach (Chapter 3) to any form of research is still not accepted in some medical and government circles – except possibly as a preliminary to embarking on 'real' or quantitative research. The contributors to this book all use or advocate qualitative methods as part of any approach to users. The strength of the qualitative approach is that it can explain processes which might otherwise be lost between the measurement of inputs and outputs. Any improvement in services is likely to depend on understanding the processes of service delivery and, for this reason alone, qualitative methods are needed when local initiatives in service delivery are being considered.

However, the most important contribution of the qualitative approach to user satisfaction is that it allows the investigation of the meanings that different services, terms or processes have for users (and staff). As many contributors to this book show, it is often easy to get users to answer questions but much more difficult to know what the answers mean. Chapter 10 shows clearly how quantitative results can leave professionals wondering why users are apparently so irrational as to want treatment which is professionally deemed to be useless. The qualitative data suggest that in a user-led service physiotherapy would be offered to stroke patients for longer. It is not clear whether this would involve a redefinition of successful outcome of treatment or whether further research would show that, even in medical terms, more physiotherapy results in better outcomes. Such research is still to be done and rather than engaging in a beauty parade for methods it is better to start with a research question and consider which methods will advance knowledge most successfully.

BOOK PLAN

The book is divided into three parts. Part One consists of five chapters which discuss key background issues in the present development of user-oriented research. Chapter 2 considers the strengths, weaknesses, pitfalls and drawbacks of quantitative methods, with particular emphasis on satisfaction surveys. Chapter 3 deals with methods and issues of validity and reliability in qualitative research. In Chapter 4 are set out the problems encountered by ethnic minorities when accessing services, and useful guidelines for the use of interpreters are suggested. Chapter 5 presents data on the relationship between poor experience of services and low expectations among older people living in the community.

Part Two considers users surveys where the emphasis is on the questions posed by service agencies and other professionals. All the contributors conclude that users are well able to answer structured questions and that they are often most at ease with closed questions with yes/no answers. Chapter 6 shows how high response rates can be achieved with a large postal survey, while Chapter 7 indicates how the demands of government sponsorship affect the design of user surveys – in this case the imposition of time constraints and the need to use quantitative methods. The use of standardized research instruments allowed comparisons with other studies and facilitated the survey of a relatively large sample of former mental hospital patients. Despite the extreme unwillingness of this group of users to criticize their services or to expand on structured answers, it is shown that former patients are suppressing many criticisms, and that they are generally in favour of community placements rather than being in hospital.

The limitations of structured data collection are illustrated in Chapter 8. User satisfaction barely dipped over the two survey periods, despite a cut of 40% in the service offered. Chapter 9 shows how a research design that expects high recall from users will fail unless users are interested in the service they were offered.

In Part Three the contributors report on user surveys which consciously attempt to see services from a user perspective. Ideally it should include research conducted by users for users, but this has not been possible. However, Part Three looks at a variety of experiences in trying to work either for the users (Chapters 14–16) or with the unequal balance of power in mind (Chapters 11 and 12). Users' views of their services and the way they make sense of their needs is shown to differ sharply from professional views (Chapters 10 and 12–14). This gap between professional and user perceptions may emerge as the data are analysed or it may be the conscious object of research. At present, professional views dominate for the reasons discussed above.

In Chapter 10 a combination of survey and in-depth interviewing is used to illustrate the difference between user and professional views. Chapter 11 uses interviews and participant observation to understand how users with learning difficulties view the aims of services they are provided with. The insights to be gained from taking people with learning difficulties and challenging behaviour seriously as respondents are discussed in Chapter 12, but with stress on the inequality of power involved. Chapter 13 shows how, working as a practitioner, it is possible to show that frail elderly hostel dwellers have strong opinions on their accommodation but little opportunity for participation.

A relatively large, mainly quantitative survey of users of mental health services is reported on in Chapter 14. The approach taken falls outside the convention of unbiased objective research and consciously aims to shift power in favour of users. An alternative way of working for user empowerment is to link users into the decision-making process, either of planning or of resource allocation. Chapters 15 and 16 report on ways of helping users influence service planning. In Chapter 15 users and potential users (as well as staff) were asked how they would like to be consulted about community care. Widespread cynicism was encountered together with a belief that professionals should do the work they are paid for and not expect others to do it for them. This is likely to be a problem with any system of continuous consultation. As shown in Chapter 16, users must see some results from their input, otherwise they will become demotivated. Once again, professionals will have to give up some power.

In conclusion, Chapter 17 considers the present state of research methods for asking users about their community care services and suggests some ways forward. More attention to issues of unequal power and to ways of allowing users to formulate their own service criteria is urgently needed.

REFERENCES

Beresford, P. and Croft, S. (1993) *Citizen Involvement*, Macmillan, Basingstoke.

Department of Health/Social Services Inspectorate (1991) *Care Management and Assessment Managers' Guide*, HMSO, London.

Finch, J. and Mason, J. (1992) *Negotiating Family Responsibilities*, Tavistock, London.

Flynn, N. (1988) A consumer-oriented culture? *Public Money and Management*, **8**(1+2), 27–31.

Flynn, N. (1993) *Public Sector Management*, Harvester Wheatsheaf, Hemel Hempstead.

Harden, I. (1992) *The Contracting State*, Open University Press, Buckingham.

Harrison, S., Hunter, D. J., Marnoch, G. and Pollitt, C. (1992) *Just Managing: Power and Culture in the National Health Service*, Macmillan, Basingstoke.

Harrow, J. and Shaw, M. (1992) The manager faces the consumer, in *Rediscovering Public Services*, (eds L. Willcocks. and J. Harrow), McGraw-Hill, Maidenhead.

Lipsky, M. (1980) *Street Level Bureaucracy: Dilemmas of the Individual in Public Services*, Russell Sage, New York.

Parry, N., Rustin, M. and Satyamurti, C. (1979) *Social Work Welfare and the State*, Edward Arnold, London.

Phillips, A. (1993) *Democracy and Difference*, Polity Press, Cambridge.

Pollitt, C. (1993) *Managerialism and the Public Services*, Blackwell, Oxford.

Pollitt, C. (1994) The Citizen's Charter: a preliminary analysis. *Public Money and Management*, **14**(2), 9–14.

Rosenau, P. M. (1992) *Post-modernism and the Social Sciences*, Princeton University Press, Princeton.

Saltman, R.B. and von Otter, C. (1992) *Planned Markets and Public Competition*, Open University Press, Buckingham.

Skelcher, C. (1993) Involvement and empowerment in local public services. *Public Money and Management*, **13**(3), 13–20.

Strong, P. and Robinson, J. (1990) *The NHS Under New Management*, Open University Press, Milton Keynes.

<table>
<tr><td>**2**</td><td></td></tr>
</table>

2	# Measurement of user satisfaction

Roy Carr-Hill

User satisfaction can be an important ingredient in service monitoring and quality assurance, but only if the problems involved in measuring satisfaction are well understood. Any measure of user satisfaction needs to be firmly grounded in theory. The basic components of models of satisfaction are set out in this chapter. Service delivery involves relationships between users and providers and these relationships, of power and knowledge, will influence the way users respond to surveys. Useful guidelines for conducting surveys are discussed, setting out common problems and ways round them.

Surveys of user views are a major and increasing activity in health and social care and are expected to perform an expanding range of functions. In particular, they are increasingly used to monitor service performance, partly because of the encouragement of consumerism throughout the public sector and the difficulty of finding other methods of monitoring performance.

In principle, if the perspective of the user were to be given more importance, this would help to counteract professional hegemony (Speedling and Rose, 1985). Indeed, a dominant political theme in the UK has been the emphasis placed on consumer sovereignty in health and social care. Community care provision is expected to be shaped by (potential) clients' demands and preferences (Griffiths, 1983), hence the requirement for a care plan to be agreed with all participants. It follows that crude effectiveness and efficiency cannot be the sole criteria of service quality; the care provided has to be socially acceptable. Consumer satisfaction is thus an outcome of the care process.

However, it is important to recognize the potential political role of results of user surveys; as will be seen, the scope for manipulating the design – and therefore the findings – of satisfaction surveys is legion.

IS THERE A CONCEPT OF SATISFACTION?

What is satisfaction? How is it defined? What does it mean to different people? What is the referent about which the client is meant to be satisfied?

Human satisfaction is a complex concept that is related to a number of factors including lifestyle, past experiences, future expectations and the values of both individual and society. The Survey Research Centre of the University of Wisconsin has tried for nearly 20 years to persuade their readers that a global index of satisfaction can be derived from responses to questionnaires designed to measure overall well-being (Campbell *et al.*, 1986), but few were or are convinced (OECD, 1974). They divide people's satisfaction into different 'life domains' and argue that each of those domains has a conceptual coherence. Regardless of one's judgement of their overall approach, satisfaction with a service is different. When the outcome of the service is relevant to a life domain, satisfaction with the service is a function of satisfaction with the domain concerned. The service itself may be a secondary consideration. In the case of community care where, given a 'choice', many users would rather not be in a position to need the service, genuine satisfaction is not to be expected.

A more fruitful approach is therefore to search for sources of **dissatisfaction**: the most frequent source of dissatisfaction about a service is the communication of information about the service and the care to be provided by the professional to the client. The relative expertise, knowledge and therefore power of professional and client have to be central to any investigation of (dis)satisfaction.

Further, because the sources of dissatisfaction can vary widely, satisfaction is likely to be defined very differently by different people and by the same person at different times (Locker and Dunt, 1978). This variability, interpersonally and over time, casts doubt on the value of attempting to define a unitary concept of a satisfaction; in addition, clients' expectations will vary according to the presumed success of a care plan and to their prior experience. It is trite to say that satisfaction has several different meanings; it highlights, however, the importance of distinguishing between the phenomenon – however defined – and its measurement.

Defining the scope

First, it is important to remember that in addition to the immediate users (clients or patients), their relatives and carers, other social service departments (the internal customer) and, where educational and promotional activities are concerned, the whole population, are also users. A sensible division is between current users and potential users and then, within each group, the service recipients, their carers and professional groups. Hence the following typology of consumers laid out below.

1. Current users:
   (a) clients of various services;
   (b) relatives and carers;
   (c) other professional groups outside the provider organization (e.g. NHS, social services, voluntary organizations);
   (d) other professional groups inside the provider organization (internal customers).
2. Potential users:
   (a) relevant population categories (children, elderly, handicapped, (ethnic) minorities);
   (b) client/consumer/customer organizations;
   (c) interested and informed people (e.g. local authority councillors, community health councils, researchers).

Aware and informed consumer

The accountant's (sorry, economist's) dream is the potential client (consumer) as the perfect market player. Floating with the tide, the National Consumer Council (1976) have suggested seven principles which might help to redress the imbalance of power between those who provide services and those who receive them. These are set out below, together with an assessment of their applicability to the community care situation.

1. *Access* – can consumers obtain the goods or use the service at all?
2. *Choice* – consumer choice will work where there is effective competition and where the balance in the market-place is fair between supplier and customer.
3. *Information* – consumers cannot make accurate judgements about what serves their best interests unless they have the information they need to do so; that information needs to be accurate and to be expressed in ways the individual can understand.
4. *Redress* – the whole process of effective choice based on fair competition is vitiated unless consumers can get redress when they do not get what they believed they were paying for.
5. *Safety* – consumers can buy with confidence only if they expect that the products they buy will not subject them to risks they cannot foresee.
6. *Value for money* – the value consumers get in terms of satisfaction for the resources used.
7. *Equity* – consumers should not be arbitrarily discriminated against for reasons which are unrelated to their characteristics as consumers.

It is clear that these basic principles of consumer rights cannot easily be applied in the community care context (Potter, 1988). The obvious non-starters are the fourth and fifth principles of *Redress* and *Safety*. Complaints can be made against professionals – and occasionally sustained – but the criteria for service provision are based on professional judgement, rather than derived from a user perspective. There are also problems in applying the other principles. When provision of a service involves redistributing costs and benefits within society, individual consumer choice cannot be the sole driving force that dictates who benefits and who pays. The first consumer principle of *Access* cannot therefore be translated into an automatic right for the consumer; equally, the sixth principle, *Value for Money*, although an important issue for the purchaser acting as an agent for the public, is not relevant to the immediate user of the service.

The applicability of the second and third principles (*Choice* and *Information*) seems doubtful: clients are in a less powerful position than professionals and clearly are not able to judge technical quality. On the other hand several studies (Hall *et al.*, 1988; Linn, 1982) show that user satisfaction ratings correlate positively with expert-developed indices of technical quality. This may be because professional staff who deliver good technical care also take pride in their work, leading to raised morale which affects satisfaction levels. Whether or not this will continue to apply is problematic.

Principles developed in an attempt to control the savagery of the market for things in the private sector are not applicable to regulating relations of service; however, the fundamental issues are very similar, as Potter (1988) concludes:

> 'Consumerism can help authorities to advance from considering individual members of their public as passive clients or recipients of services – who get what they are given for which they must be thankful – to thinking of them as customers with legitimate rights and preferences as well as responsibilities. But it will rarely be enough to turn members of the public into partners, actively involved in shaping public services ... . Consumerism is fine as far as it goes, but it does not go far enough to affect a radical shift in the distribution of power.'

Despite the difficulties of applying the seven consumer principles to the care market, they do provide a coherent framework for discussing the various aspects of satisfaction which should be considered in a survey. But consumer feedback surveys in Britain have only consistently addressed *Access*, *Information* and overall quality of the process (Dixon and Carr-Hill, 1989). Operationally, therefore, not only are user surveys obviously inappropriate for addressing the issue of equity (a different kind of study is required), in practice they do not address problems of *Choice*, *Redress* or *Safety*. On a more detailed level, the lack of attention to psycho-social problems and satisfaction with outcomes is a major weakness.

Individual care versus collective consumption

A **customer** may be seen as an individual service user. The term **consumer**, on the other hand, has the connotation of a social category which usually refers to the individual as being part of a group of users, as in a consumer organization. Correspondingly, the term **consumer view** can either refer to an aggregate of views (as in a market research survey) or to a collective view (as in a joint decision). The latter (a collective decision) is more usually associated with participation in decision making. That is, the involvement of service users in making decisions about the provision of services (Chapters 12 and 16). All three aspects – individual customers, consumer views and collective participation – are relevant. This chapter is obviously concerned mainly with the second aspect, although the other two should not be ignored.

AN INDEX OF USER SATISFACTION

Assuming that distinct dimensions of satisfaction can be defined (Chapter 8), the researcher is now forced to take several backward steps. For in order to produce an overall satisfaction score, the scores on the different dimensions have to be weighted (Chapter 13). Unless they are prepared to make arbitrary assignments of weights, then weights have to be determined in a prior separate exercise.

The fundamental issue is how people's views about the importance of the different dimensions of satisfaction are to be taken into account. People can be asked to assign a weight or value directly to each dimension. Sutherland *et al.* (1989) argue that raters tend, in this method, to assign unitary or equal weights to each dimension. The alternative approach is to use judgements made by respondents to a range of questions, which may combine the dimensions, scenarios or vignettes; Froberg and Kane (1989) argue that this approach is also suspect. Many use some statistical reduction technique (such as factor analysis, Chapter 8), presuming that there is an underlying unity to 'satisfaction'. Given there is very little evidence for this, it is preferable in general to retain separate measures of satisfaction with different aspects of the care received in addition to (or in place of) an overall score.

Importance of a conceptual model

Respondents to a standard questionnaire in the UK are typically 80%–90% satisfied (Raphael, 1972 and 1979), as in most of the chapters in this book. One must doubt the utility of any measure of satisfaction which commands such levels of assent and is undifferentiated through the population. Indeed, even when patients report high levels of satisfaction, Carstairs (1970) showed how the volume of comment was a more sensitive indicator for management purposes. Most people, especially current or former patients, are very obliging and will complete a questionnaire to the best of their ability even if they are having difficulty with the questions. There are two main reasons for this. First, questions may be relevant and intelligible, but the response options are not sufficiently precise or detailed to detect changes. In Chapter 7 it is noted that patients said yes to a question asking if they had enough privacy even though they did not have a single room when in hospital. Secondly, the questions do not make much sense to your respondents so the results are unreliable. Both can be hard to detect, especially in self-completion or highly structured surveys, unless the questionnaire is piloted with interviews and open-ended questions.

Once it is agreed that satisfaction is multidimensional, the next issue is how should each of the separate dimensions of satisfaction – for example, those enumerated on page 18 – be measured? The naive approach:

> 'How satisfied were you with access to/choice given by the social worker, nurse etc.'

will not do. This is partly for practical reasons. The uniformly high levels of satisfaction which will be recorded are obviously of limited use to a service manager except for public relations purposes: they need to know what is wrong, not what is right (Chapter 6 gives an analysis that stresses negative responses).

Moreover, satisfaction expressed in response to such a bald question is a relative judgement which will vary according to user expectations of the service. However, the requirement to assess people's expectation of care is complex: it means taking into account

1. the goals of those seeking care in each specific instance;
2. the level of experience or use of care;
3. the socio-political values upon which the particular care system is based;
4. the images of community care held by the lay population.

Such a model (Calnan, 1988), whilst conceptually comprehensive, poses considerable (impossible?) demands upon a questionnaire. Moreover, the first item is not unproblematic. First, no clues are given as to how to pose questions on goals; secondly, the extent to which people have clearly defined goals will depend on their prior knowledge and their capacity for independent action. Varying expectations are thought to have most impact on general questions of the type 'What did you think of the social workers (very satisfied – very dissatisfied)'. However, there is evidence to suggest that no matter how specific the questions may be, the responses recorded will have a lot to do with the way people are feeling about their condition and their consequent expectations of the service.

Autonomy, control and satisfaction

Despite the introduction of goals (expectations or aspirations), the model remains mechanical: clients arrive with goals; professionals do something (or not); and the 'satisfometer' registers the result. The reality is surely different: whatever satisfaction really means, it should reflect, at least in part, the **relationship** between professional and client. That relationship, structurally, is characterized by differences in expertise and knowledge and, therefore, potentially power. The extent to which the client perceives themselves to be powerless will influence the way in which they frame their expectations. Crudely, in situations where the client has, or perceives themselves to have, more control, they are more likely to pursue their own goals; where the client sees themselves as powerless, then expectations will be redefined to match the probable outcome.

Goals cannot, therefore, be measured in a vacuum: they have to be situated in the context of the structural relationship between the patient and the care agents. The following issues arise:

- how to record expectations;
- how to take account of factors such as the state or phase of a client's condition which may give rise to uncertain expectations;
- how to compare outcomes with expectations;
- how to take account of the socially structured relation between clients and care agents, and the socio-political values of the associated care system.

Also, because the connection between expectations, outcomes and satisfaction is neither mechanical, nor does it take place in a vacuum:

- how to allow for the ways in which expectations of both services and outcomes are influenced by lay models of care.

These are difficult issues that are vital to the systematic interpretation of data on client satisfaction. The additional complexities mean that those who set out to measure satisfaction in global terms are probably on a hopeless quest. It is for this reason that the remainder of this chapter, which is concerned with methodological and practical issues, is confined to the measurement of aspects of (reactive) client satisfaction.

DESIGNING SURVEYS TO MEASURE ASPECTS OF SATISFACTION

First, it is necessary to be clear about the objectives. Then there are several technical issues to consider.

Different objectives

Many user surveys seem to lack definite objectives and have not clearly identified how the information they collect will influence decision making. The motives for conducting a survey will usually be some combination of the following:

- to identify problems with an existing service or to highlight areas for service development;
- as a public relations exercise;
- in response to some contractual or other requirement (because it must be done);
- to monitor service performance.

Identify problems and draw up plans for service development

To pinpoint problems and plan services requires more detail than is normally provided by short user questionnaires. This type of information is usually obtained through qualitative techniques and by activities that do not directly involve users, such as management inspections, although the short questionnaire may collect useful comments or indicate areas for more detailed investigation.

Improve public relations

User surveys may be a relatively expensive and inefficient method of promoting public relations. They may even be counterproductive if users' views cannot be acted on.

Respond to some contractual or other requirement

A workshop of NHS managers suggested this as a major and increasing reason for doing these surveys. There are obvious problems and dangers with the coerced survey.

Monitor performance

Performance monitoring takes many different forms and is based on many types of information. The question here is: what can the results of satisfaction surveys tell us about service performance? This has two parts:

- What aspect of performance is monitored by these surveys?
- Can the surveys provide a genuine monitoring function, rather than merely a one-off snapshot of the service?

ASPECTS OF PERFORMANCE

User satisfaction can be treated as an objective in its own right. It can reasonably be argued that service-sector industries have the maximization of customer satisfaction as one of their legitimate objectives. In retailing, and increasingly in community care, the argument is that satisfaction encourages customer loyalty. For example, screening programmes will be more effective if high satisfaction levels encourage higher reattendance rates. Also, satisfaction with care may increase the likelihood of compliance with treatment regimes.

Alternatively, satisfaction can be treated as a proxy for other aspects of service performance:

- as an indicator of the perceived quality of the service, regardless of any other outcomes;
- as a measure of user appreciation of the outcomes – whether or not these are the outcomes that the service providers most value;
- as a measure of user perceptions of the ways in which the service works to achieve its own or the users' objectives.

Questionnaires can be devised specifically to address each of these themes, although most user surveys are open to several interpretations, both by respondents and researchers. It must be remembered that different groups will have different interests.

Monitoring

As a form of evaluation, monitoring can be contrasted with the one-off snapshot. Monitoring implies first, repeated data collection and, second, comparisons between services or against targets. Monitoring may have several aims. It may try to be indicative – to point out major differences between services or over time that need further investigation – or it may aim to provide quantitative measurements of performance.

Monitoring involves the following, either singly or in combination:

- repeatedly measuring the performance of the same unit – taking existing standards as the target, working towards some predefined target or simply recording any variations;
- regular or infrequent comparisons of performance across units, with or without targets;
- one-off or infrequent evaluations against predefined targets.

Most user surveys that want to monitor performance assume that satisfaction ratings are a proxy for quality. As far as arrangements for monitoring are concerned, the most usual forms are one-off or regular comparisons across units or repeated surveying within the same unit(s). There are many one-off surveys, but they cannot be regarded as monitoring exercises unless they involve comparisons with predefined targets, and this is rare.

QUESTIONNAIRE CONTENT

In the health care context, Hall and Dornan (1990) argue that the essential conceptual features of user instruments are directness, specificity, type of care and dimensionality. **Directness** refers to whether the patient is asked to give a satisfaction rating or whether the research infers satisfaction levels from answers to questions about the care. **Specificity** is a continuum from a specific referent event (e.g. a particular visit) to the evaluation of health services in general. **Type of care** refers to the kind of care or service being evaluated. **Dimensionality** refers to the different aspects of medical care inquired about. Most studies measure only a few aspects of care.

Choosing a topic

Who chooses which topics to include in a survey and the way they are presented? Even the smallest surveys, consisting of a few simple questions on specific aspects of services, will involve decisions on how the questions are to be worded and what topics are prioritized. In health care it is becoming more acceptable to include questions on user satisfaction with the quality of the professional care they receive, but surveys still tend to be biased towards the hotel aspects of the service (e.g. the comfort of the office accommodation) and issues of convenience and access.

Basically, there are three approaches to selecting the issues and framing the questions:

- Let the people being surveyed identify their own concerns (not a simple matter, as shown in Part Three of this book).
- Use factor analysis or similar techniques to construct a statistical picture of the issues underlying the replies to previous surveys.
- Organize the questionnaire and data collection around the ideas and issues suggested by some predefined framework.

Users' priorities

Service users' priorities and definitions can be explored with a range of techniques that are predominately qualitative, and can be time consuming (Chapter 3 provides a fuller discussion). Suitable methods include open-ended interviews, problem-oriented techniques and focus groups. Results from these techniques can be used as the basis for constructing standard questionnaires (as in Chapter 10), but it is easy to lose some of the user centredness in this process.

The alternative of allowing individual users to use their own priorities as a basis for assessing quality presumes a certain level of articulateness.

Factor analysis

Factor analysis and related statistical techniques can be used to reveal underlying response patterns and establish thematic groupings (Chapter 8). The resulting themes can be used in summarizing the results or adopted as section headings in subsequent surveys. It must be emphasized that, however sophisticated the analysis and despite the apparent rigour of the approach, the themes are completely dependent upon the range and type of questions in the original survey on which the analysis is based. A differently based questionnaire could lead to quite a different list of themes.

Professional frameworks

Care professionals and service managers have their own ideas on the issues that should be covered by feedback and user surveys. These service-led views of topics for user comment inform many user questionnaires, but are not often subject to systematic scrutiny. They risk being self-confirming and missing key concerns. If they purport to address the client's perspective their validity should at least be tested by an independent interviewer asking clients whether they think that the questions cover the most important issues. This is one of a number of simple basic tests of validity that is all too infrequently applied.

TECHNICAL ISSUES IN CARRYING OUT A SURVEY

The results of user surveys are sensitive to specific design features. There are some basic and avoidable design problems that frequently recur:

- questionnaires with in-built biases;
- information in a form that cannot be easily analysed;
- surveys that miss crucial data.

These can usually be avoided by referring to standard texts or expert advice, though there is often a problem of inadequate resources.

Many design issues are harder to address. Five crucial parameters are considered below, each having a major influence on the results and making comparisons extremely difficult. They all contribute to the sense of unreliability of the findings of user surveys.

Choice of population

The choice of population is crucial. Some argue that surveys should be limited to those who are actually currently using a service. Others say that, as community care services are public, the reaction of those who are not immediate or recent clients/consumers is also very relevant (see the list on page 18). Even if only current clients/consumers are considered, there can be wide variations in the type of client interviewed; for example, recipients of district nursing services (Chapter 8), people with learning difficulties (Chapters 11 and 12), ex-mental hospital patients (Chapters 7 and 14).

How much data should be collected?

There are two parts to this question. First, how many topics are being covered by a single questionnaire? Overlong multitopic questionnaires are frequently a sign of a project with no clear objectives that will probably be inconclusive. Secondly, what type and size of sample should be used (Carr-Hill, 1987)?

Sampling methods are grossly underused in most service-sector surveys. There is often no need to contact every patient seen in a unit, and attempts to contact everyone are notorious for systematically excluding particular groups. Better to target a well-defined sample and try to get higher response rates and use whatever techniques are necessary to try to establish whether non-respondents have distinctly different perceptions of the service.

Timing

The timing of surveys may also be of critical importance. The longer the gap between the use of services and the interview (or the questionnaire), the greater the chance of recall bias, of respondents overlooking matters that affected them during the episode of care, and of changes in their appreciation of services (Chapter 9). Such considerations led Rees and Wallace (1982) to conclude that factors relating to the timing of research interviews 'make it difficult to interpret the "meaning" of the results and once again suggest caution in accepting some research conclusions about client satisfaction'. For example, in the NHS context, there appears to be a clear decay in satisfaction from being on the spot to being interviewed at home.

Rating satisfaction

Using ratings chosen from 'Very Satisfied, Satisfied, Dissatisfied, Very Dissatisfied' is problematic. High levels of dissatisfaction on one aspect of the information given could be masked by high levels of satisfaction on other aspects. And a change from satisfaction to dissatisfaction may be due to small cumulative shifts in each of the component aspects or to a large shift in just one of them.

Suppose that conditions improve in one respect but deteriorate in another. Groups asked before or after will almost certainly give different weightings to the two aspects. It will be possible to calculate satisfaction rates but it will not be possible to know how different users rated each aspect of the service or whether individual users would agree with the overall rate. Action taken on the basis of expressed dissatisfaction could be inappropriate. (Chapter 8 discusses components of service satisfaction.) Any proposal for monitoring users on a regular basis must be sensitive to the multiplicity of ways in which satisfaction is expressed and felt by both clients and professionals.

Type of questionnaire

Perhaps the most important methodological consideration relates to the type of questionnaire used to acquire data. It is axiomatic that the questionnaire should not distort the consumers' views, but achieving this is not an easy task when provider perceptions are taken as paramount.

Simple questions are relatively insensitive, with responses tending to fall into narrow bands, superficially indicative of high satisfaction levels. Where a substantially different level of satisfaction is obtained, the cause is likely to be glaringly obvious – such as a new management – obviating the need for the questionnaire in the first place.

Respondents can be asked to talk about or comment on the services they have received (Chapter 5) or to answer a series of direct questions about different aspects of those services (Chapter 6). These different types of question clearly generate different kinds of data: the first is based on accounts of what happened from which we infer satisfaction; the second generates direct evaluations but the researcher does not know the precise referent.

Unstructured and structured questions produce different results. Individuals will report satisfaction or dissatisfaction when asked directly about different aspects of care in a structured or semistructured questionnaire. In an unstructured interview they might not have given the same issues sufficient priority to mention them spontaneously. Direct questions appear to function as probes for eliciting dissatisfaction with the aspects of care which have less impact than those mentioned in response to open-ended questions. Both kinds of questions should be included to avoid underreporting and to assess users' priorities.

The range of questionnaires and other techniques for collecting clients' views can be grouped into four basic types. Each type of instrument has strengths and weaknesses according to the type of application considered.

1.   *Short instruments for routine and/or widespread use*

- less than 20 questions (limited space for comments);
- may be machine readable;

- predominantly self-completion;
- full range of topics (but little detail on each);
- simple to analyse – dedicated software may be included in the package;
- results simple and well-presented (e.g. graphs);
- continuous or regular use;
- might be administered to all service users.

2. *In-depth questionnaires*

- more than 50 questions;
- may need interviewer assistance;
- full range of topics (considerable detail on each);
- can be difficult to analyse – suppliers may offer analysis service;
- one-off use or infrequent use;
- likely to be applied to a sample.

3. *User group/specific instruments*

- shorter than a detailed general questionnaire;
- may need interviewer assistance;
- service-specific topics;
- moderately simple to analyse;
- frequency of use depends on objectives – might be one-off audit or continuous monitoring;
- might be used with a sample or population depending on objectives and numbers seen.

4. *Qualitative methods, including: critical incident techniques, semistructured interviews, diary records and focus groups*

- employ many and varied techniques with few common methodological features;
- require some type of personal involvement in the data collection;
- range of topics can be open or limited;
- may require extensive analytical effort – others require very little;
- usually only applicable to relatively small numbers.

WHAT DOES IT ALL MEAN?

Reliability

The reliability of the findings of user surveys is frequently questioned. There are four issues. First, the level of criticism or dissatisfaction expressed by clients depends on the context and the way in which questions are asked. Apart from the strictly technical considerations above, data on consumer satisfaction are only comparable across environments to the extent that service consumption coincides. For example, community nursing services will be perceived very differently in rural and urban areas. Similarly, it is important to check the respondent's present level of consumption because standards of practice change and those without recent experience may be basing their responses on socially stereotyped conceptions of providers or services.

The second issue is that the general perspective adopted by most studies (i.e. the type of questions asked and the topic areas included) has implied that clients do not, or should not, evaluate professional practice. This is partly because most studies are designed from the perspective of the providers, and it is presumed that clients do not have the required knowledge. On the other hand, we know that clients can become 'expert' – more critical of, and less satisfied with, the care provided (Calnan, 1988; West, 1976). Indeed ethnographic studies show that clients have clear criteria both for judging the ability of their professionals and for evaluating the care provided (Calnan, 1987).

Thirdly, the characteristics of the intended and achieved samples are rarely compared. Ideally, sampling should be from lists of clients as they enter the system but this is rarely feasible. In a study of retrospective opinions, it is difficult to obtain undistorted views on the organizational and psychological experience of the care process or on the psychological needs of long-term clients. In practice, the response rates are, frankly, often appalling. One gem of an exercise involved the distribution of 105 700 questionnaires with 38 responses; nevertheless, a report was written. Those commissioning studies seem content with very low response rates: a study by the Audit Commission (1991) of patients' opinions of day-care surgery made no apologies for a response rate of 50%, which, it stated, 'are common for this type of study' (no source cited). In fact, response rates can be quite high (Dixon, 1991).

Practice in calculating response rates is often bizarre. Variations in the way groups of clients are intentionally or unintentionally excluded in the reporting of results makes interpretation of the response rates very difficult. The example below shows the importance of clearly specifying both denominator and numerator:

> 400 registered clients
> 130 prescreened as ineligible
> 40 refuse the questionnaire
> 200 are returned

As 230 have accepted the questionnaire, a high response rate of 87% is suggested from the 200 returned. But the 40 who refused to accept the questionnaire ought, of course, to be included, giving a response rate of 74% (200/270). Moreover, if the intention had been to reach all clients the correct figure is 50% (200/400).

However, even when the target numbers originally sampled and the size of the achieved sample are clearly reported, it is rare to find an adequate commentary on the characteristics of the achieved versus the target sample and a discussion of factors related to non-response. This is bad practice: positively good practice would involve the interviewing of a small sample of non-respondents.

Fourthly, it is striking how little is known about the operating characteristics of even the most widely used satisfaction questionnaires. It is neither easy nor cheap to comprehensively evaluate these instruments, but there is still no excuse for the general lack of interest in their properties. At a very minimum, any instrument that is to be considered for performance monitoring should be tested to see how responsive it is to change and how suitable it is for different groups of users. There should also be discussion of the meaning of the results and what interpretations are valid. The devisers of questionnaires have a responsibility to provide this type of information for any new instrument.

OTHER DATA SOURCES

One approach to the problem of finding sufficient variation in the data for management purposes is to actively seek out dissatisfaction. This can be done via probing the satisfied response more thoroughly in an interview situation or by employing one of a range of other qualitative techniques described in Chapter 3.

In the first place, service managers should become more aware of the informal data collection that may already be part of their daily routine. Thus, customer opinions are registered in a variety of forms such as magazines and radio phone-ins. Obviously, these are likely to represent the most vocal end of the spectrum of patient opinion, but they can be used to decide upon the range of possible complaints and dissatisfactions. Even the traditional complaints box is not the only method of trapping opinion; special telephone lines can be made available, and more effort can be made to ask family and friends of users what they think about services.

In some circumstances, it is worth investigating the possibility of ensuring that these observations and conversations are systematically reported. It often makes more sense to extend these informal methods, rather than conduct an expensive and potentially inconclusive survey. This is not only because of the expensive and uncertain payoff of full scale surveys. It is also because the questionnaire method only gets replies to a series of preset questions, not the clients' considered (or spontaneous) views on the issues which concern them (Chapter 10), whether as current users or as members of the public. Once the fieldwork is over, there is a considerable temptation to forget that what are confidently described as respondents' views are only their replies to questions devised by the researcher and are not necessarily the clients' own views and priorities.

Thus, it is commonplace to observe that service policy has been steered by providers' perceptions and definitions of good practice. It is important that those engaged in consumer research, in order to obtain systematic information about consumer views, do not fall into a similar trap (Carr-Hill et al., 1989).

INTERPRETING THE RESULTS

So, you have a survey, some well-planned questions based on a qualitative pilot, and a strategy for service monitoring. The results start to appear – but what do they mean? The widely accepted assumption is that recorded satisfaction levels will principally reflect the quality of the services. However, this is not necessarily the case. As already shown, there are a number of factors that can have a significant impact on the results:

- quality of services;
- expectations of clients/consumers;
- hopes and concerns surrounding the situation and its possible outcomes;
- expectations and prior experiences of care – likely to be related to age, gender and culture;
- respondent's situation;
- responsiveness of the measuring instrument.

It is one thing to list these potential influences on responses to a user questionnaire; it is quite another to control them.

The last of these topics – the responsiveness of the measuring instrument – needs addressing by better design and piloting.

The influence of expectations on satisfaction is more difficult to resolve. Great care is needed when comparing results for groups that are likely to have different expectations. You may need to carry out further research into the effects of varying expectations. Good comparative data on the responses of different population groups will be a starting point. It may then be possible to unpack the influences with multivariate techniques. However, this may be so difficult that, rather than try to take them into account, you will have to limit the analysis so that possible confounding influences are minimized or at least made more manageable. Common sense and a good text book will help. Alternatively, qualitative approaches can try to collect people's first-hand accounts of what influences their attitudes to services and how they express them in responses to user surveys.

Even when a single unit is being surveyed, it is necessary to check that neither the users of a unit or their expectations are changing. There are many factors that could have an effect: the unit may take on a different group of clients that were previously cared for elsewhere; national or local media might highlight an issue that influences client expectations of a particular service; there could be expectations of new forms of care being introduced; the local population might be changing; political campaigns may have changed the ways people view public services. Some of these effects are very visible and easily understood, some are long-term and cannot explain sudden changes in satisfaction ratings, but they all need bearing in mind. The same factors will also influence attempts to compare the satisfaction ratings for different types of units caring for different types of clients. The principal issue is whether the satisfaction level will be intrinsically different because of the nature of the conditions and clients. In principle it should be possible to adjust for casemix. In practice, so little is known about the precise ways in which expectations and satisfaction vary with conditions, cultures, etc. that cross-unit, cross-condition comparisons are unlikely to be valid.

The use of satisfaction data as a performance indicator should probably be limited to looking at the results for a single unit over time and then only when the casemix is known to be static and there are no reasons to assume that patient expectations will have radically changed. Even very big differences in satisfaction levels may not indicate differences in the quality or effectiveness of services. This is not to say that such differences should be ignored. Possible explanations should be sought. There may be a case for increasing satisfaction level in the less popular units simply to improve future cooperation or compliance.

CONCLUSIONS AND RECOMMENDATIONS

It would be utopian to suppose that a uniform set of guidelines on consumer surveys could be agreed; however, the following points should be considered more widely.

Reporting

There has to be more complete reporting of the characteristics of the sample studied as well as of the results obtained. Too often, it is simply impossible to know who was the target population (see list on page 18) or to understand how satisfaction varies among the population.

Response rate

It seems not to be realized that the response rates have to be high to give credible results. First, as with other surveys where the response rate is low, there is an inevitable risk of bias; second, because overall levels of satisfaction are usually quite high, only a small fraction of the population can potentially express dissatisfaction and they may also be non-respondents.

Standardized instruments

Any service manager should be wary of standardized instruments. The reason is simple: standardized instruments are based on studies which are specific in context and objectives. There is no guarantee that they will provide accurate results when context and objectives differ.

Minorities

There have been very few studies of minority groups whether defined in terms of users or of treatment characteristics. For management purposes, it would be inappropriate to simply assume that results obtained on a general population are transferable to minority groups.

Coverage of satisfaction

The theory underlying existing satisfaction studies is inadequate. Partly in consequence, several aspects of satisfaction simply have not been studied.

Method

To date, nearly all the studies have been one-off cross-sectional studies of customer satisfaction with a particular service, with a few before and after studies. There have been no properly randomized control trials.

TOWARDS GUIDELINES

The increase in survey activity and the successive restructurings of the public sector have meant that many surveys are not conducted by suitably qualified staff and that any developing centres of expertise have tended to be dispersed. There is an increasing tendency to employ professional survey agencies to run some of the bigger initiatives, but the general quality of survey work is poor. Nevertheless there continues to be great pressure to collect 'user satisfaction data' – especially because of the lack of other 'outcomes' information for use in performance monitoring.

If user surveys are to play a useful role in performance monitoring they require very precise planning:

1. They need clear aims and positive arguments for including each topic in the questionnaire. There should be an intended use for every piece of information.
2. When it comes to collecting the data, this should be planned and not just happen. Issues such as the frequency of data collection and the size and type of sample should not be ignored.
3. In using and interpreting the results any comparisons should be cautious and controlled or limited to minimize probable casemix effects associated with the different expectations of different groups.
4. In any event, the results may have to be treated as indicators, not precise measurements. More needs to be known about the working characteristics of survey questionnaires, not least their sensitivity to variations in expectations and other factors not directly related to the quality of service received.

5. Monitoring programmes should include mechanisms to assess their own effectiveness in meeting or improving quality. These assessments should consider whether the same results could be achieved more effectively or economically by methods other than user surveys.

Hundreds of thousands of user questionnaires are being completed in the NHS and Social Services every year, but there is relatively little discussion, let alone evaluation, of how the results are interpreted and used. It may be that we need to be much more selective and strategic in using these methods. It may be that other techniques, especially more intensive qualitative methods applied to strategic samples, are a more effective means of getting the information we require.

REFERENCES

Audit Commission (1991) *Measuring Quality: The Patient View of Day Care Surgery*, NHS Occasional Paper No. 3, HMSO, London.

Calnan, M. (1987) *Health and Illness: The Lay Perspective*, Tavistock, London.

Calnan, M. (1988) Towards a conceptual framework of lay evaluation in health care. *Social Science and Medicine*, **27**(9), 927–933.

Campbell, A., Converse, P. E. and Rodgers, W. L. (1976) *The Quality of American Life: Perception, Evaluation and Satisfaction*, Russell Sage, New York.

Carr-Hill, R. A. (1987) When is a data set complete: a squirrel with a vacuum cleaner. *Social Science and Medicine*, **25**(6), 753–764.

Carr-Hill, R. A., Dixon, P. and Thompson, A. G. (1989) Too simple for words. *Health Services Journal*, **99**(5155) 728–729.

Carstairs, V. (1970) *Channels of Communication*, Scottish Health Service Studies 11, Scottish Home and Health Department, Edinburgh.

Dixon, P. (1991) *Response Rates on Postal Questionnaires*, Centre for Health Economics, University of York.

Dixon, P. and Carr-Hill, R. A. (1989) *Consumer Feedback Surveys: A Review of Methods*, (The NHS and Its Customers, No.3), Centre for Health Economics, University of York.

Froberg, G. and Kane, D. G. (1989) Methodology for measuring health state preferences – I Measurement strategies. *Journal of Clinical Epidemiology*, **42**(4), 345–354.

Griffiths, R. (1983) *Working for Patients*, The NHS Management Inquiry, DHSS, HMSO, London.

Hall, J. A. and Dornan, M. C. (1990) Patient sociodemographic characteristics as predictors of satisfaction with medical care: a meta analysis. *Social Science and Medicine*, **30**(7), 819–828.

Hall, J. A., Roter, D. L. and Katz, N. R. (1988) Meta analysis of correlates of provider behaviour in medical encounters. *Medical Care*, **26**, 657.

Linn, B. S. (1982) Burn patients' evaluation of emergency department care. *Annals of Emergency Medicine*, **11**, 255.

Locker, D. and Dunt, P. (1978) Theoretical and methodological issues in sociological studies of consumer satisfaction with medical care. *Social Science and Medicine*, **12**(4), 283–292.

NCC (1986) *Measuring Up: Consumer Assessment of Local Authority Services – A Guideline Study*, National Consumer Council, London.

OECD (1974) *Subjective Elements of Well-Being*, Organisation of Economic Cooperation and Development, Paris.

Potter, J. (1988) Consumerism and the public sector: how well does the coat fit? *Public Administration*, **66**(2), 149–164.

Raphael, W. (1972) *Psychiatric Hospitals viewed by their Patients*, King's Fund, London.

Raphael, W. (1979) *Old People in Hospital*, King's Fund, London.

Rees, S. and Wallace, P. (1982) *Verdicts in Social Work*, Edward Arnold, London.

Speedling, E. J. and Rose, D. N. (1985) Building an effective doctor-patient relationship: from patient satisfaction to patient participation. *Social Science and Medicine*, **21**(2), 115–120.

Sutherland, H. J., Lockwood, G. A., Minkin, S., Tritchder, D. L., Till, J. E. and Llewellyn-Thomas, H. A. (1989) Measuring satisfaction with health care: a comparison of single with paired rating strategies. *Social Science and Medicine*, **28**(1), 53–58.

West, P. (1976) The physician and management of childhood epilepsy, in *Studies in Everyday Medical Life,* (eds M. Wadsworth and D. Robinson), Martin Robertson, London.

FURTHER READING

Carr-Hill, R. A. and Dixon, P. (1989) *The NHS and Its Customers*, Vol. II Customer Feedback Surveys – an Introduction to Survey Methods, Vol. III Customer Feedback Surveys – a review of current practice, Centre for Health Economics, University of York.

Fitzpatrick, R. (1991) Surveys of patient satisfaction. II – designing a questionnaire and conducting a survey. *British Medical Journal*, **302**, 1129–1132.

Wykes, W. *et al.* (1992) *Listening to Local Voices: A Guide to Research Methods*, Nuffield Institute, University of Leeds.

<table>
| Exploring users' views | 3 |
</table>

Exploring users' views

3

Julie Dockrell

Qualitative research is often thought to be unscientific and a soft option. In this chapter Dockrell considers the place of a range of qualitative methods in research on user views. She discusses how to go about collecting and analysing data and using it to understand belief structures and the underlying processes that influence behaviour. Credibility and confirmability replace concepts of validity in qualitative research but rigour is still needed in designing and executing projects.

SETTING THE AGENDA

Customers' views are an important way for businesses to develop and enhance their products. As customers, we are regularly consulted in formal and informal ways. Consider the last time you went into a fast food restaurant. There is a high probability that your views were sought. You may have been asked to fill in a form. From the ticks in the boxes the owner could tabulate the views of the customers. Did you fill in the form? Alternatively, the waiter or waitress might have asked you whether everything was to your liking. Staff were trying to get a feel for the views of the clientele and make amendments if necessary. Now consider your response. How poor did the service or the food have to be before you complained? Despite the present ethos of letting service providers know our views, it is not always easy for them to get an accurate reflection of how the consumer actually feels. Sometimes this lack of awareness by the providers arises because there are problems with the way the user is asked. In other cases providers fail to understand the complexity of the issues underlying the user view.

Service users are not in a strong position to clarify the misconceptions that arise. In the restaurant example the customer is in a position of power; you have chosen to go there, you have the money to pay for the service, and you expect a certain standard. You may not complain to the waiter, but you have the option of going elsewhere next time. Consumers of health services are rarely in this position and it becomes much harder for them to challenge the service provided. If, instead of sitting in a restaurant, you were 85, frail and sitting in a residential home, your ability to complain would be severely constrained. In this situation if you were asked 'Is everything to your liking?', what could you say? Inaccurate measures of consumer satisfaction can arise through poorly worded questions, but also when people believe criticism will be held against them or there may be a negative effect on the service provided (Lebow, 1982). It is important that the beliefs, values and needs of service users are explored in a way that elicits credible and informative data.

This chapter examines some approaches to exploring user views. These methods differ from surveys but may be used in conjunction with them. Researchers using these approaches attempt to tap an individual's belief structures in a detailed way, with the aim of clarifying the underlying processes that influence behaviour. The chapter begins by considering some of these different methods and proceeds to practical applications and handling the data that arise. In order to draw worthwhile conclusions from qualitative approaches it is essential that a rigorous approach is taken to the design, data collection, analysis, interpretation and reporting of the results. The extent to which such approaches produce reliable and valid results will be discussed in the conclusion.

ASKING USERS' VIEWS

A central theme in community care provision in the 1990s is the role of users' views in service development and evaluation. The routine requirement to monitor users' views was a major feature of the Griffiths report. The management board of the NHS was requested to:

'Ascertain how well the service is being delivered at local level by obtaining the experience and perceptions of patients and the community: these can be derived from community health councils and by other methods, including market research and from the experience of general practice and community health service.' (DHSS, 1983)

This statement makes it clear that the task should be approached in several different ways. Two questions arise:

- What are these different ways?
- Why should one method be used above another?

It is important to acknowledge that there is no best method overall. The selection of methods should be driven by the kind of research or service development questions that are being asked. A research question is the expressed focus of a project or investigation. Research questions limit the focus of the enquiry by highlighting the key dimensions of the research agenda. If, for example, the interest is in studying service provision, there is a need to begin by structuring the project either through intuition about what is occurring or through the results of other similar studies. This might lead to a more specific focus which could be the ways in which service users and service providers work together to provide a service. The next step would be to define what activities would be included in working together. This way of devising the research question narrows down the focus of the enquiry.

Research questions should be articulated clearly at the beginning of the project. At that point the investigators need to consider (a) the type of data that will be collected, (b) the inferences that can be drawn from the data set, and (c) the reason the information is required. This means that the questions or issues driving the study must be formulated so that data can be collected which will answer the initial questions that were posed. The question 'Is the service successful?' is unanswerable. It is not known who the service needs to be successful for, nor what the criteria of success are. Reformulated as 'Does the service enhance individual ability to live independently', the initial vague question becomes an answerable research issue.

The kind of information that will be collected will vary according to the research focus. For example, service planning will highlight the need for different information from service evaluation. The latter case is commenting on the strengths and weakness of an existing entity, the terms of reference are set. In the former situation the terms of reference need to be identified. Planning requires that a need be defined. This means the concept of need must be clarified and the range of options available to meet the need considered. Inappropriate services may be designed if service options are specified without consultation with the user.

Let us consider two examples. A consultation to discover whether residents in sheltered accommodation prefer showers to baths will be different in kind from a consultation aimed to establish the needs of bereaved widowers. In the former case the limits of the exercise are already prescribed. The decision, for whatever reason, is to investigate washing preferences. In this case a closed question, such as

CIRCLE YOUR RESPONSE
I prefer a bath to a shower. YES NO

might suffice. Note that this is an extremely unsophisticated approach. Preferences for washing are likely to vary according to time of day, time of year or state of health. However, the second case, that of the bereaved widower, is much more complex. Even identifying the issues that are relevant to defining the problem may need a pilot project. Considerable demands will be placed on the researcher to go beyond individual cases to identify implications for service development. A database that is more detailed and client centred will be required. A preconstructed questionnaire will not provide the requisite information since we do not know the key issues. The investigator will need to distinguish the key dimensions of the information collected.

QUALITATIVE APPROACHES

Methods that provide in-depth understanding of the perspectives, attitudes and beliefs of target populations have an important role to play in understanding users' views and behaviour. The field of health education provides a relevant illustration. Calnan (1989) argues that the initial stage in any health campaign is to find out the various sets of beliefs held by the individuals involved. As an example consider the present concern over the lack of compliance with medication for tuberculosis. The implication is that in order to increase compliance with medication it is essential to know why people are failing to follow their regimes. The reasons are likely to vary markedly across the groups at risk, such as the homeless, people who are HIV positive, and immigrant populations.

The focus of this chapter is qualitative approaches to investigating service users' views. Qualitative analysis can be used to examine critically data that occur as words and in other non-numerical forms. The focus is any information, gathered during research, which has not (yet, at least) been quantified in any rigorous fashion. Quantitative analysis, on the other hand, is restricted to numbers or data that can be translated into numbers (Chapter 2). Qualitative data generally originates from case studies or combined methods of tackling a research question. Such work draws on a type of investigation traditionally used by social anthropologists and includes such methods as participant observation, unstructured or informal interviewing, and the use of documentary methods. It is important to realize that it is the method of data collection that permits the different types of analysis. Questionnaires can only be analysed quantitatively, whereas interviews, group discussions, media messages and so forth can be analysed quantitatively or qualitatively. Quantitative analysis consists of counting the occurrence of some variable in the study and embarking on some form of statistical analysis.

Qualitative analysis considers the content and processes involved in the study. Bruner and Kelso (1980) provide a clear illustration. These authors investigated graffiti in toilets. Graffiti could have been examined by counting occurrences in particular situations. This would have been a quantitative project. Bruner and Kelso opted for a qualitative approach. They analysed the **content** of the messages. Their results demonstrated that women's graffiti was more interpersonal and interactive tending to contain questions and advice about love relationships and commitment, whereas men's graffiti tended to be egocentric and competitive, concentrating on conquests and prowess. The authors argued that the graffiti reflected different gender-based stereotypes in society. Counting alone would not have provided this insight. When we use qualitative approaches in service related research, we are concerned with achieving greater insight into the nature of the problem under investigation.

ENQUIRY NATURE

Enquiry scope

Many people in hospitals, waiting rooms and so forth will have received this courtesy request: 'There's nothing else you need, is there?' Failure to respond with a list of requirements does not mean that all is well. Asking questions and getting informative answers is a skill. Despite the apparent simplicity of asking for users' views, the task is not straightforward. As has been noted in Chapter 1, users of health and social services are often disempowered. Many individuals accept services that are far below an adequate standard (Chapters 4 and 8). This occurs for several reasons: users are often grateful to receive any service at all or they fear that by complaining they will jeopardize their chances of receiving further help. Disempowered users are in a vulnerable position and this means that they may be less likely to express their true views. Sheppard (1994) found that criticizing the ward was something which ex-patients would never have dared to do while they were still patients. It would have been disappointing to the nurses.

The introduction of the *Patient's Charter* has led more people to expect requests for their views and forces practitioners and researchers to consider the different ways that users can be consulted. The first option for many is to use a survey. A well-constructed survey can address a range of predetermined issues and dimensions (Chapter 2). What the survey gains in numbers, it often loses in depth of analysis. Preset standards for health services can easily be translated into a structured questionnaire. It is harder for a questionnaire to identify the importance of a delay between appointment time and being seen, in comparison with other delivery issues such as courtesy. Britten and Shaw (1994) used quali-tative data to examine whether the standards set out in the *Patient's Charter* were appropriate to patients admitted through accident and emergency depart-ments. The qualitative approach highlighted the finding that 'the rights and standards outlined in the *Patient's Charter* are generally appropriate to these patients' experiences but that they are too narrowly defined'. The methodology used allowed the researchers to identify several important issues for the patients which were not mentioned in the *Patient's Charter*: pain relief, giving and receiving information, the attitude of reception staff and so forth. The authors concluded that patients want rather more than recent government documents suggest. If the research questions had only addressed the issues contained in the

Patient's Charter, accident and emergency users would have appeared more satisfied than they actually were. The inclusion of the subjects' broader perceptions allowed a more accurate consideration of service satisfaction.

In addition to surveys, ongoing responses about the service can be provided through regular meetings of groups of service users (Chapters 15 and 16). Such groups require careful planning if they are to include a broad range of users and if they are to allow open expression of views (discussed in the section on group interviews below). Results of such group discussions will rarely be quantified but the discussions can be considered in a qualitative manner. Views can be included at a strategic level, with service users being represented on steering groups and so forth. Different conceptual and practical factors will act as barriers to accessing the point of view of the user in these different contexts.

THE CASE STUDY

Various changes, such as the *Patient's Charter* and demands for accountability, have compelled practitioners and researchers to consider users' views. There are several tools that can be used to meet this goal. Many qualitative techniques can be subsumed under the case study approach. A case study is an empirical study that investigates a contemporary phenomenon within a real-life context. The specific concern of this chapter is consumers' views.

It is important to realize that a case study is a strategy rather than a method (Robson, 1993). The unit chosen may be a person, a small group, a community, an event or an episode. Case study methods are inherently more suitable for such tasks 'as describing an individual's experience ... developing idiographic interpretations of that experience and developing context-specific predictions, plans and decisions' (Runyan, 1982). The ways in which cases are identified will limit or extend the generalizability of the phenomena.

In case studies, users' views can be collected both directly and indirectly. **Indirect** information can be collected through monitoring of services: information on waiting times, appointments procedures, and the general quality of the service provided, such as staff behaviour. Indirect information can also be acquired through anecdotal evidence. Anecdotal evidence is information collected from personal/social sources. This might include information reported at coffee mornings, in day centres and in other informal settings. There is no need to assume the information is generalizable. Rather, such data reflect a view or perception felt by the individuals who generate it. It can serve as the basis for further investigations. For example, speech therapists developed a group for parents of the children they were seeing on their courses. The development of this group arose from anecdotal evidence. The therapists had noticed that, while waiting for their children, the parents expressed a need to talk to each other and to receive more information without the children present. These overheard conversations led to a formalized series of meetings for the parents that were further continued by the parents themselves (Dockrell, 1989).

Direct access to consumers' views and wishes entails consulting them personally. However, personal requests on their own do not guarantee reliable responses. The methods used to make the requests will critically affect the reliability and validity of the data generated. Complaints are direct evidence of service users' views. As has already been mentioned, complaints generally only occur when there is serious cause for concern. Consequently complaints and compliments are unlikely to tap the depth and extent of users' views. They may provide indications of service adequacy but they cannot be a reliable basis for planning and developing provision.

Indirect information collected from service monitoring will generally reflect the professional view of what makes an acceptable service. This may not necessarily coincide with user views. So while these direct and indirect approaches serve particular purposes they are not, on the whole, appropriate means of addressing the **expectations**, **perceptions** and **requirements** of users. Instead of introducing preconceived ideas about services or allowing preconceptions to intrude, we need to let participants voice their own views if we are to get information that will take us beyond the surface. Qualitative methods, which tap into lay constructions of service provision and individual service requirements, offer a means of addressing some of these issues. They allow for in-depth exploration of matters in a way that large surveys cannot accomplish.

ELICITING INDIVIDUAL BELIEFS

Qualitative studies, according to Cronbach (1975), should describe and interpret the particular practices of the individual in their unique context. They focus upon the decision making of the individual rather than upon modal effects (Chapter 2 discusses the problems of measures of central tendency). As the following chapters in this book show, individual and group interviews can play a role in extending the understanding of the range and diversity of issues that are relevant to user views and requirements. Besides the interview format, qualitative studies use the analysis of case records from which various types of information can be extracted. More recently, details of key events have been used to reveal tensions that may otherwise remain undetected. For example, problems in service coproduction can be highlighted when practitioners are requested to keep note of joint planning activities between provider and service user.

HOW TO ASK THE USER, OR: WHICH QUESTION AND WHEN?

Bromley (1986) emphasizes the need to keep in mind three questions when embarking on a case study:

- What is the issue?
- What other relevant evidence might contribute to understanding the issue?
- How are the data to be obtained?

Setting the research agenda and defining the scope of the enquiry

The methods which produce qualitative data, such as interviews, focus groups and diary studies, will be used by a wide range of professionals but the data collected can be used to focus on different issues. Staff specialists and managers may rely on qualitative information as a routine part of their work to clarify organizational issues. This information will be used to enhance the efficient running of the organization. Service evaluators can use qualitative data to address the adequacy of the service under consideration (Dockrell *et al.*, 1990). Academic researchers may be concerned with the broader issues generated from their data and the ways in which this approach can be taken further to explore the nature of the phenomena under investigation. In all instances the investigator will be collecting information to arrive at underlying principles that are likely to apply (be generalized) to the particular case under investigation and may, under certain circumstances, apply to other similar situations.

The need to clearly identify the scope of an enquiry has already been addressed. The key is to decide what the investigator thinks should be done and what the relevant features are for the study. The questions asked will depend on these initial decisions.

Selecting the sample

There are two main approaches to selecting appropriate samples – representative and purposive. A representative sample is smaller in numbers than the total population but has the same characteristics as the total sample, such as socio-economic group (class), education, gender and so on. In such cases there should be an exact correspondence between the attributes of the sample and the total population. Representative samples are drawn using various sampling techniques including random sampling, e.g. every fifth admission to the hospital, or quota sampling where there are set targets, e.g. a certain number of pregnant females. Purposive sampling, on the other hand, occurs when the researchers specify the types of subjects that are of interest. This approach is more common in case studies. Purposive sampling maximizes the researcher's ability to select samples related to the research questions and the local conditions and values. For example, one might purposively select unusual cases, critical cases or problematic cases. Sampling requires the researcher to articulate the basis for the selection of the participants in the study. This is important for others to interpret the results and to judge the acceptability or otherwise of the study.

COLLECTING THE DATA

Individual interviews

How the data are obtained is very important. Qualitative data that are collected through the means of open interviewing have the following in common:

- the aim of eliciting the informants' views in the informants' own terms;
- an attempt to make the interviews resemble natural conversations as far as possible;
- the desire to impose as little as possible of the researcher's ideas on the conversations.

The manner in which the interviews are executed can influence the quality of the data generated. The interview format is particularly important with vulnerable or disempowered groups. Interviews require interpersonal skills of a high order. Oppenheim (1992) identifies the following – putting the respondent at ease, asking questions in an interested manner, identifying the key issues for the respondent, and developing these in a sensitive fashion.

The initial contact will establish the basis (or not) for easy communication. Respondents may feel easier and freer to discuss issues in their own home (possibly elders) or in an anonymous cafe (possibly the homeless). The respondent's willingness to respond may be affected by others who are present, such as a partner or carer, or by the knowledge that the information will not be anonymous and may be shared with others, as in a case conference. Equally important is the consideration of the age, gender and ethnic background of the respondent and the interviewer. The interviewer is either limited or helped by their gender, apparent age, background, skin colour, accent and so forth. Failure to take such factors into account may lead to an unwillingness to respond or a superficial response from the respondent (Matsuoka, 1993).

The structure of the interview format will vary but usually the interviewer has some agenda and specific issues will need to be covered. Given that we are concerned with getting individuals to express their own beliefs and views it is important not to ask questions which are subtly leading. In some interviews pictures, scenes or objects can be introduced for discussion or sorting. This can be a particularly useful technique with individuals who are reticent or unable to communicate verbally, such as some people with learning disabilities (Chapter 11). There is considerable scope for developing techniques of this type to identify desires and beliefs. For example, pictures of ideal meals could be used with frail elders in residential accommodation to help them identify their preferences. Having something concrete to respond to often enables the participant to air their own views more explicitly.

Qualitative interviews often require the interviewer to frame questions on the spur of the moment. They need to be framed in an understandable manner and in a way that will elicit detailed responses and not simply a yes/no response. If you ask a widower whether he was happy with the service he received after his wife's death the response could easily be yes or no without further expansion. Rewording the question and asking about what happened after his partner's death allows for the development of many more themes to discuss. Further, there is a need to establish what is central and salient to the respondent. Some authors have referred to tapping these ideas as identifying the irreducible core of the respondent's beliefs. The aim is to investigate beneath the clearly structured life view that is commonly presented. Often skilful probing will be essential to seek elaborations, details and clarifications. It is important to realize that the flexible approach used in some interviews will limit the generalizability of the data. This kind of exploration serves as a technique for improving our conceptualization of a problem or considering the process involved in a particular situation.

Specific probing often yields different responses to the more general responses with which respondents begin. In a recent study (Dockrell *et al.*, 1993) carried out concerning safer sex most of the respondents stated spontaneously that they always practised safer sex. However, when respondents were carefully probed with questions referring to their own reports, many respondents recalled at least one recent encounter in which they had not managed to have safer sex. Examination of the social influences upon these unsafe encounters lead to an increase in understanding of the issues under investigation. A focus upon the gap between individuals' general attitudes and their specific views extends our understanding of the central themes. As a further example consider a recent investigation of a night sitting service for frail elders. Although it was a service that everybody was 'grateful to receive', only specific probing showed that some individuals needed to be visited in the night to be helped to the commode.

How faithful are the verbal reports provided in such interviews? Does the depth and subtlety that they provide allow for a reflection of the beliefs of respondents? Some cognitive psychologists have argued that verbal reports are not a good indicator of real thought processes (Nisbett and Wilson, 1977). It is argued that the reports are a biased, generalized reconstruction. However, more detailed examination has shown that verbal reports can be accurate reflections of the process under investigation if the individual is recounting a specific event or set of events (Ericsson and Simon, 1990). A parallel argument has been made by some social psychologists. Billig (1987) proposes that both the general and the specific levels of verbal data are useful since they investigate social interpretations and real situations, respectively. Accordingly the data that are collected serve different kinds of purposes. If we are interested in service users' views of specific activities then we must ask about specific activities; if we are interested in the extra support someone needs to manage in the community then we must ask them to describe a typical day and to document a specific case when things went wrong. A comment by a 95-year-old such as 'I'm so lucky with my GP, it's a shame I don't see him more often' should not be accepted as satisfaction with the GP service but clarified by identifying, in an uncritical fashion, what limits contact with the GP.

Gaps in interviews can be as informative as inconsistencies. Are topics being selectively omitted because of fear, embarrassment or politeness? A strength of qualitative analysis is that these gaps can be noted and analysed.

Inaccuracies of memory also should be considered. They can manifest themselves in various forms. As the lapse of time between an event and the interview increases, there is often an increase in the underreporting of information about the event. Omission is coupled with **telescoping**: an event is often reported to have occurred more recently than it did owing to the compression of time. Inaccuracies in memory may also reflect the importance of the events to the individual. Events which are highly salient to the individual tend to be reported more accurately than less salient events (Cannell *et al.*, 1977). It is extremely difficult for the researcher to decide *a priori* what is a salient event. There is likely to be individual variation with respect to saliency.

Group interviews

Many of the issues discussed above are also relevant to group interviews or focus group discussions. Group interviews are widely used in market research for testing reactions to new products. They allow the possibility that the discussions between individuals will spark off new ideas, criticism or developments (Chapter 15). A serious problem with group interviews is that one person dominates either by restricting the topics for discussion or dominating the discussion themselves. Minority members of the group may be hesitant to offer a different or alternative perspective. Oppenheim (1992) suggests that leading such groups requires special talents and experience to allow a lively discussion to occur without excluding any of the group members. Collecting the data from group interviews requires planning. If someone is taking notes they will have difficulty participating. Special microphones will be required if the interview is being taped.

Observations

A final word must be said about observational data and the collection of field notes. It can be argued there is no better way to understand a problem or issue than to observe it oneself. There are a variety of approaches to observation and participant observation. Wolcott (1988) distinguishes three different kinds of participant observation styles: the active participant, the privileged observer, and the limited observer. According to this framework the active participant has a job to do in the setting in addition to the research, the privileged observer is someone known and trusted and given easy access to information, and the limited observer asks questions and attempts to build trust over time but does not have a public role other than researcher. There are, in addition, attempts at observation where participation is actively avoided. In these cases observation occurs using standardized observation tools (for example Beasley *et al.*, 1989). However, even in these cases the observer is likely to influence the nature of the interactions that are being observed.

The important point to raise here is that while observation can provide rich data for interpretation, **how** one collects those data, **what** situations one chooses to observe, and the **position** one takes as an observer will critically influence both the data and the behaviour of the participants. Consider a case of observing nursing care on a hospital ward. Collecting data between 9 am and 5 pm will produce a different kind of information from that which is collected between 5 pm and 9 am. Choosing to observe in a residential home for the elderly but eating meals with the staff may equally provide a skewed view of what kind of service is being provided and what kinds of experiences the users have. Coming in as the head of a service to record the practices of day-care staff will elicit different data to an unknown observer. Each of these contrasts highlights the fact that the notes taken and situations observed will depend both on the observer and the observed.

ANALYSING THE TEXT OR: WHAT DO I DO NOW?

The qualitative approach produces a mass of data and there are few shared ground rules among researchers about how to proceed with analysis. Unlike the questionnaire, qualitative material is not structured. The structure that follows is imposed on it or drawn out of it by the researchers themselves. Most researchers agree that some analysis of data should occur during, rather than after, the collection stage. This can direct the research towards issues that were previously not considered. Initially there will be an attempt to categorize the data in some meaningful fashion. If, for example in a study examining professional contact with vulnerable clients, it is found that certain types of professional gain access more often, an attempt can be made to try to understand the processes that lead to this occurrence.

As in all stages of the study the initial themes to be identified in analysing the data will depend on the purpose of the enquiry. Impressions will be gained and subheadings decided upon. Typically the researcher will look for concepts or categories and try to map the relationship between categories. With qualitative data one can preserve the chronological flow, assess local causality and derive fruitful explanations (Miles and Huberman, 1984). Some basic rules for dealing with qualitative data are listed below:

- Analysis of some form should start as soon as data is collected.
- Make sure to index what is collected.
- Identify themes and codes as they emerge, putting in more rather than less as a first stage.

- Try not to be mechanical; keep notes and memos on why codes are added or eliminated.
- Use a filing system to sort the data (preferably a computer package for qualitative analysis). In any case, be prepared to recode extensively.
- There is no right way to analyse data so a rigorous and defensible system is essential.
- The aim is to take apart or dispose of the data under various themes and codes, and then reassemble it to give a picture which is useful to the enquiry. (After Robson, 1993.)

Qualitative data can be analysed in several different ways. Tesch (1991) has identified a range of different types of analysis; three are pertinent in this context. The first she describes as **language orientated**. Here the research is focusing on the usage of language and the meanings of words or the content of text as a process of communication. How are situations described? What examples are chosen to provide information? There are other methodological considerations to analysing texts, be they in the form of diaries, case notes or critical incidents. Content analysis is a way of analysing material that is recorded, sometimes for another purpose, such as the minutes of meetings. It is a way of extracting meaning from text and has been used to identify biases and prejudices. For example, Stockdale (1994) presented an analysis of charity posters. Her analysis identified perceptions of handicap and the differentiation between forms of physical and mental disability and the implications that exist for behaviour towards individual disabilities which society deems as handicapping.

The second type of analysis is characterized as **descriptive**. Here the research intent is to gain insight into the phenomenon or situation under study and provide a systematic and illuminating description of it. This is the most common use of qualitative techniques in user interviews. Chapter 11 uses this approach to discover how users felt about the transition from family home to individual living. Descriptive approaches allow us to consider in greater depth how different interests and actors conflict. Analysis of the mismatches that occur in the text and identification of hidden messages are important analytic tools in such cases. Wilson (1993) identified the following examples:

User (referring to nurses on a geriatric ward): 'You could see they didn't enjoy their work. They were not dedicated, not dedicated.'

Interviewer: 'How was it in ... ward?'
Son: 'Oh she won't want to talk about that.'
User: 'They're all very nice in there and they do their best. That's the answer you want dear.'

In these cases the emphasis is on the meanings inherent in the text rather than the words per se.

The third type of analysis identified by Tesch is described as **theory building**. Here the aim is to identify connections and explain the reasons for these connections. The interpretation is not restricted to an analysis of what is the case, but also why it is the case. This allows development of a set of explanatory propositions. Explanatory propositions are statements about relationships, such as: X exists because Y; given X, then Y will follow; X is necessary but not sufficient for Y to occur; X causes Y (Miles and Huberman, 1984). Consequently, the researcher's first goal in such an analysis is to find the entities that will be called X or Y. In fact the whole point of theory construction is to 'produce concepts that seem to fit the data' (Strauss, 1987). If we consider models of compliance with health messages, we know that knowledge about a particular risk factor or illness is necessary but not sufficient for the key behaviour to change. Besides accurate knowledge, attitudes and beliefs are critical factors in altering behaviour. There is, for example, ample evidence that although people tend to be able to describe widely known risk factors for HIV and may be moderately well-informed, they tend to weigh these factors differently in applying them to their own and other's behaviour. Moreover, the likelihood of taking further action to reduce 'risky behaviour' is influenced by the social nature of HIV-risk behaviours. The careful mapping of respondents' statements allows connections to be identified.

EXTENDING THE ANALYSIS

The qualitative techniques outlined above provide the basis for considering service users' perspectives, needs and beliefs. Mixed methods provide us with a means of extending our analysis and interpretation. These designs generally include at least one quantitative method (designed to collect numbers) and one qualitative method (designed to collect words; Greene *et al.*, 1989). Mixed method investigations can serve several purposes – triangulation, complementarity and development. In the classic sense triangulation seeks convergence, corroboration and correspondence of results across different method types. A complementarity purpose is suggested when qualitative and quantitative methods are used to measure overlapping but distinct facets of the phenomenon under investigation. Results from one method are meant to enhance, illustrate or clarify results from the other. In development designs the different methods are used sequentially; that is, a study might begin with in-depth interviews, go on to use a large scale survey and finish with participant observation. The results of one method are used to help develop or inform the other (Chapter 10 provides an example of this approach).

Another technique for extending our interpretation is **negative case analysis**. This is a situation where a single case does not fit the patterns identified so far and thus challenges the accepted explanations of the phenomenon under investigation. Each of these approaches allows for a more comprehensive view of users' beliefs and perspectives to be developed. Such studies would serve as a good basis to service planning and development.

CONCLUSION

This chapter has considered some ways users' views can be investigated. Case studies give an entrée to variables and research questions concerning individual naturally occurring entities, whether these are individual people, groups, organizations or whatever. They allow an examination of current events and concerns and provide theoretical generalizations. Qualitative techniques provide the researcher and practitioner with a set of tools that allow consideration in depth of the views and attitudes of service users in these situations. However, the richness of data and depth of understanding which such data allow hide the complexity of the techniques and analysis. There is no prescriptive formula for the analysis of qualitative data and this very fact often leads to objections of reliability and validity. While there are presently many aids to data analysis and interpretation the investigator needs to be aware of the different ways of drawing conclusions and the acceptability of the chosen approach.

How can the investigator be sure that the processes identified are worthy of consideration? The concepts of reliability and validity that dominate quantitative analysis have been, to some extent, replaced in qualitative analysis by alternative notions (Lincoln and Guba, 1985). Particularly important for understanding and interpreting the results of investigating service users are the notions of **credibility** and **confirmability**. Credibility entails that the enquiry was carried out so that both the description of the study and the selection of the topic were adequate. Throughout, this chapter has considered the ways in which qualitative studies can be evaluated as credible or not. Confirmability means that it is possible to assess whether the conclusions from the study flow from the data and to decide whether the findings are consistent with other data sources. Much important information can be gained from good qualitative studies both in understanding a particular situation and generating ideas for further studies. The research enterprise must be carefully considered in advance to avoid useless and possibly wrong analysis and interpretation.

REFERENCES

Beasley, F., Hewson, S., and Mansell, J. (1989). *MTS: Handbook for Observers*, Centre for the Applied Psychology of Social Care, University of Kent, Canterbury.
Billig, M. (1987) *Arguing and Thinking: A Rhetorical Approach to Psychology*, Cambridge University Press, Cambridge.

Britten, N. and Shaw, A. (1994) Patients' experience of emergency admission – how relevant is the British Government's Patient Charter? *Journal of Advanced Nursing*, **19**, 1212–1220.

Bromley, D. B. (1986) *The Case-study Method in Psychology and Related Disciplines*, Wiley, Chichester.

Bruner, E. M. and Kelso, J. P. (1980) Gender differences in graffiti: a semiotic perspective. *Women's Studies International Quarterly*, **3**, 239–252.

Calnan, M. (1989) Control over health and patterns of health related behaviour. *Social Science and Medicine*, **29**, 131–136.

Cannell, C. F., Oksenberg, D. and Converse, J. (1977) *Experiments in Interviewing Techniques*, Report 78/7, National Centre for Health Services Research, Hyattsville, MD.

Cronbach, L. (1975) Beyond the two disciplines of scientific psychology. *American Psychologist*, **30**, 116–127.

DHSS (1983) *National Health Service Management Enquiry* (Griffiths Report), Department of Health and Social Security, London.

Dockrell, J. E. (1989) Meeting the needs of the parents of children with speech and language difficulties. *Journal of Child Language Teaching and Therapy*, **5**, 146–156.

Dockrell, J., Gaskell, G., and Rehman, H. (1990) Challenging behaviours: problems, provisions and 'solutions', in *Treatment of Mental Illness and Behavioral Disorder in the Mentally Retarded*, (eds A. Dosen, A. Van Gennep and G. J. Zwanikken), Proceedings of the International Congress, 1990, Amsterdam, The Netherlands. Logon Publications, Leiden, The Netherlands.

Dockrell, J. E., Joffe, H., Blood, L., Dockrell, W. B. and Dockrell, M. (1993) Sex, HIV and AIDS: behaviours and beliefs of sexually active young people – heterosexuals, gay men and male sex workers, in *Talking About It: Young People's Sexual Behaviour and HIV*, (eds A. Glanz, D. McVey and R. Glass), Health Education Authority, London.

Ericsson, K. A. and Simon, H. A. (1990) Verbal reports as data. *Psychological Review*, **87**, 215–251.

Greene, J. C., Caracelli, V. J. and Graham, W. F. (1989) Toward a conceptual framework for mixed-method evaluation designs. *Educational Evaluation and Policy Analysis*, **11**, 255–274.

Lebow, J. (1982) Consumer satisfaction with mental health treatment. *Psychological Bulletin*, **91**, 244–259.

Lincoln, Y. S. and Guba, E. G. (1985) *Naturalistic Inquiry*, Sage, London.

Matsuoka, A. (1993) Collecting qualitative data through interviews with ethnic older people. *Canadian Journal on Aging*, **12**, 216–232.

Miles, M. B. and Huberman, A. M. (1984) *Qualitative Data Analysis: A Source Book of New Methods*, Sage, London.

Nisbett, R. E. and Wilson, T. D. (1977) Telling more than we can know: verbal reports on mental processes. *Psychological Review*, **84**, 231–259.

Oppenheim, A. N. (1992) *Questionnaire Design, Interviewing and Attitude Measurement*, Pinter Publishers, London.

Robson, C. (1993) *Real World Research*, Blackwell, Oxford.

Runyan, W. M. (1982) *Life Histories and Psychobiography*, Oxford University Press, New York.

Sheppard, B. (1994) Homeward bound. *Health Service Journal*, **104**, 5425.

Stockdale, J. E. (1994) The self and media messages – match or mismatch, in *Representations of Health, Illness and Handicap* (eds. I. Markova and R. M. Farr), Harwood.

Strauss, A. L. (1987) *Qualitative Analysis for Social Scientists*, Cambridge University Press, Cambridge.

Tesch, R. (1991) Software for qualitative researchers: analysis needs and program capabilities, in *Using Computers in Qualitative Research*, (eds N. Fielding and R. Lee), Sage, London.

Wilson, G. (1993) Users and providers: perspectives on community care services. *Journal of Social Policy*, **22**, 507–526.

Wolcott, H. (1988) Ethnography research in education, in *Complementary Methods in Research in Education*, (ed. R. M. Jaeger), American Educational Research Association, Washington DC.

<table>
| 4 | # Working with interpreters: access to services and to user views |
</table>

Working with interpreters: access to services and to user views

Rosalind Edwards

Using interpreters is an essential first step in allowing service users who do not speak English to express their views and needs, but it is not a simple uncomplicated procedure. Issues of power and meaning present problems in collecting and analysing data. Racism may be combined with differences in class, age and gender to limit access to services and affect the way user views can be gathered. There are also important differences in language and belief systems within ethnic minority groups which need to be taken into account. This chapter combines practical advice on ways of using interpreters as a resource (acknowledging the interpreter) with an extended discussion of the situation of service users with limited competence in English.

This chapter highlights language competence in two ways. Outlined first are some of the ways that, in Britain, speaking little or no English can affect both people's use of and participation in services. Secondly, the ways in which language competence can affect evaluations of services that draw on user perspectives on service design, delivery and quality are examined. Researchers need to be aware of the ways that lack of a shared language between themselves and interviewees can combine with their own preconceptions to distort their understanding of interviewees' accounts. This happens when gathering in-depth qualitative accounts, and also when framing quantitative survey questionnaires, although the former is concentrated on here.

In Britain (other than in parts of Wales and Scotland perhaps), English is the language of general communication and, importantly, the language of access to many resources, such as education and employment, as well as to health and social services. The world of those with little or no English is significantly structured by the possibilities of communication. As Ahmed (1991) notes:

'Unfortunately the language barrier has been one of the most oppressive factors in denying many black and minority ethnic families their right to services, simply because the service agencies are not able to communicate with them in their own languages ... . Linguistic skill is an essential pre-requisite of social work and other caring professions, without which they can neither communicate nor provide an effective and sensitive service.'

Where service provider and service user, or researcher and interviewee, do not speak the same language, verbal understanding cannot take place. Communication is only possible with the presence of an intermediary – an inter-preter.

Here, language competence is considered together with the need for working with interpreters on a variety of levels: national and local, familial and male/female, and also within the research process. It is argued that a thoughtful consideration of the issues involved in working with an interpreter, whether as a service provider, practitioner researcher or outside evaluator, can greatly enhance service delivery and evaluation. Specifically, a model is put forward that treats interpreters as active and key informants within the research process.

LANGUAGE, POWER AND ACCESS TO SERVICES

In Britain, service providers and researchers are usually white English-speakers, and those who do not speak English well, or at all, are likely to be refugees or immigrants from a variety of minority ethnic groups. There are over 1.5 million adults in Britain whose first language is not English, and about one-third speak little or no English. Some areas of the country have greater concentrations and ranges of minority ethnic groups and languages than others. For example, Pakistanis form 1% of the population of England but 17% of this group live in the West Yorkshire area (forming 4% of the area population). Nearly 60% of these live in the Bradford district (forming just under 10% of the district population). Bangladeshis form nearly one in four (23%) of the population of the London Borough of Tower Hamlets, with a broad range of other minority ethnic groups. The North Norfolk district, however, has no recorded Asian population and only 0.1% of each of a small range of other minority ethnic groups (OPCS, 1993).

LANGUAGE COMPETENCE

More specifically with regard to language diversity, research in the London Borough of Merton revealed an identified need for interpreting facilities for at least 17 different languages (Baker *et al.*, 1991). The London Borough of

Lambeth conducted a survey of all pupils in nursery, primary, secondary and special schools, which revealed a range of 115 different languages among children whose first language was not English (Lambeth Education Department, 1992). Sixteen of these languages were each spoken by over 100 pupils.

The Lambeth survey also indicates how the distribution of languages in an area may change over time. Between 1983 and 1991, the number of Yoruba-speaking pupils rose by over 400%, to become the most common language other than English, while those speaking Greek almost halved.

Britain, however, like many other Western countries, is not a multilingual society in the pluralist sense. As has been said of Australia:

> '... it is simply not true that there is a colourful equality to languages here. Language and society cannot be separated. Language is always an integral part of the social process and, as such, most obviously in terms of effective social participation, the dominant language of state and public participation is more than equal to other languages in any particular national or local context.' (Kalantzis *et al.*, 1989)

The interaction between languages (and dialects within these) is social and political – part of the establishment and maintenance of hierarchical relations. Access to the dominant language gives individuals and groups power over their own affairs and an ability to define and influence the affairs of others. They are able to shape society to serve their own ends. Competence in the English language (and particular forms of it) is one of the ways dominant groups in society are able to retain their powerful and authoritative position, and maintain groups with little or no access to resources, including English language competence, in a subordinate position. Those without access to the dominant language have difficulties in defining and drawing attention to their needs and influencing society to meet them (Cameron *et al.*, 1992; Corson, 1990).

RACISM

Racism and language disadvantage can combine to place disproportionate numbers of those who do not speak English in deprived sections of the population. There are links between English language disadvantage and social inequality and deprivation in terms of income, employment, housing, health and educational achievement. As a result, there are 'strong indications' (Baker *et al.*, 1991) that welfare services are faced with an increasing need to work with people who have little or no English. Yet language competence affects the takeup and effectiveness of benefits and services that may, to an extent, alleviate social deprivation. Those who most need to register with and draw on the services of health practitioners, housing and social security departments, and so on, may be least able to do this because of language difficulties (Baker *et al.*,

1991; Edwards, 1993a; Kalantzis *et al.*, 1989; London Research Centre, 1992 give examples).

Of course, difficulties with communication cannot be reduced to little or no English language competence alone (Chapters 10–12). Poor communication between service providers and users can be a source of dissatisfaction for members of any ethnic and language group. Even proficient English speakers can feel they are not listened to by professionals (consult Ley (1983) and Chapter 5 of this volume with regard to hospital and GP patients). Moreover, competence in the English language is no shield against racism for groups such as Afro-Caribbeans.

Nevertheless, people with limited English who are also members of racialized minorities are likely to be doubly disadvantaged. An inability to communicate in a language that is not their own can make them even more vulnerable to institutional racism than are English-speaking members of ethnic minorities. Such racism in service provision is argued to include inadequate interpreting facilities (Rocheron, 1988). Additionally, little seems to be done to rectify such language disadvantages in Britain in terms of English as a Second Language tuition. Public funding for such language and literacy classes is patchy or poor (House of Commons Home Affairs Committee, 1986). In April 1994, the government cut by a quarter its contribution to the Section 11 programme, which enables local education authorities to provide specialist teaching to children whose first language is not English (*The Guardian* 15.3.94).

Moreover, other European languages are accorded greater prestige and status than, for instance, Asian or African languages spoken by large resident minorities. There are numerous examples of this. Baker and colleagues (1991) report that the ability to speak both English and, say, Urdu was not recognized as a potential vocational asset under the British government's Employment Training Scheme, and training for bilinguists to develop interpreting skills and obtain professional interpreting qualifications was not forthcoming. There was also an original intention not to include minority ethnic languages such as Gujerati or Tigrinean on the list of modern foreign languages for the National Curriculum, as opposed to the inclusion of French, German and Spanish. The ability to communicate in languages other than those of Western industrialized nations is often seen as an obstacle to integration rather than a useful skill – one reason for the cut in government funding, in America, for first-language education other than English (Kalantzis *et al.*, 1989).

DIVISIONS BETWEEN AND WITHIN MINORITY LANGUAGE GROUPS

English language competence is not equally distributed within minority ethnic groups for whom it is not their first language. Among Asians in Britain, for example, there are substantial numbers of people who are poorly educated, but there are also very well-educated segments. In one large-scale national survey, around a quarter of Asian adults overall were found to have left school before the age of 13 or had no schooling, while another quarter had continued their education into their 20s (Brown, 1984).

Variations within the Asian language groups are also striking with, for example, over 60% of Bangladeshis having been found to speak little or no English, as opposed to under 30% of Indians (Brown, 1984). (While the most comprehensive data on language competence are around a decade old (Brown, 1984), more recent smaller studies of particular localities show there has only been a slight improvement in the situation – for example the Linguistic Minorities Project data cited in Baker *et al.*, 1991). These differences primarily reflect the variable socio-economic background, education and status opportunities available to them both in their countries of origin and in Britain. They do not appear to be mitigated by the length of time spent in Britain either (Brown, 1984).

Gaps in social class and position between members of ethnic groups are often overlooked. A conception, for example, of Asians as a whole, which can be an aspect of racism, can lead to such divisions being ignored. It is from amongst the well-educated within a particular minority language group that we usually draw interpreters. As Rocheron (1988) points out, a sizeable number of doctors from the Asian subcontinent are, and have been for many years, working in the NHS. While Asian professionals have had to deal with racial discrimination within services, they have also formed alliances with their while middle-class counterparts, sharing the same values and concepts. As mentioned below, this can raise difficulties when recruiting and working with interpreters in research exploring service users' experiences and perceptions.

AGE AND GENDER

There are also other divisions in circumstances and experiences within minority ethnic groups. These are often related to social class, but they are also related to gender and age. Even within families where men have good jobs and there is adequate income and housing, women may be disadvantaged and controlled by their inability to speak English. In fact, there is a parallel between language distribution and the literature on the inequitable distribution of other resources within households (e.g. Brannen and Wilson, 1987). Within minority ethnic and language groups, it is men who are likely to speak, read and write English better than women. Three-quarters of Bangladeshi women were found to speak little or no English, as opposed to half of Bangladeshi men, for example (Brown, 1984). Additionally, younger people are likely to be more proficient than older people. Just under half of those in linguistic minority groups who speak little or no English are aged 56 or over (Baker *et al.*, 1991).

It is largely women as mothers, daughters-in-law and so on who care for others within the home. They also may need to mediate with state and other (English-speaking) health and social services on behalf of those they care for or for themselves as carers. Family and caring responsibilities and notions of a woman's place, as well as fear of racist attacks outside the home, can mean that women are consigned to the domestic sphere. This limits their ability to attend what few English language classes there are, more so than men. Compounding this, the home can be regarded as the place where their 'mother-tongue' is kept alive for children, rather than English competence being passed on to mothers and older family members (Brown, 1984; Kalantzis *et al.*, 1989). Sexual politics also play their part: men can be threatened by their wives' desire to learn English (Rockhill, 1987). (Seeing women who gain an education for themselves as threatening to their male partners is not confined to minority ethnic groups (Edwards, 1993b).)

AVAILABILITY AND USE OF INTERPRETERS

From the above considerations it can be seen that if service planners and providers, and researchers evaluating services, are to hear the voices of some of the most disadvantaged members of British society (particularly women and elders), they will usually need to work with interpreters.

There is, however, an acute lack of permanent in-house interpreters in primary health care services (Edwards, 1993a; Mayall and Foster, 1989), in antenatal services (Mayer, 1983), in housing departments (London Research Centre, 1992), and social services departments (Baker *et al.*, 1991), as well as the criminal justice system and immigration appeal hearings (Council on Tribunals, 1991). Users may be asked to return to a service, either at a time when an interpreter can be brought in on a sessional basis or when they can bring somebody to interpret for them. The latter course is dependent on service users having a network of bilinguists available to them. Again, men and younger people are more able to meet people outside the home and cultivate such networks. Women and elders may have to rely more upon other family members. The latter, as mentioned below, are often regarded as least suitable to act as interpreters.

Apart from an increased availability of interpreters, several solutions to language competence difficulties have been put forward, particularly within the health field. While it is important for non-English speakers living in Britain to learn English, it is felt that more professionals could be recruited from linguistic minorities (Fuller and Toon, 1988; Karseras and Hopkins, 1987). Additionally, it is suggested that those service providers who are not from these groups should be encouraged to learn minority languages. There are also moves towards having interpreters who take on a more active advocacy role, not only aiding interpersonal communication but also representing particular ethnic groups of service users in identifying problematic institutional procedures and resource allocations (Baker *et al.*, 1991; Rocheron, 1988).

RESEARCH LITERATURE

Within the social research field, there is very little discussion of either the use of interpreters in specific research projects or in general. Yet, as Mayall (1991) has pointed out, few academic researchers are from minority ethnic groups. This is also the case amongst service providers, including practitioners who have turned researcher in order to consult groups of service users about their views. The design and execution of evaluative research projects is thus unlikely to be in the hands of those who can speak minority languages, let alone incorporate particular minority group perspectives into the work. Indeed, researchers some-times omit minority ethnic groups from studies for the sake of homogeneity, whether they speak English or not. Those examining aspects of caring for chil-dren, elders or disabled people who do include minority ethnic groups, may or may not interview English-speaking respondents only; it is often difficult to tell from the accounts of their research. Exceptions which mention that non-English speakers have been included and that interpreters or sessional bilingual inter-viewers have been employed do exist (Currer, 1986; Mayall, 1991; Mayall and Foster, 1989; Mayall and Grossmith, 1984; Rockhill, 1987).

When researchers, other than anthropologists, have used interpreters, they do not appear to have written much about the experience. (The anthropological literature largely refers to situations where the interviewee's mother-tongue was the dominant language in the region or country concerned.) However, there is a small body of literature concerned with interpreters in the welfare services, especially that related to delivering health services (including Baker *et al.*, 1991; Freed, 1988; Fuller and Toon, 1988; Karseras and Hopkins, 1987).

CHOOSING AN INTERPRETER

Most of the available advice on using interpreters focuses on choosing them and managing their use in specific provider–user situations. There is much concern over the accuracy of interpreters' translations. Interpreters are regarded largely as a necessary evil (Fuller and Toon, 1988) – not used out of choice but because there is no alternative. Later, this chapter puts forward another view of the inter-preter's part in the process of gaining access to user perspectives in research; one that is more akin to the active and positive role of advocacy in service provision.

A hierarchy of the suitability of the social characteristics of interpreters is often provided by those writing on the subject (Freed, 1988; Fuller and Toon, 1988; Karseras and Hopkins, 1987). In particular, there is stress laid on interviewee and interpreter being of the same sex, as well as on the interpreter having a non-familial relationship with the interviewee – children are regarded as especially unsuitable. The aim is to ensure the confidentiality of the interview; to avoid the interviewee feeling constrained in discussing particular family or personal details; and/or to avoid misrepresentation of the interviewee's account by the interpreter because they feel it is embarrassing or discreditable. Obviously much of this will depend on the topic under discussion and the particular social conventions concerning the areas of life that are appropriate for discussion with particular categories of people in terms of sex, age and so on. For example, women may find it difficult or shameful to talk about aspects of their health and bodies with male interpreters or, indeed, with male service providers.

PROFESSIONAL INTERPRETERS

Trained interpreters and qualified professionals are often seen as most effective in avoiding many of the potential problems of confidentiality or misrepresentation just outlined. However, as discussed earlier in this chapter, there are likely to be wide educational and social class differences between interpreters or professionals and service users. These could affect users' ease or confidence in discussing certain issues. They may feel that some of their beliefs or practices are frowned upon by those of a higher social class or status within their ethnic group.

Where no service in-house interpreters are available, interpreters can be employed on a sessional basis either via agencies that provide interpretation services or bilingual professional workers or key people in a locality can be drawn on from the particular ethnic groups being studied. There are pros and cons to each source. On the one hand, for example, an outside (e.g. agency) interpreter may have to spend time establishing their credibility with interviewees. But on the other hand, interviewees are not dependent on maintaining a good relationship with them in some way, which may be disrupted by or disruptive to the research process. Professional workers or prominent people can have a lot of power within an ethnic group in a local area, and, for better or worse, they have specific sorts of investments in a relationship with users of services or those living in a particular locality. On the one hand, a local community worker may have a strong commitment to finding out about and promoting the interests of those they work with, whatever these may be. On the other hand, they could threaten to withdraw support from an individual or family if agreement to taking part in research is not forthcoming, and may have strong and known views on the appropriate interests of those they seek to represent. Viewing the interpreter as a visible and active part of the research process, however, as elaborated below, can allow for this and can have positive aspects.

INTERPRETING SKILLS

Whoever is to act as interpreter, bilingual skills are important. Those who hold a brief for the development of recognized training and qualifications for interpreters in low-status languages are especially concerned to point out that the ability to hold conversations in two languages is not the same as an ability to act as an interpreter:

> '... listening for meaning and conveying it accurately, fluently, clearly and at the appropriate speed are skills which have to be learnt and developed over time.' (Baker *et al.*, 1991)

The conventional way of testing such language skills is by means of a process known as **back translation**. In this, a text relevant to the research is prepared in English and is then translated into, say, Somali by one interpreter, and the Somali version is subsequently translated back into English by another interpreter. The two versions are then compared and discussed (Baker *et al.*, 1991; Mayall and Grossmith, 1984). It is also possible to apply a similar procedure to taped interviews, with different interpreters producing their own version of the exchanges.

MATCHING CONCEPTS

All of this begs the question of matching languages generally. No single correct translation from one language to another is possible; rather, there are only more or less approximate versions. Even the best approximation may be difficult to produce in the heat of an unstructured interview. The relationships between language, knowing, agency and self, which are integral to people's accounts of their perceptions and experiences, are variable constructions, and form a whole field of study in themselves. For example, it is difficult to imagine a correspondence between Marathi in which there is no concept of generalized people, i.e. 'they' (Fielding, 1993), and languages that do have such a conception.

Evaluations of services may also impose the cultural framework of assumptions that one language embodies upon another framework. The notion of faithfulness of translation can ignore the hierarchical status and power relations between languages and their respective speakers, referred to above, and between their conceptual schemes of reference (which may have gendered aspects; Chamberlain, 1988). For example, Western principles of self-determination and individualism can often be inappropriate in understanding the perspectives of service users from India. Corporate notions of mutual obligations and duties are more likely to be stressed than individual rights.

So, the very logic of service users and of participation, embodied in much evaluative research, may carry assumptions that can be inappropriate and misplaced. This is true in both asking questions of particular minority language speakers during interviews, and in representing the data collected from them within such a conceptual framework. For example, teachers or doctors may be held in high esteem and viewed as having a duty to perform a service which users have an obligation to receive, an attitude which is a way of maintaining the social relations within a community. Individual decision-making over, and evaluations of, the content and delivery of a service in this context is inappropriate; it is the overall maintenance of group social relations that is the issue.

INTERPRETERS IN QUANTITATIVE SURVEYS

The matching of interpreter and interviewee referred to earlier, in terms of social characteristics, may not be regarded as such an important issue when drawing up questionnaires. Nevertheless, many of the points made above with regard to matching languages and conceptual frameworks – as well as many of the points made below – are relevant.

Interpreters – or, more correctly, translators – are obviously necessary when a postal questionnaire is to be translated into several languages. However, they may also play a role when the survey is to be conducted in English. In both cases, interpreters/translators can check whether or not questions are framed with ethnocentric assumptions that could be (mis)understood in varying ways within different cultural conceptual frameworks. This may be the case for those respondents who have enough language competence to answer an English language survey, as much as it is for those who will require a questionnaire delivered in their mother-tongue. For example, asking respondents from minority ethnic groups whether or not they should be treated in a special way when accessing health and social services does not take account of varying meanings that may be attached to the notion of 'special treatment'. Nor does it take account of what this may imply for respondents within the context of a racist society.

Careful piloting of survey questions (Chapter 2) is even more essential when they are to be delivered to a range of ethnic groups. In framing survey forms, the assumptions underlying questions must be critically examined prior to distribution, as well as in analysis. This is all the more important in the context where surveys and numerical presentation of data may be regarded as carrying indisputable hard scientific weight. However, as Oakley (1992) has shown, using the illustration of infant birthweight, the nature of such quantifications is intimately linked, conceptually, with qualitative judgements. The wider role for interpreters described below is thus as relevant for quantitative user surveys as it is for in-depth qualitative studies.

INTERPRETER ACTIVITY/PASSIVITY

In addition to linguistic abilities, and even if the interpreter is a professional, there is usually mention within the literature on working with interpreters of the need to understand that their role is to assist. A continuum of interpreter activity/passivity in the interview or consultation process is often posited. There are the two extremes, whereby the interpreter either acts completely independently and controls the interview or simply translates words and nothing more. The ideal is said to fall between the two extremes, although nearer to the passive end:

> 'The interpreter is a conduit linking the interviewer with the interviewee and ideally is a neutral party who should not add or subtract from what the primary parties communicate to each other. At the same time, the interpreter must inform the interviewer or interviewee when a question or comment is unclear or is culturally unacceptable. In addition, the interpreter must select carefully the words to use.' (Freed, 1988)

The presence of an interpreter adds a third person to what, typically, is a one-to-one provider–client or interviewee–researcher relationship, but the idea seems to be to bypass or disguise this. The view of the interpreter as, variously, a conduit, mouthpiece or agent for transferring messages is widespread. It is exemplified both in the commonly used phrase 'working through an interpreter' and in much of the model picture of the interview situation. For example, a triangular seating arrangement is recommended for interviews, so that the service provider (or researcher) remains a part of the exchanges non-verbally and psychologically, with the provider or researcher addressing remarks and questions directly to the interviewee and not to the interpreter (see, for example, Freed, 1988; Fuller and Toon, 1988). Additionally, interpreting in the first person (I am satisfied) rather than the third person (She says she is satisfied) is regarded as the mark of a trained interpreter (Baker *et al.*, 1991). Interpreters **are** a presence, and an essential one, where service provider or researcher and service user do not speak the same language, and their role can be viewed more positively.

ACKNOWLEDGING THE INTERPRETER

While not dismissing much of the valuable advice given on using interpreters, an alternative perspective on this is to work with, rather than work through interpreters. Many feminist researchers (for example Oakley, 1981) and others have criticized the unconscious bias of the paradigm of traditional interviewing practice. In this the interviewee is regarded as an object of study – a collection of social data variables, as determined by the researcher – and the interviewer is held to be a depersonalized and uninvolved data-collecting instrument, without social characteristics. They have called for a recognition of both the researcher (or service provider) and the subjects of research as parts of a larger social whole. That is, as people with social characteristics that give them particular positions in society, and which place them in a socially structured relationship to each other.

This call for the social relations of research to be acknowledged and made explicit can be extended to encompass and understand interpreters not only as an interactive part of the interview situation but as part of the whole research process. Rather than regarding the interpreter as a necessary but unwelcome mediary, whose effect must be ignored or minimized as far as possible, their presence can be made clear – not as a form of apology for an inability to conduct research in the conventional one-to-one manner, but built upon in a positive manner to add further insights to analysis. The same can be said for many interviews conducted by health and social care staff as part of service delivery or service evaluation.

PUTTING ACKNOWLEDGEMENT INTO PRACTICE

Working towards giving the interpreter personhood and visibility can take place in a variety of ways. It is important that interpreters feel able to translate fluently in whatever class of personal pronoun comes most easily to them – whether this is first or third person or a mix of the two. Translation in the third person, however, does not allow the interpreter to be a hidden part of data collection, especially when directly quoting from a user's account in written material in order to illustrate a point. In addition to making it clear that an interpreter was part of the process of gathering user views, this practice also has the advantage of highlighting an important aspect of such users' access to and use of health and social services and many other social resources and public services – that for the most part they can only do so with the aid of another person who speaks both their own language and English. The medium for their use of services (an interpreter) becomes reflected within the evaluation when the presence and role of an interpreter in the research is made explicit.

Interpreters' activity during the interview does not necessarily have to be regarded as something to be damped down as far as possible and confined only to pointing out cultural transgressions, as appropriate, during interviews. When working with or researching the perspectives of ethnic and language groups other than their own, service providers and researchers may define a topic (but as many chapters in this book indicate, they will do better to incorporate user perspectives early in the research process). Nevertheless, during the exploration of that topic, the bases on which providers and researchers make decisions as to which avenues of a user's account are relevant, and which to pursue or follow up, are not necessarily more informed than those of the interpreter.

In fact, this point applies to any research concerned with people's perceptions, and to any social interactions. There can be misjudgements and misunderstanding on the basis of differences in terms of language and ethnicity, and because of racism. However, distorted understandings can also be related to differences based on age, gender, sexuality, class and professional training, as well as individual factors. Listening carefully to people's experiences and perceptions, on their own terms, is a skill that requires careful and reflective development (Chapter 3). But the lack of a shared language and the need to work with interpreters points up this issue especially clearly.

With regard to interpreter interventions or activity during interviews, an induction or training process for interpreters is often advised. This is to arrange the format of interviews (who does the introductions, initial explanations and so on), and to sensitize interpreters to their role and to the aims and objectives of interviews. Similarly, at the end of each interview a debriefing process, where the interview is jointly reviewed and evaluated, is recommended (Baker *et al.*, 1991; Freed, 1988; Karseras and Hopkins, 1987). The fact that researchers and others who need to work with interpreters might also need some training in this is not usually posited (Baker *et al.*, 1991, being an exception to this), other than using the induction to gain knowledge of relevant cultural factors from the interpreter.

Trust in the interpreter's skills, as well as a more relaxed stance towards their role in the interview process, is likely to develop if researchers or service providers work regularly with particular interpreters. As already mentioned, however, interpreters are most often employed as short-term sessional workers, both in service areas and on research projects, which can militate against building such relationships.

INTERPRETERS AS PART OF THE RESEARCH PROCESS

The ways that an interpreter's role can be built upon within the wider research process are now considered. Interpreters need not only work in narrow behind-the-scenes ways, as in merely interpreting during interviews or providing relevant cultural feedback. They can form an overt part of the research process, as key informants.

All interpreters, as well as researchers, bring their own assumptions and concerns to the interview and research process, whether they are professionals or not – as indeed do the interviewees whose views and experiences are sought in research or service evaluation. Interpreters' own priorities and understandings need to be made explicit, not only as part of the process of making their involvement visible. They can provide pointers to, and can be explored as, part of the social context in which service users live their lives. This can be especially relevant in terms of interpreters' own contact and negotiations with service providers. Are there particular issues in access to or receipt of services that interpreters come across repeatedly in the course of their interpreting work?

Are there any difficulties that they experience for themselves in accessing or receiving services, despite their English language competence?

Interpreters themselves should be interviewed as part of the research and asked about their own experiences, their relationships to the ethnic groups they work with, and the issues they see as important in relation to the research questions. Treating the interpreter as a key informant can enrich research. Here, however, the confidentiality and anonymity usually extended to research participants should also be extended to interpreters. When it is likely that an individual can be identified by others as the person who was acting as interpreter for a particular project, their consent should be obtained before reproducing any details about them or their views in writing within a report or publication.

CONCLUSION

In research on service users, the framing of research questions, the design and method of collecting data and their analysis are largely integrated processes. Research goals, and the consequent use of particular methods of gathering data, depend on particular assumptions about what knowledge is – the way we come to know about and understand people's views and experiences on a certain topic.

The ideal, therefore, would seem to be to build the employment of interpreters into the duration of a user survey. Such a step is expensive and one of the costs most likely to be omitted in attempts to gain funding. In any case, working with interpreters will mean time and money. At the very least, as suggested above, interpreters should be enabled to make a far wider contribution to research than that of merely being present for interviews. This can only enhance attempts to gather together and understand user perspectives on service design, delivery and quality.

REFERENCES

Ahmed, B. (1991) Preface, in *Interpreters in Public Services: Policies and Training*, (eds P. Baker, Z. Hussain, and J. Saunders), Venture Press, London.

Baker, P., Hussain, Z. and Saunders, J. (1991) *Interpreters in Public Services: Policies and Training*, Venture Press, London.

Brannen, J. and Wilson, G. (eds) (1987) *Give and Take in Families: Studies in Resource Distribution*, Allen and Unwin, London.

Brown, C. (1984) *Black and White Britain: The Third PSI Survey*, Policy Studies Institute, London.

Cameron, D., Fraser, E., Harvey, P., Rampton M. B. H. and Richardson, K. (1992) *Researching Language: Issues of Power and Method*, Routledge, London.

Chamberlain, L. (1988) Gender and the metaphorics of translation. *Signs*, **13**(3), 454–472.

Corson, D. (1990) *Language Policy Across the Curriculum: Multilingual Matters*, Clevedon, Avon.

Council on Tribunals (1991) *Annual Report 1990/91*, HMSO, London.

Currer, C. (1986) Concepts of mental well- and ill-being: the case of Pathan mothers in Britain, in *Concepts of Health, Illness and Disease: A Comparative Perspective*, (eds C. Currer and M. Stacey), Berg, Leamington Spa.

Edwards, R. (1993a) *Evaluation of the Department of Health's New Under Fives Initiative Homeless Families Projects*, Report for the National Children's Bureau, South Bank University, London.

Edwards, R. (1993b) *Mature Women Students: Separating or Connecting Family and Education*, Taylor and Francis, London.

Fielding, N. (1993) Interviewing, in *Researching Social Life*, (ed. N. Gilbert), Sage, London.

Freed, A. O. (1988) Interviewing through an interpreter. *Social Work*, July/August, 315–319.

Fuller, J. H. S. and Toon, P. D. (1988) *Medical Practice in a Multicultural Society*, Heinemann Medical, Oxford.

House of Commons Home Affairs Committee (1986) *Bangladeshis in Britain*, First report from the Home Affairs Committee, Vol. 1, HMSO, London.

Kalantzis, M., Cope, B. and Slade, D. (1989) *Minority Languages and Dominant Culture: Issues of Education, Assessment and Social Equality*, Falmer Press, London.

Karseras, P. and Hopkins, E. (1987) *British Asians' Health in the Community*, Wiley, Chichester.

Lambeth Education Department (1992) *Pupil Survey 1991*, Policy and Planning Unit, London Borough of Lambeth.

Ley, P. (1983) Patients' understanding and recall in clinical communication failure, in *Doctor–Patient Communication,* (eds D. Pendleton and J. Hasler), Academic Press, London.

London Research Centre (1992) *Refugees and Asylum Seekers Accepted as Homeless by London Local Authorities*, Housing Information Supplement No. 4, LRC, London.

Mayall, B. (1991) Researching childcare in a multi-ethnic society. *New Community*, **17**(4), 553–568.

Mayall, B. and Foster, M-C. (1989) *Child Health Care: Living With Children, Working For Children*, Heinemann Nursing, Oxford.

Mayall, B. and Grossmith, C. (1984) *Caring for the Health of Young Children Vol. II*, Department of Health and Social Security, London.

Mayer, L. (1983) *A Pregnant Pause? Communication Between Women Whose First Language is Not English and Antenatal Clinics in Paddington and North Kensington*, Paddington and North Kensington Community Health Council, London.

Oakley, A. (1981) Interviewing women: a contradiction in terms, in *Doing Feminist Research*, (ed. H. Roberts), Routledge and Kegan Paul, London.

Oakley, A. (1992) *Social Support and Motherhood*, Blackwell, Oxford.

OPCS (1993) *1991 Census: Country Reports*, OPCS, London.

Rocheron, Y. (1988) The Asian Mother and Baby Campaign: the construction of ethnic minorities' health needs. *Critical Social Policy*, **22**, 4–23.

Rockhill, K. (1987) Literacy as threat/desire: longing to be SOMEBODY, in *Women and Education: A Canadian Perspective*, (eds J. S. Gaskell and A. T. McLaren), Detselig Enterprises, Calgary, Canada.

Low expectations reinforced: experiences of health services in advanced old age

5

Gail Wilson

This chapter reports on user experience rather than user satisfaction. Experiences are important since they can influence the propensity to complain. If a service is known to be bad why expect it to be otherwise? The aim of the project was to listen to older people as they spontaneously reported their experiences of health services. The group interviewed ranged in age from 75 to 96. They were fitter than the average for the area, but as a group they were high users of health services compared with younger people. Very few people had any complaints but the majority recounted experiences which appeared to the researchers to indicate poor service. Insensitivity and ignorance were commonly encountered when dealing with professionals. Poor communication, lack of respect and failure to understand the living situations of people in advanced old age were reported as widespread among hospital and primary health care staff. Ageism appeared to be very common and to contribute to the experience of poor services in many different ways. Most staff are presumably unaware of this aspect of their practice. Surveys of users based on the staff perspective are thus unlikely to pick it up.

This last chapter in Part One provides background detail on the way that one group of users experience health services. In this study users were not asked directly about their services. Instead they offered information spontaneously in the course of discussions of their everyday life. In the total sample (67 households composed of people over 75), 20 (29%) were not interested in health or were neutral in their views of health services, five (7%) were wholly positive and 42 (63%) were negative, but these included six people who had also had positive experiences. It is possible that service users from younger age groups in the same area might have recorded more positive experiences, but equally they might not. Certainly they would not have been as vulnerable as these high users of health services.

The report is confined to a small group of people over 75 but there is no reason to believe that the experience of people in the other main community care client groups would be very different. People with learning disabilities or with mental health problems suffer from negative stereotyping by society in much the same way as older people. The problems of access and communication recounted are likely to be even greater for some members of ethnic minorities (Chapter 4) and for people with learning difficulties (Chapters 11 and 12).

The aim of this chapter is to illustrate, through individual accounts, a reality which accompanies the low expectations so often found in research on elderly service users. It has first to be said that health services in London are widely acknowledged to be worse than in many other parts of the country. As Martin *et al.* (1992) point out, the effects of the Resource Allocation Working Party which redistributed funds away from London between 1976 and 1988, combined with years of general underfunding of the NHS (Robinson and Judge, undated), have reduced morale throughout the London health services. In addition, the mismatch of beds and needs, caused by the presence of large teaching hospitals and shifts in population, has resulted in acute services which are not well adapted to their local populations. In primary health care the number of small practices and older doctors also worked against a quality service (Acheson, 1981). The experiences of elders in other parts of the country may therefore be better than those reported below. It seems unlikely, however, that they will be **very** much better because ageism and resource shortages are common in virtually all parts of the health service.

The research contrasted two different areas (wards). One of the wards was almost entirely middle class and the other was a large council housing estate developed in the 1920s and 1930s. A sample of households consisting only of people over 75 was selected by calling on every fifth dwelling and asking if the occupants met the sampling criteria. Basic information on household composition, age, tenure and social class were collected about each eligible household and they were asked to join the study. Reasons for refusal were noted. In each area those who refused did not differ from those who accepted in terms of age, class or ethnicity, but refusals were concentrated among the very frail, the most disabled and the most angry. Working class elders were more likely to fall into those categories and more likely to refuse (48% as against 33% in the better off area). The resulting sample is therefore biased in favour of those in better health, with more money and more content with their lifestyle. Table 5.1 shows the number of households in each area and the breakdown by sex.

The only ethnic minorities in the sample were from Europe. This reflects long residence and low housing mobility among elders in both areas and the fact

Table 5.1 Composition of households interviewed

Households	Men	Women	Total
Working class area	11	25	30
Middle class area	14	32	37
Total	25	57	67

that most ethnic minority elders were still below the age of 75 in 1991 when the study began.

The results set out below can be taken as representative of the experiences of very old people in the two areas, except that differential refusal rates have worked to make the picture more positive than a completely random sample would produce. Greater ill health and greater poverty were associated with worse experiences of health services so the responses are biased in favour of the experiences of middle class healthier service users. Since the sample was small and London health services are poor the results are not directly applicable to the rest of the country. They may, however, be taken as pointers to the possibility of poor services for people from socially disadvantaged groups across the country. The experience of poor services makes complaints less likely because it is hardly worth complaining about something that is not going to be changed.

THE INTERVIEWS

The interviews recorded one aspect of consumer response to health services. The subject of the interview was daily life and coping strategies. Interviews were semistructured and allowed respondents to talk about the things that they thought were important. In 61 cases out of 67 recent experience of the health services was mentioned as one aspect of daily life. The interviewers did not initiate any discussion on GPs, hospital treatment or any other aspect of the health services. Direct questions were confined to whether a respondent had slowed down in the last year and whether their home was conveniently sited for getting to the GP's surgery. However if any aspect of health or treatment was spontaneously mentioned it was followed up. Stories of recent experiences were encouraged.

The interviews were transcribed and analysed using the Nud*ist computerized qualitative analysis package (Richards and Richards, 1991). This package is a great advance on cut and paste methods of content analysis. Blocks of text can be grouped in a complex series of ways, in this case concentrating on health, hospitals, doctors and other medical personnel. Secondary processing enables the text to be recategorized or regrouped into concepts or classes such as positive, negative or neutral. Theories can be developed and rigorously checked against the data.

SERVICE PROVISION

The sample in the working class area (30) was served by a number of practices of varying sizes, a health clinic with a geriatric health visitor, and a small district general hospital with an off-site geriatric ward. Specialist treatment was available in inner London teaching hospitals. The middle class sample of 37 households was served by a large and prestigious health centre and a number of smaller practices. Most in-patients went to one inner London teaching hospital.

CLASSIFICATION OF RESPONSES TO HEALTH SERVICES

As other chapters show, older people are usually recorded as being extremely content with the services they are offered. Such findings are highly likely when direct questions are asked (Chapter 2). However, even in unstructured interviews positive responses should not always be taken at face value. As Cornwell (1984) pointed out, there are conventions in the way the health services (or any free service) are spoken of. Middle class researchers can usually be identified with some aspect of the welfare state. They are likely to be treated according to social conventions of politeness and hospitality and will be told that services and staff are good or very good. In this analysis such expressions of approval were taken as being neutral unless they were backed up by an example, a comparison or in some other way that showed that what was being expressed was real approval rather than politeness. The response categories of no interest, positive, neutral and negative are defined below.

Older people with no interest in the health services

In seven out of 67 interviews there was no mention of health or medicine other than to note that the GP was nearby. In one of these cases a widower was suffering from long-term depression but had not mentioned the fact to his GP and appeared to have no other health problems. In one a retired GP insisted that he had no health problems, and his wife was unwilling to talk about hers. In the other five cases the respondents were more concerned with other things and were fit enough to pass over any discussion of health. These interviews where health was not mentioned offered no way of interpreting the attitude of respondents to their doctors or other health services. They may have been completely satisfied or they may have been among those who tried never to go to a doctor.

In addition to those who made no spontaneous mention of health services, the sample contained six cases who stated that they never went to a doctor or tried not to go to the doctor (including one who had given in and found that she could be helped). Although these are negative cases they cannot be counted as being critical of the service because it is possible that their attitude would be maintained however good the service and however positive their experiences.

Approval (positive and neutral)

In 12 interviews nothing but approval was voiced in relation to doctors or other aspects of the health service. However, the praise was specifically targeted rather than polite in only five of these cases. Possibly more people intended their remarks to be taken as approving but there was no way of knowing whether they were being polite or positive. They are counted as neutral. All but one of those who were clearly positive were in the middle class area. One couple explained how good the health centre was and specifically mentioned that the personnel were friendly and did not tick you off so there was no need to feel nervous going there. Another stressed that having tests at the centre was good because it saved the journey to the hospital. One woman singled out a successful cataract operation carried out at a specialist hospital as the best thing that had happened to her in the past year. Another who had long been registered as disabled praised the physiotherapy she had been given.

Ranges of discontent

Discontent with health services was expressed in different ways. These have been classified below into: outright and specific criticism; unpleasant experiences recounted without comment; and approval followed by criticism. The respondents themselves identified lack of satisfaction only in relation to the first category – the specific complaints. Others may have intended to register dissatisfaction, but it was not the aim of the interview to insist on their being specific when they showed no wish to do so. Also, as with direct questions on satisfaction, there is no guarantee that the answers would not have been polite. The second and third categories of non-specific criticism are therefore research-led definitions which depend on the judgement of the interviewer.

Specific complaints

Complaints which were specifically attached to a service or a professional were rare. Some were relatively minor, though they could be important to individuals. For example one man identified:

> 'The only thing I'm really against with our GP ... we have to put our prescription in after 11 o'clock, but I really think you could put it in before. Sometimes I go out early you know and I usually bus home. You can collect it at any time but you can't put it in till after 11. Otherwise they're very good.'

In this case administrative convenience, perhaps unthinkingly, has been put before the convenience of patients.

Other such complaints were more serious. A daughter reported that she had changed her mother's doctor 'because I am convinced Dr — is really anti old people'. One local hospital is described as 'diabolical, it really was. I didn't have a bath all the time I was in there, which might not have bothered some people but it bothered me.' Another daughter was convinced that her mother's dementia had been caused by long-run barbiturate addiction, supported by a GP from outside the area.

Unpleasant experiences

Much more common than specific complaints were stories of encounters with health professionals or with hospitals which were not identified as complaints by respondents. For example, one woman was admitted with very high blood pressure and her husband had to follow because he could not stay alone. She said:

> 'So the ambulance came twice, first for me and then for him ... . Every afternoon they brought him in a wheelchair to visit me. It caused quite a stir in the ward, especially when he came in with the nail clippers and put his feet up on my bed. I've got a thing up me nose, something in here and for me to do his toenails. Cos you know he didn't think. He knew I was there and his toenails hadn't been cut. ... then of course instead of giving me a chance to recuperate, when they decided **I** was fit enough to come home, **he** came home. You know, if I could have had a couple of days to re-establish myself, but we both came home together.'

'No complaints'

There was another group of patients who specifically said they had no complaints or praised the services they had received and then went on to recount unpleasant experiences. For example, an 80-year-old woman explained what happened following a hip fracture:

> 'They took me in [to hospital] then and there, because I'd been under them for 9 years and they've been very very very good. Very good, short of nurses, but the doctors do try. And they're still very good, fortunately, and being an old patient they do try. ... I was keen to come home. More or less towards the end I couldn't take it. Eight weeks is such a long time. It was just like a nightmare to me and um although when I go back, I have periodical appointments and I went for an infusion just for 6 hours and which is a great help, but I don't think they could do that very often with all the, with the injections I have ... . They just go by the book and what the book says they try. They go by their medical book, but it doesn't help a lot, it doesn't help everybody. However they were nice, they soon got me back, they tried with a frame and it got worse, they soon got me back to bed and I got a sore bottom and sore heels and it was all very sad.

Gradually over those weeks, because I spent Christmas in there and I got food poisoning on top of it. It was a lovely turkey dinner and I was very unfortunate. Two or three got a little food poisoning but I was worse, everything attacks me worse. And they thought at first it could have been salmonella but however it lasted three or four days with certain capsules they gave me and um, that wasn't very nice, Christmas day ... .'

In another case an 82-year-old man fell in the snow and was taken in to casualty but later sent home. He said:

'But um the treatment there was quite good I had no complaints. They said it was a hairline fracture [in casualty] first of all. I went in and came out, and after a week it was so painful that I had to go back. At the end of the week I said to the sort of doctor I saw, a young man, I said this is driving me crazy I said, there's something wrong here. So I had some more X-rays and he came back and says "Well it's a little worse than what we thought but we'll have to put it into plaster" so down I went and put in plaster and have an arm stuck out like this (horizontal, bent at the elbow), came home and I said to my wife, I said to her, "There's something wrong". I couldn't sleep. I said "There's something wrong here, something badly wrong".

So I stuck it for the week when I had to go back and soon as I walked in I saw Mr — then, a tip top feller that. "Oh" he said "Operation right away", downstairs and in ... . And then after the operation I got into bed. They had these irons, that's the only complaint I had, they had these irons on the side. They were too high so I said to the sister, "Can we have one of these irons off?". So she said "No they're there in case you get out of bed". So I said I want to get out of bed. Me feet and my legs are all right, it's me arm. I said I can go to the toilet, I can wash, I can have a shower, I can manage meself, I said, without anybody, but they wouldn't do it. She wouldn't do it. So consequently when I wanted to get up in the night, by the time, to get out of bed with these irons, it took all the skin off me legs, [laughs] so – and once you knock skin off when you get old it takes a long time to get it back, doesn't it. So I thought to meself well this is it. So instead of going to bed at the night time I used to get a, I had a eiderdown thing, and wrap it round my shoulders and sleep in the chair, couldn't be bothered about the bed. [I. Didn't they mind?] Nobody came. At the — [Hospital]. Nobody came, nobody.'

He went on to recount how after a week of inattention he had threatened to discharge himself, how he lost weight because the food was delivered in plastic containers and removed before he had time to open them with one hand, and how he was finally discharged at 8 am on a Saturday morning with no transport. The treatment had left him permanently crippled, unable to raise his arm above shoulder height and unable to use his right hand properly. It is impossible to know whether his condition was inevitable or whether a correct diagnosis at the outset would have enabled him to continue the active life he had previously led.

A variant on the theme of no complaints was the backhanded compliment. For example one woman said:

'It annoys me when people will pull — Hospital to pieces ... . They can't stand and listen to all your history there like some of these do want. They can't do it. Now at — [geriatric] they could stand and have a chat with you, see, but you don't get that kind of help from — Hospital. But I've always found over the years they've been very kind.'

Aspects of poor service

Experience of general practice has been analysed separately from experiences of other health services. Table 5.2 shows that only four interviews produced wholly positive responses about GPs.

Table 5.2 Experience of GP services

Response	Working class area	Middle class area	Total
Not mentioned/not recorded	12	14	26
Neutral	7	9	16
Favourable	0	4	4
Unfavourable	11	11	22
Total	30	38*	68*

* Includes one interview where good and bad experiences were recounted.

Inaccessibility and fear of deregistration

GPs who were inaccessible, either because their patients had become increasingly frail or because patients had been assigned to them following the retirement of a previous GP, were tolerated. The reason usually given was that it was impossible to change doctors in advanced old age. There appeared to be a widespread belief, even in the middle class area, that GPs would not accept new patients in this age group. It was not always borne out by experience. As one single woman of 78 said:

'I talked to people about it, and they said, oh the centre, the health centre down there, is full up and you won't get in, and they don't take you if you're getting on in years, and I thought, blimey I've listened to all these people all this time and now I'm going to find out for myself.'

She had no problems.

Evening surgery meant that the doctor was inaccessible in winter for older people, particularly women, who would not go out in the dark. One woman had managed to change doctors for this reason. It was not clear what others did when they needed to see a doctor in winter.

The feeling that old people were not wanted and should not impose was even more prevalent in the working class than the middle class area. The view that the doctor should not be bothered for the inevitable ailments of old age was reinforced by a fear of being taken off a GP's list. A very arthritic woman in constant pain said:

'The doctor, it just seems as if she can't be bothered. I haven't seen her for about 6 months. They can't be bothered with old people. I'm afraid to go to her because I'm afraid she would take me off the books and that, and who else would take me on at 87? [laughs] No one. Oh if you're too much trouble they cross you off.'

INSENSITIVITY TO SOCIAL CONDITIONS

As well as being unable to communicate or receive information, doctors or hospitals were also recorded in four cases as being out of touch. For example, one GP did not apparently realize that a blind 80-year-old woman might have difficulty in taking herself to casualty in an inner London hospital on a Sunday. GPs assumed neighbours would rally round after early discharge or when a patient was to some degree homebound. GPs were also recorded as being ignorant of Social Service procedures and hence ineffective at getting community care support. As Table 5.2 shows there was relatively little difference in response patterns between working class and middle class areas. Such differences as there were indicated more experiences of poor service in the working class area. People who spontaneously praised their GPs were all in the middle class area. It is impossible to know whether these differences are the result of chance, of genuine variations in service standards or whether they reflect different propensities to complain in the two samples. Other research that indicates poorer services in working class areas would support the finding of differences in standards of service (Anderson and Mooney, 1990).

HOSPITAL AND COMMUNITY HEALTH SERVICES

Table 5.3 summarizes responses on other aspects of health services, mainly experiences of hospitals but also of physiotherapists (two favourable mentions) and community nurses.

As can be seen, other aspects of the health services, particularly hospitals, attracted more comment than did GPs. This was especially true of the working class area. Negative experiences were more numerous. Positive experiences, where they existed, were in all but one case balanced by negative experiences.

Table 5.3 Experience of hospital and community health services

Response	Working class area	Middle class area	Total
Not mentioned/not recorded	7	16	23
Neutral	4	5	9
Favourable	6	3	9
Unfavourable	18	13	31
Total	35*	37	72*

* Includes five interviews where good and bad experiences were recounted.

AREAS OF POOR SERVICE

Table 5.4 Key areas of poor service identified by respondents

Poor service category	Working class area	Middle class area	Total
Misdiagnosis/Chronic iatrogenic disease	8	8	16
Poor communications	10	5	15
Long waits	5	4	9
Ageism	3	5	7
Poor discharge procedures	2	5	7
Total mentions	28	27	55
Total households	30	37	67

Note: some respondents identified more than one area of poor service. Some mentioned good aspects of services.

Table 5.4 shows that experiences of poor service were common to both working class and middle class areas but that working class households either had more to complain of or were more likely to mention bad experiences. The data might also be interpreted as indicating that the more complex health problems and lower personal and community resources in the working class area imposed a greater burden on services. The added burden may then be reflected in higher rates of negative comment.

Table 5.4 shows 16 cases of misdiagnosis or medically induced chronic conditions which were spontaneously reported. Some of these cases would probably not have been classified as iatrogenic by medically qualified personnel, but the focus in this paper is on the patient's interpretation of events.

Equally, since this was not a health status survey, some examples of iatrogeni-cally induced conditions or of poor diagnosis will have been overlooked.

One example where the patient's view might well have been contradicted by a clinician was a man whose leg had been amputated. He felt that the hospital ought to have tried removing only his toe first, as they had on his other leg. The quality of his life had been very greatly reduced and he had been given no acceptable reason for such a major operation. In another case a woman was convinced she had picked up her oral thrush (which caused great misery and restricted her diet) at a dental hospital and had found it was incurable. Two women suffered from ulcers brought on by earlier medication. Another had recurrent internal bleeding as the aftermath of radiation treatment.

Poor communication exacerbated many of the problems that these older people had with the health services. Working class respondents mentioned prob-lems of communication with health professionals more than twice as often as middle class patients. In 15 cases, poor communication was mentioned as caus-ing extra worry or worsened health. One man, who stopped taking his medica-tion, said that the doctor only told him that he had to take pills for his heart condition for the rest of his life after he had a second heart attack. It seems likely that a computerized prescription system would have indicated when such a prescription was not being renewed, but the practice did not have one.

In at least four cases patients were unable to communicate their needs to their doctors. One who could barely walk because of pain in his feet struggled up to surgery when called for his annual old age health check:

'He wanted to test my health, to see whatever was right you know. But the thing I was asking him about was my feet, you know, but he was not interested in that. No. He had a book there and there were questions on the book and he asked me one question after another ... . I could answer all the questions but the soles of my feet are dreadful. You'd think a doctor would try, innit, send me to the hospital for things, examine you.'

This man was further upset because the doctor asked him his next of kin and he felt the health check was measuring him up for his coffin. He reported that the doctor did look at one of his feet but made no comment. Another woman, nursing a dying husband, had been greatly relieved to leave communication with the doctor to the district nurse. She herself felt too intimidated to bother the GP but had confidence that the nurse would call him when medically necessary.

Waiting

Long waits were accepted but nine cases were recorded with three mentioned as being particularly stressful. A woman had waited with her husband for 8 hours outside a ward after he had been admitted as an emergency but no bed was available. Another woman had been 8 hours in casualty after a locum had prescribed aspirin although she was unable to speak and had a splitting headache. A stroke was diagnosed in due course. Her daughter had insisted that she went to hospital and remained with her. Another emergency admission needed 9 hours in casualty and the daughter, possibly unfairly, dated her mother's deterioration from that time. She felt that her mother's growing panic attacks and loss of memory had been caused by the great stress of being in casualty so long with no information and an inability to eat or drink (the reason for admission).

Ageism

Ageism is hard to pin down. Almost all the experiences classified in Table 5.4 and many of the other complaints about the services could be linked to ageism. However, it can also be argued that old people are subject to the same shortages and effects of low morale as any other consumers of health services. For this reason ageism was only recorded when it was specifically mentioned or when it was clearly implied. First, there was a widespread belief among respondents that doctors could not be bothered with old people and (among some middle class respondents) that they did not give the service they used to. Respondents had been denied treatment on grounds of age. Perhaps more important, there was evidence that they supported their own marginalization and failed to bother doctors or remained registered with inaccessible GPs when they could have changed. The data do not allow charges of ageism on the part of health services to be proved or disproved but they give evidence that ageism was seen by patients as a problem.

The class difference in experience of ageism might well be significant if it were repeated in a larger sample. It could be argued that working class elders have never experienced social power or very much respect from health professionals and hence record no change. On the other hand, many members of the middle class have had high social status and better treatment from the health service. When, in old age, they fail to get it they may notice and recount the difference.

PATIENTS, CONSUMERS OR SERVICE USERS

It is fair to ask whether very old people have access to an adequate health service. There was no evidence that people over 75 in the two survey areas did. Deficiencies in one or more areas of communication, discharge from hospital, confidence that they would be respected by professionals and access to some forms of treatment were reported by two-thirds of the sample. The incidence of bad experiences and the very wide variety of discontents suggested that the NHS was not providing the type of service that people needed in advanced old age.

Health services, either in the community or in hospitals, were not developed with an ageing population in mind. The very old belong to one of the patient groups that have made up the 'Cinderella services' since the early years of the NHS. This sample illustrates, in individual terms, the suffering and incapacity caused by the long-term failure to meet the needs of this growing client group.

CONCLUSIONS

The interviews were not in any way a survey of patient satisfaction. Internal evidence strongly suggests that most respondents would have said they were satisfied with the health services if the question had been asked directly. Information on health services was spontaneously presented, with and without comment. The data highlight the effects of ageism in society and indicate the handicaps of access and communication which affect disadvantaged groups – handicaps that are largely taken for granted by all. The accounts given make it possible to argue that it is not surprising that older people have low expectations of services. The data show that, for one group of users at least, poor service was the norm and that there was little to raise their expectations and, if they had previously been used to better service, a great deal to lower them.

Rapid discharge from hospital is likely to be a problem for any group of users but possibly more serious for elders. Difficulty of access to services affects all users who are not fully mobile or who do not have access to good publicity material for any reason. Problems of communication with profession-als are likewise felt by nearly all non-professionals, but are probably more acute for people in disadvantaged groups. Status differences are related: while the people in this sample looked up to doctors, they still wished to be treated with dignity by health and social care workers. However, when their experiences were bad they made allowances rather than considered complaining or chose to suffer in silence.

The study showed that the method of wide-ranging semistructured interviews is unlikely to be much use to those researching user satisfaction or trying to improve services. The broad focus threw up a very wide range of researcher-defined problems, but not all of them would have been listed as sources of dissatisfaction by the users. Also, the range was so wide that it would be hard to focus on one aspect of service and justify prioritizing it for improvement. A more targeted or focused approach would be needed, say to consider all aspects of hospital discharge or to work towards setting up procedures for a better chiropody service.

If, as seems likely, the experiences recounted above make up the reality of poor services for marginalized groups, it is not surprising that community care recipients are so often able to overlook poor service and answer satisfaction questionnaires positively. A range of sayings can describe the situation: 'It is no used crying over spilt milk', 'What's least said is soonest mended', and so on.

In other words why add to the stress of an already stressful existence by complaining about things that are perceived as unalterable? Researchers who get positive answers from service users should be aware of this background to their work.

In addition, a user survey that starts from the point of view of service providers is likely to miss the bad experiences that users regard as inevitable. The study suggests that only a very narrow range of users' experiences are accessible to satisfaction surveys. Work which really wants to find out about experience should start from a different point.

ACKNOWLEDGEMENT

The field work on which this chapter is based was financed by the Nuffield Foundation.

REFERENCES

Acheson, D. (1981) *Primary Health Care in Inner London: Report of a Study Group*, London Health Planning Consortium, London.

Anderson, T. V. and Mooney, G. (1990) *The Challenges of Medical Practice Variations*, Macmillan, London.

Cornwell, J. (1984) *Hard Earned Lives*, Tavistock, London.

Health Advisory Service (1983) *The Rising Tide: Developing Services for Mental Illness in Old Age*, HMSO, London.

Martin, P., Wiles, R., Pratten, B., Gorton, S. and Green J. (1992), *A User Perspective: Views on London's Acute Health Services*, King's Fund, London.

Richards, L. and Richards, T. (1991) The transformation of qualitative method: computational paradigms and research processes, in *Using Computers in Qualitative Research*, (eds N. G. Fielding and R. M. Lee), Sage, London.

Robinson, R. and Judge, K. (undated) *Public Expenditure and the NHS: Trends and Prospects*, King's Fund, London.

PART TWO

Service-Oriented User Surveys

Patients' opinions of hospital care and discharge

6

Dee Jones and Carolyn Lester

Surveys of large numbers of users can be expensive, particularly if they deal with complex issues. This chapter shows how a postal survey can be used to gather a large amount of basic information on user satisfaction relatively cheaply. As pointed out in Chapter 2, large-scale surveys need to achieve high response rates if they are to be valid and useful. The authors show that reminders and face-to-face visits for the few non-responders who have difficulty filling in the questionnaire can produce very satisfactory response rates at low cost, even with frail elders who have recently been discharged from hospital.

User surveys routinely produce very high levels of satisfaction and if managers are to get useful information from the results they need to start with areas of reported dissatisfaction. The authors show that even with highly satisfied users this approach allows areas for potential improvements to be identified.

STUDY BACKGROUND

The government's health service reforms (DHSS, 1989a) provided the impetus for this 1990 study of older patients' opinions of hospital care and discharge. The aim of the reforms was to run the NHS on efficient business lines, whilst at the same time improving the quality of patient care, with particular emphasis on choice, provision of information, communication between staff and patients, participation in decision making, and appropriateness of care both on admission and after discharge back into the community. Users' and carers' opinions of health and social services have been of increasing interest to policy makers as well as service providers in order to enable the development of primary and secondary care which are client-centred and more closely meet the needs of individual clients (Thompson, 1988; Cm 849, 1989).

The demands of efficiency require that patients should not remain in hospital longer than is necessary, and it has been recommended that many frail older people who currently reside in residential or nursing homes or long-stay hospital wards could and should be adequately cared for in the community among their family and friends (DHSS, 1989a). For frail older people to be maintained effectively in the community, it will be necessary for patients' ability to cope at home to be assessed thoroughly before being discharged and for appropriate and adequate home support in the form of nursing and home help/care services to be available in the community.

The interface between primary (community) care and secondary (hospital) care has been of particular concern, and criticisms of coordination and communication between them expressed. Clients should be able to be admitted into hospital and transferred back into the community with the minimum disruption of their care. Quality of transfer from hospital to the community has been a theme addressed by many studies (Skeet, 1970; Waters, 1987). Practice guidelines have been produced in order to implement seamless care, where users can transfer smoothly from one sector to another.

Previous research has used various methods including home interviews, hospital in-patient questionnaires, telephone and postal surveys. Some routine patient care questionnaires are oversimplified so as to be machine readable (Carr-Hill et al., 1989; Carr-Hill, 1992), and fail to give the users an opportunity to express their concerns fully. Telephone interviews, although they may achieve higher response rates (Kershaw 1987), may be socio-demographically biased because they are based on telephone ownership. Interviews and postal questionnaires have the advantage of enabling the researcher to use open-ended questions rather than satisfaction scales, which can overcome the tendency for the vast majority to appear satisfied because there is no opportunity for individual problems to be aired (Chapter 2).

Postal studies sometimes have such low response rates that they risk being unrepresentative of the total population they seek to investigate. This may be caused by an officious or impersonal covering letter, a questionnaire that seems irrelevant or an inefficient reminder system. If these pitfalls are avoided it is possible to achieve high response rates from postal questionnaires, particularly if help is offered to those who have difficulty in reading or completing forms.

This chapter describes a study which aimed to examine user and carer views of hospital care and transfer back into the community.

STUDY DESIGN

This study was based in three South Wales health authorities. It investigated older peoples' opinions of their recent experience of hospital care, discharge procedures and provision of after-care in the community. A random sample of 400 patients was drawn for each district, consisting of patients aged 65 years and over, who had been discharged from hospital in the previous 3 months. They were mailed a letter and a 12-page questionnaire. The letter explained the purpose and intention of the study, the possible benefits of the findings to service providers and future patients, and assured respondents of the independence of the research team and complete confidentiality and anonymity of the information they provided. A reminder letter was mailed to non-responders 3 weeks later, and those who had not replied by 6 weeks were visited and offered help with completing the form.

The questionnaire covered many different aspects of patient care: time on the waiting list, admission procedure, hospital cleanliness, hospital food, communication with staff, discharge procedure and provision of help after transfer to the community. Patients were also invited to comment in their own words on what they had liked and/or disliked about their care in hospital. They were also asked about the timeliness and appropriateness of the assistance they received at home from health and social services and voluntary organizations. Their unmet needs for assistance were also investigated. Open-ended and closed questions were used in the questionnaire; open-ended questions were mostly used to explore their opinions.

Patient response

Questionnaires were completed and returned by 960 (89%) respondents, of whom 438 (46%) were male and 522 (54%) female. There were no differences between the responses of those who were visited by a member of the research team and those who were not. The age range was 65 years to 93 years for men (mean 74 years) and 65 years to 98 years for women (mean 76 years). After being visited by a fieldworker 194 (20%) completed their questionnaire; these respondents were mostly visually or physically impaired so unable to read or mail the questionnaires. The main specialities from which respondents were discharged were: geriatric medicine (21%), general medicine (21%), general surgery (16%), ophthalmology (9%), trauma and orthopaedic surgery (7%) and urology (6%); the remaining specialities each comprised 2% or less of the total.

STUDY FINDINGS

Waiting time

Half of all respondents were categorized as emergency admissions but, of the remainder, 38% were admitted within a month of being told that they would need hospital treatment. The mean reported time on the waiting list was 5 months, but 34 patients reported waiting more than a year to be admitted.

Information and communication

The amount of notice of admission given to people who were non-urgent admissions ranged from 1 day or less to more than 1 week, and most patients said they were satisfied with this. It has been recommended that patients should be provided with more written information about the hospital before or on admission. Of the non-emergency patients three-quarters remembered receiving information about visiting times, and half remembered receiving information about the availability of optional extras which could be purchased. Other items of information recalled were: what patients should bring to hospital (64%), complaints procedures (30%), and procedures for making suggestions (27%). Some respondents commented that as they were admitted at regular intervals, it was unnecessary to provide information which they knew already.

Communication with staff, and the provision of medical information was much better, only 14 patients reporting that they had been given no medical information about their condition at all. Of those who had been given medical information, 73% thought that it was appropriate to their needs (as opposed to too little or too much) and 79% had found the information easy to comprehend. Nearly all patients considered nurses easy to communicate with, easier than doctors; only 3% finding difficulty with nurses and 5% experiencing difficulty communicating with doctors.

Hospital food

Hospital food has long been a subject of criticism and complaint and patients in this study were no exception. In closed questions on opinions of food, ratings of poor or very poor were given by 14% of respondents for quality, 18% for choice and 21% for suitability. In response to open-ended questions on likes and dislikes about their hospital stay (Table 6.1), 35 respondents were of the opinion that the food was unpleasant or poorly presented, and six diabetic patients claimed that their condition had been adversely affected by an inappropriate diet.

Some illustrative comments that were typical of many were:

- *Quality* – 'The food was cold by the time it reached B block – too far from the kitchens.' (Female aged 67)
- *Choice* – 'Until I asked for the menu, we were given what they thought we would like.' (Female aged 79)
- *Suitability* – 'Food was not appropriate for a diabetic and my blood sugar went up. There was lack of communication between ward and kitchen.' (Male aged 69)

Table 6.1 Patients' negative hospital comments (N = 960) – no negative comments were received from 70% of all patients

Comments	Number	Percentage
Just being in hospital	46	5
No medical explanation	14	
Poor medical care	13	
Delay in medical care	10	5
Attitude of doctors	7	
Poor pain relief	3	
Lack of nursing attention	17	3
No help with bath/toilet	15	
Unpleasant food	35	
Unsuitable food	6	4
General conditions on wards	27	
Night noise/lights	27	
Dirty or inadequate toilet	16	9
Dirty or inadequate bathrooms	8	
Mixed wards	7	
Day room conditions	3	
Disturbance by other patients	23	
No mental stimulation	14	
Cut-backs (short-staffed)	10	10
Privacy/students	10	
Visitor disturbance	7	
Miscellaneous	32	

Hospital cleanliness

Of those patients who expressed an opinion on cleanliness, 8% rated lavatories as poor or very poor, although only just over 2% thought that ward areas did not come up to standard. There were 16 patients who made specific comments about dirty or inadequate lavatory or bathroom facilities and the following is one of the more detailed comments:

> 'The toilets were clean every morning, but with patients unable to bend and sit after operations, they got very dirty by the end of the day. Also, bins got overloaded. I feel the toilets should be cleaned more than once daily.' (Female aged 68)

Negative comments about the hospital stay

When asked if they had disliked anything about their time in hospital, 30% of respondents made criticisms, some of which were attributed by them to cutbacks (Table 6.1). Some aspects of care about which respondents complained were lack of nursing attention and, more specifically, no help with bathing or toileting. One such complaint, which was typical, was:

'I would have liked my hair washed and I only had one bath in 2 weeks. I rang for help for toilet at 4.30 am and had to wait until 5.45 am until a nurse came.' (Female aged 74)

Several complaints related to organizational and environmental issues such as poor decor, uncomfortable beds, ward temperature, night noise and lights or poor day-room facilities. Some people were nursed on mixed-sex wards and eight of these had strong objections to this. There were also complaints about disturbances by fellow patients, for example general noisiness, smoking, and inconsiderate use of televisions. Other patients were also thought to have too many noisy visitors. The general opinion among those who complained of other patients and visitors was that nursing staff did not always ensure that hospital rules were obeyed.

There were a total of 47 complaints (under 5%) about aspects of medical care, including lack of explanation, poor or delayed medical care, attitude of doctors to patients and inadequate pain relief. Some examples of complaints relating to doctors were:

'Other patients could hear the consultant summing up your case – very embarrassing.' (Female aged 70)

'I particularly disliked the feeling of being ignored or being treated as if I were a young child.' (Female aged 67)

A more serious complaint about medical treatment was made during an interview with a lady who had failed to respond following mailed reminders. This was a 76-year-old whose discharge diagnosis was cancer of the uterus.

'I disliked the doctor's attitude. I had a very rough internal examination and was told that the pain was all in my mind. I bled for 3 days afterwards. Dr — said that he would explain everything before discharge, but he sent a junior who said that I was too old for the operation. Doctors should be gentle and have a better attitude. If someone says he will come back to see you, then he should do. My condition was not fully explained until I got to — hospital [radiotherapy centre].' (Female aged 76)

It would seem from this person's account that her cancer was probably too advanced for surgery, and that there was a reluctance to explain this to her. However, the first complaint about the insensitivity of the examining doctor seems reprehensible. It must be said that this type of complaint was very much in the minority.

Positive comments about the hospital stay

Most respondents (72%) took the opportunity of making positive comments about their time in hospital (Table 6.2), but the majority of these were very general, and referred to the kindness of staff and being well cared for (47%). There were 126 positive comments about medical treatment and a further 86 who said that the hospital was good or excellent.

Table 6.2 Patients' positive hospital comments (N = 960) – no positive comments were received from 265 (28%) of all patients

Comments	Number	Percentage
Caring to patient	448	47
Medical treatment	126	13
Generally good	86	9
Company of others	71	7
Hospital environment	40	4
Atmosphere	38	4
Rest	26	3
Short stay	15	2
Explanation to patient	11	1
Grounds, view	9	1
Near home	3	<1
Miscellaneous	16	2

Other aspects about which respondents made positive comments were companionship, pleasantness of the environment, good atmosphere, shortness of stay and good medical explanations. Some typical positive comments were:

'I felt I was afforded excellent treatment before, during and after my operation.' (Male aged 68)

' — [private hospital] is very expensive, but no better.' (Female aged 86)

'Nursing staff would do anything to make sure her stay was comfortable. Doctors would always explain any problems.' (Proxy for female aged 72)

ON LEAVING HOSPITAL

Discharge planning

Patients who discussed how they would cope at home usually did so with a nurse (35%) or doctor (20%), but just over a third did not recall discussing their discharge with anyone. Other members of staff reported as discussing discharge were social workers (11%) and occupational therapists (4%). In 52 instances, patients' homes were visited by hospital staff before discharge to assess suitability of their home environment and needs for care, and the majority of those visits were by an occupational therapist or social worker.

Notice of discharge and transfer home

Many patients had very little notice of discharge, with a third being told on the same day and 16% after visiting time the night before. There were 23% who were told before the previous evening's visiting time, 21% had up to 3 days' and 5% more than 3 days' notice. Some respondents (4%) felt that their relatives and friends had not had enough notice to make the arrangements necessary for discharge, and seven patients had to delay going home because notice was so inadequate. Most patients thought that they had been discharged at the right time, but 98 (10%) thought that it was too soon, and 27 (3%) thought that they had been kept in hospital too long. On leaving hospital, most patients made their own transport arrangements, but 151 were taken home by an ambulance or hospital car, the majority of whom (69%) were aged 75 years and over. Some examples of negative comments about the transfer home were as follows:

'They just told me I was going out and put me in an ambulance.' (Female aged 93)

'They tried to discharge him too soon, without fully explaining how to use the stoma bag.' (Wife of male aged 78)

Coping at home

Most patients were discharged to their own home (where they had lived before admission), but 41 respondents were transferred to long-term care (residential or nursing home). Other patients did not return to their previous residence: 7% went to live with a son or daughter, and 1% with other relatives or friends. Of those who were discharged home, three-quarters of the men but only 39% of the women lived with their spouse; the spouse was also more likely to be the main source of help for men. This reflects the lower life expectancy of men and hence the slightly higher age of women in the study. Women were more likely than men to live alone or with a daughter or son, and women were more likely to have a daughter as their principal source of help after leaving hospital. Patients also named other relatives and friends as sources of help. Very few (7%) named a statutory service as their principal source of help in the first week home from hospital, with 3% naming a home help and 2% a community nurse (or health visitor). There were 110 patients who reported receiving no help at all during their first week home, but many of these said that they had not needed help. Three months after discharge the proportions of those not receiving help had increased slightly to 16%, and the principal sources of help named were similar to those of the first week, but slightly more people were receiving assistance from the home help service.

Many respondents had encountered problems in coping since leaving hospital and help was not always provided. Some respondents who had received help before hospital encountered difficulty in having the service reinstated when they came home. Those who did receive help were often very appreciative, as were their carers. These are some examples of respondents' responses to open-ended questions about the after-care they received (or did not receive):

'We'd rather manage on our own. Don't want strangers in the house, but we could have done with some help with transport.' (Female aged 88)

'I can't get in and out of my bath, so I go to my daughter's three times a week for a shower, but have to be helped upstairs.' (Female aged 81)

'I had home help before hospital, but when I really needed help after discharge, I had to wait 2 weeks for it to start.' (Female aged 73)

'I liked the district nurse's prompt arrival and good supply of aids (e.g. sheepskin, special cushion).' (Wife of male aged 74)

STUDY CONCLUSIONS

In a previous study of hospital in-patients of all ages (Raphael, 1973), 90% had found hospital food satisfactory compared with the 86% of our elderly sample. Raphael also reported that 14% thought that lavatories were not clean enough compared to 8% in the present study but in the study contentment with all aspects of the hospital rose with age. One would therefore expect that this study of elderly patients would show greater contentment than studies of all ages. Where lower or similar rates of satisfaction were found, it is possible that standards for this sample were lower than in previously surveyed hospitals. Younger patients in this study more frequently made negative comments, the majority relating to organizational and administrative aspects. However, there were a few serious complaints about quality of nursing and medical care.

Notice of discharge was shorter for patients in this study than in some studies carried out several years ago, but this may be a function of the shorter length of hospital stay which is now normal. In 1984, Bowling and Betts found that 24% were notified on the day of discharge compared to 33% in this study. A more recent study of elderly people in Wales (Victor and Vetter, 1988) found that 39% were given less than 24 hours' notice, but this compares favourably with reported notice on the same day or the day before for 72% of current patients. A similar proportion of respondents in Victor and Vetter's study, as in this study, reported that they had been discharged too soon or had not discussed their return home with staff.

Considerably fewer people in this study (7%) named their primary source of help as health or social services compared with the 13% reported by Victor and Vetter. There are an increasing number of very elderly women living alone but a declining number of available carers. An increasing proportion of daughters are currently employed outside the home or are elderly themselves and family members may no longer live within the vicinity of their older relatives. Shorter length of stay and short notice of discharge exacerbate the problems of those who have to provide care in the community; the proportion of people recently discharged from hospital receiving help from formal services appears to have declined. As the proportion of very elderly people in the population increases, and length of stay decreases, the deficit in community care can only be overcome if resources are increased appropriately.

This study demonstrates that high response rates can be achieved with large random samples of older people by using postal questionnaires. It also indicates that older patients can successfully complete quite lengthy questionnaires that contain open and closed questions. The content of the explanatory letter, the design of the questionnaire and the instructions for completion are crucial. The offer of assistance to those who are visually impaired and have difficulty reading the questionnaire and who cannot easily post the questionnaire improves the response rate and hence the representative nature of the respondents (Chapter 2 discusses the importance of good response rates). Although the response rate was higher than for a study where forms were distributed to patients while still in hospital (Raphael, 1973), it did have the disadvantage of being carried out 3 months after discharge and this time-lag may have led to some problems of recall. However, a 3 month delay enabled the collection of useful information about the timeliness, appropriateness, adequacy and coordination of after-care. The method allows large amounts of data to be collected relatively cheaply. If it is analysed with special attention to negative findings (Chapter 2) it produces information which enables health and social services to improve the appropriateness and quality of services provided to clients.

REFERENCES

Bowling, A. and Betts, G. (1984) From hospital to home: communications on discharge. *Nursing Times*, **2**, 31–33.
Carr-Hill, R. A. (1992) The measurement of patient satisfaction. *Journal of Public Health Medicine*, **14**(3), 236–249.
Carr-Hill, R., Dixon, P. and Thompson, A. (1989) Too simple for words. *Health Service Journal*, **99**(5155), 728–729.
Cm 849 (1989) *Caring for People: Community Care in the Next Decade and Beyond* HMSO, London.

DHSS (1989a) *Working for Patients*, HMSO, London.

Kershaw, G. (1987) Don't call us ... . *Health Service Journal*, 30 July, 883.

Raphael, W. (1973) *Patients and Their Hospitals*, King Edward's Hospital Fund, London.

Skeet, M. (1970), *Home from Hospital*, Dan Mason Florence Nightingale Memorial Committee, London.

Thompson, A. G. H. (1988) The practical implications of patient satisfaction in research. *Health Services Management Research*, **2**, 112–119.

Victor, C. R. and Vetter, N. J. (1988) Preparing the elderly for discharge from hospital: a neglected aspect of patient care. *Age and Ageing*, **17**, 155–163.

Waters, K. R. (1987) Discharge planning: an exploratory study of the process of discharge planning on geriatric wards. *Nursing*, **12**, 71–83.

7

Users' views of care in the community 6 months after discharge from long-stay psychiatric care

Michael Donnelly and Nicholas Mays

Researchers, and practitioners doing research, may often have very little time or resources. They may also find that funding bodies are firmly convinced that quantitative research is the only real or valid research. In such circumstances standardized instruments which have been tested on other populations and are known to be easy to administer may be the easiest way to proceed. Users from disadvantaged groups can easily complete questionnaires which demand simple yes/no answers. People with communication difficulties may be helped by selecting pictures (such as line drawings of happy and unhappy faces). The validity of all these measures is unknown but they have a clear ability to generate responses which can be compared across different groups and over time. This chapter illustrates how interviewers with relatively little training can gather large amounts of data using mainly quantitative methods. It then shows that sensitive analysis can produce results that go beyond simply tabulating the data to pose fundamental questions about the nature of service provision.

INTRODUCTION

Implementation of community care policies has come later and more slowly in Northern Ireland than in England. More care is still being provided in long-stay hospitals than in England. In 1987, the Regional Strategy for Northern Ireland Health and Personal Social Services set a target reduction of at least 20% in the numbers of people in long-stay psychiatric hospitals by 1992 (DHSS(NI), 1986). The current Regional Strategy for 1992 to 1997 aims for a further reduction of 30% in long-stay residents with a chronic mental illness by 1997 (DHSS(NI), 1991). The effects of moving former long-stay residents – people who had spent at least 12 months continuously in hospital – to care outside hospital in Northern Ireland has been the subject of a research evaluation. The study is similar to studies in England of the implementation of the change from hospital to community-based care (Knapp *et al.*, 1992; Wills *et al.*, 1990) in that users' views before and after discharge form a central part of the evaluation and a key criterion by which the success of the change in the pattern of care is judged. The early views of people who had moved from the six long-stay psychiatric hospitals in Northern Ireland in the course of the evaluation are reported in this chapter, together with an account of the methods used.

METHODS OF OBTAINING USERS' VIEWS

To a great extent the methods chosen for the research were dictated by the requirement by the commissioning body, the Department of Health and Social Services (NI), for multiple assessments at repeated intervals before and after discharge of all long-stay residents discharged from the six psychiatric hospitals to care in the community. The period covered was 1990 to 1992 and the receiving communities were spread throughout Northern Ireland. It was not possible, therefore, to carry out the sort of open-ended interview which involves building up a rapport over a long period with those to be interviewed. Instead, a shorter, structured interview was used to elicit residents' views on the effects of community care. This was complemented by information collected by the professionals responsible for looking after each resident. This source of data is not discussed here.

The principal source of information from users themselves came from the Residents' Interview (RI), formerly known as the Interview for Morale and Life Satisfaction which was developed by the Personal Social Services Research Unit (PSSRU) at the University of Kent in its evaluation of the Department of Health-funded Care in the Community Demonstration Programme in England (Knapp *et al.*, 1992). The Residents' Interview was chosen because it provides an opportunity to make direct comparisons between the Northern Ireland study and the evaluation of care in the community in England by PSSRU. As Knapp *et al.* (1992) have noted, many different approaches to measuring outcomes have been developed, but there is some consensus on which domains of outcome should be assessed, including living environment, daily activities, social contacts, morale and life satisfaction (Chapter 2 pages 20–21 discusses the importance of defining domains). These are all included in the RI.

However, the interview has the limitation that it was constructed by researchers without direct client input. It was not generated through extensive qualitative investigation and piloting with users of mental health services, and, therefore, the relative importance to users, as opposed to experts, of the areas covered in the RI is unclear. Although the interview consisted mainly of closed questions with three possible answers (e.g. yes, no and don't know), in practice it was conducted flexibly and in a conversational style and lasted, on average, 30 minutes. In addition, several open-ended questions were included.

The first section of the RI elicited the individual's views and opinions about their living environment. This part of the RI comprised two question-naires one of which was originally designed by Seltzer and Seltzer (1988) to ask people with moderate learning difficulties about their satisfaction with their living circumstances in the community. The second questionnaire was devised by Wykes (1982) who measured patients' attitudes to aspects of life in a psychiatric hospital and in a hostel-ward. The questionnaire covered things such as the food, staff, other patients, free time, privacy and attitudes to discharge. Soon after the Northern Ireland study had begun, it was noted by members of the research team that the RI did not contain any specific ques-tions on personal space – perhaps a reflection of its origins! So two questions about the degree of privacy available to each individual were added to this section of the interview schedule. As a result, 82% (91/111) of people were asked and subsequently provided responses on both occasions to the questions summarized in Table 7.1.

Table 7.1 Questions on privacy (91 respondents)

Question	Environment	Response		
		Yes(%)	No(%)	Don't know(%)
Do you have some place to go if you want to be on your own?	Hospital	74	25	1
	Community	92	4	3
Do you have a place to go if you want to be alone with someone?	Hospital	72	24	3
	Community	91	4	5

The number and perceived value of social contacts are important to the inte-gration of clients in the community (Renshaw *et al.*, 1980). The Residents' Interview contained a section on social contacts which is an abbreviated version of the 52-item Interview Schedule for Social Interaction (Henderson *et al.*, 1980). Prior (1991) found that some clients may feel the need, due to perceived social norms, to pretend to have friendships. The section on social contacts, therefore, asked residents to give the first name of each friend and relative with whom they were in contact. The validity of this information was checked in the course of conversations with key carers, always mindful of the promise of confidentiality given to the client. A score combining the number and frequency of contacts could then be calculated for comparisons over time.

The degree to which clients engage in meaningful activities also has an important bearing on the quality of their lives (Knapp *et al.*, 1992). The activities section of the Residents' Interview contained clients' own descriptions of their patterns of activity and their preferences for different sorts of activity. This information permitted the plotting of changes in the type and level of activity which occupied clients in hospital and later in the community. It was again modelled on the earlier work by Wykes (1982) who had described and quantified the activities of people with mental health problems resident in a hostel-ward. Wykes recorded each client's behaviour at half-hourly intervals between 8 am and 10 pm on two selected days each week: one a Tuesday, Wednesday or Thursday, the other a Saturday. Observations were assigned to the following six categories: in bed, meals and toilet, work and Occupational Therapy, television and radio, active leisure, and nothing. Wykes's observational categories were adapted for use with individual clients in a one-to-one interview as part of the RI.

The Residents' Interview also contained three instruments measuring morale and life satisfaction. An advantage of using scales employed by others is that there is an opportunity to compare experiences and findings. First, Cantril's Ladder (Cantril, 1965) was included as an easy-to-administer, brief, global measure of morale. The top of the ladder represents 'the best of all possible worlds'; the bottom represents 'the worst'. Each client was asked to point to the stage on the ladder which indicated how they felt at the time. In addition, people with poor communication skills were shown seven simple line drawings depicting three happy faces, three sad faces and a face with a neutral expression and asked to point to the facial expression which best indicated how satisfied with life they were at the time of the interview (Simons *et al.*, 1988).

Secondly, the two subscales of the Psychosocial Functioning Inventory (PFI; Feragne *et al.*, 1983), developed for use with psychiatric patients, provided the interviewee with an opportunity to report how often in the past month they had experienced a range of negative or positive emotions such as boredom, loneliness, restlessness, sadness and happiness. The frequency with which these occurred was recorded (as never, sometimes or often) with a potential score ranging from 0 (low morale) to 51 (high morale). According to Feragne *et al.* (1983), the development of the scales was guided by previous research on the measurement of affective states which had found that subjective well-being, or global satisfaction, comprised at least three components: positive affect, negative affect and background life satisfaction (Beiser, 1973; Bradburn, 1970). The nine-item life satisfaction scale consists of questions such as 'Looking back to the last several years, would you say: (1) things are much better now; (2) things are somewhat better now; (3) things are the same; (4) things are somewhat worse; (5) things are much worse'. The easy-to-comprehend and to administer

Cantril's Ladder was considered to be a more appropriate way of tapping feelings about life satisfaction than the background life satisfaction scale of the PFI. The PFI was primarily designed for outcome research with the full range of adult psychiatric conditions rather than specifically with people with chronic conditions.

Thirdly, the Depression Inventory (DI) (Snaith *et al.*, 1971), consisting of 12 items representative of the symptoms of depressive illness, was included in the RI. The frequency with which respondents experienced the symptoms was recorded on a four-point scale (definitely, sometimes, not much, and not at all). The potential range of scores is 0 to 36 with high scores indicating a less depressed state.

Following notification by hospital staff of the client's impending discharge, the client was then interviewed by a member of the research team at a time and a place chosen by the client. The majority of interviews were conducted in private, without staff and other residents present. The interviewer explained to the interviewee that the purpose of the research was to evaluate services and not to assess individual clients. Each interviewer explained in straightforward language that all answers would be treated in confidence and anonymized. The interviewer then explained that the research team had a genuine desire to hear the viewpoint of the client and invited each client to participate voluntarily in the interview. It was made clear that clients were under no obligation to be interviewed and that a refusal would in no way affect their care or lifestyle. This reassurance is particularly important to clients who are living in care settings. Most clients welcomed the opportunity to talk to someone in private and in confidence. In a review of studies of consumer satisfaction with mental health treatment, Lebow (1982) reported that an interviewing approach of the kind used in this research conducted by independent researchers rather than by service providers tends to improve the rate and accuracy of user responses. In the present study, only 15 people out of 188 refused to be interviewed.

The interview began with a series of standard questions such as the respondent's full name, age and previous place of residence. This served two purposes. It was intended to provide the resident with a gentle introduction to the interview and to more difficult questions. It also gave the interviewer an opportunity to consider how well the interviewee understood the questions and, therefore, an indication of the amount of explanation and probing needed and the pace at which the interview might be best conducted. At the end of the first interview, clients were asked if they had any questions and whether or not the interviewer could make contact again in their new home 6 months later to invite them to be interviewed a second time. The majority of clients were interviewed by the same interviewer at follow-up. This helped reduce inter-interviewer variability and improved the rapport between interviewer and interviewee. The interviews were conducted by a team of research interviewers (two full-time, two part-time), none of whom had had previous experience of interviewing people with mental health problems. This lack of experience was counterbalanced by training interviewers in the use of the RI. The preparation and training comprised 2 hours of instruction about the content, format and structure of the RI, two or three observed interviews conducted by experienced interviewers, and a small number of practice interviews of fellow interviewers. Since the interviewers were not experienced in mental health they did not have a particular professional interest nor ideological bias towards one or other system of care. Over time, the research interviewers became a familiar sight around the psychiatric hospitals and community settings and, after an initial period of suspicion when the research was perceived as a DHSS monitoring exercise and staff were worried about job security, staff welcomed the interviewers. The consistency between interviewers' ratings was discussed at regular meetings held throughout the evaluation to ensure standardized recording of responses.

Residents' Interviews were completed by a member of the research team for approximately 60% (111/188) of clients before they left hospital and 6 months later in the community. Of the remaining 77 residents, 27 (14%) had been readmitted by the time of the 6 month follow-up. Two per cent (4/188) had died and a further 2% provided incomplete interviews due to their inability or reluctance to continue the interview. Only 15 people (8%) refused to be interviewed at any stage and 14% (27/188) were discharged to the community before an interview could be arranged. A comparison of people who remained in the community with those who were readmitted and those who refused an interview revealed no differences in terms of age, length of stay in hospital, sex or diagnosis. Thirty per cent of former hospital residents discharged to private nursing homes (6/20) had been readmitted by the time of the 6 month follow-up interview, whereas 23% (9/40) had been readmitted from statutory hostels. Sixteen per cent of those discharged to live independently (4/25) were in hospital within 6 months. The main reasons for readmission given by staff in the community were a client's deterioration or relapse in mental state and behavioural problems (for example, sexual deviance and aggression). Unfortunately, the views on care in the community of the readmitted clients were not obtained. The analysis and discussion presents the views of 111 people or 70% of the 157 'movers' still resident in the community 6 months after discharge who provided completed interviews at both points in time. In other words, the study is biased towards obtaining the views of people who stayed in the community.

The 111 former long-stay hospital residents (58% male) ranged in age from 18 to 89 years. Twenty-seven per cent (30/111) were under 40, 37% (41/111) were aged between 40 and 59, and 36% (40/111) were 60 years of age or more. Approximately 60% (64/111) had spent at least one continuous period of between 1 and 5 years in hospital. Similar proportions were recorded for each of the following periods: 6–10 years (14%), 11–20 years (13%) and 21 or more years (16%). Schizophrenia was the most frequently noted diagnostic label, being recorded for approximately 80% of people. According to questionnaire assessments of social functioning and problem behaviours completed by staff, residents had a moderate to high level of ability to perform the activities of daily living and had relatively few behaviours which would make successful adaptation to community living a difficult goal. In other words, the leavers were perceived as the more able people in hospital. Furthermore, they had received a period of preparation in anticipation of their discharge to community care.

Results were analysed using the PC version of the Statistical Package for the Social Sciences. The McNemar test was used to assess the significance of any change between the frequency of particular responses given in hospital and in the community to questions about the living environment, daily activities, social contacts and the proportion of people who scored above or below 15 on the Depression Scale. Paired sample *t*-tests were used to assess the significance of change for Cantril's Ladder of Satisfaction, the Psychosocial Functioning Inventory and the Depression Scale. The following presentation of results uses the term significant only when a statistically significant result at the 0.05 level was found.

The final methodological point to make on the study concerns the dissemination of findings on users' views to the staff responsible for purchasing and providing mental health services. The DHSS(NI) has recognized the importance of disseminating research findings by providing support for the feedback of users' views from the study to staff in different types of community settings. In due course, specific reports will be prepared for each.

RESULTS

Accommodation

At 6 months, most people (73%) were living in homes which provided a high level of supervision and support, such as nursing homes (6%), residential homes (29%) and hostels (38%). Only 13% had returned to live on their own or with their families. The remaining 14% were resident in low-staffed accommodation such as sheltered housing (4%) and group homes (10%).

The first section of the Residents' Interview was introduced as follows: 'I am going to ask you what you think about where you live, whether you like or dislike certain things or whether they're good or bad'. A list of the main questions and the proportion of people who endorsed each response are summarized in Table 7.2.

Satisfaction ratings with the various specified aspects of the living environment were consistently high, with only one item – income – being positively rated by less than 80% of residents. Approximately 66% of residents in hospital and 58% in the community reported that they were satisfied with the amount of money they had to spend. More than 50% (58/111) in hospital received less than £10 per week, 36% (40/111) received £10–20, with the remaining 12% (13/111) having a weekly income of between £31 and £50. When interviewed 6

Table 7.2 Users' views of their living environment before and after leaving hospital (111 respondents)

Item	Hospital care			Community care		
	Satisfied (%)	Dissatisfied (%)	Unsure (%)	Satisfied (%)	Dissatisfied (%)	Unsure (%)
Ward, home, hostel	86	13	1	94	5	1
Comfort	98	2	0	99	1	0
Bedroom	97	2	1	99	0	1
Enough space	91	8	1	96	3	1
Food	81	18	1	97	3	0
Surrounding area	85	10	5	87	8	5
Access to shops, PO, etc.	79	15	6	90	4	6
Rules of establishment	88	12	0	95	5	0
Enough money	66	31	3	58	35	7
Feelings about personal possessions	89	10	1	89	11	0
Enough possessions	87	12	1	88	12	0
People living in the establishment	88	10	2	89	4	0*
Staff in the establishment	98	2	0	85	0	0†

* Eight people were living on their own.
† Seventeen people were living on their own or with their families.

months later, 26% (29/111) had a weekly income of less than £10, 44% (49/111) received £10–20, 20% (22/111) received £31–50, and 10% (11/111) received £51–90. Although incomes had risen, satisfaction had decreased indicating the contextual nature of client satisfaction.

Despite the high levels of satisfaction with the hospital environment in which clients were resident before discharge, overall there was an increase in the proportion of people who reported positive views about their new home in the community. In particular, there was a significant increase in the number of people expressing satisfaction about the food and the accessibility of public amenities.

Compared to the hospital environment, there was a significant increase (from 74% to 92%) in the proportion of people afforded basic privacy 6 months later in the community. The bedroom was the most frequently noted place of privacy in the hospital (42/91; 46%) and in the community (59/91; 64%). However, only 20 out of 42 people in hospital who reported that their bedroom was the place they went to when they wanted to be alone had exclusive use of their own bedroom. The remaining 22 shared a bedroom with four or more residents.

As Table 7.3 shows, approximately 70% (79/111) of people at 6 month follow-up stated that they wanted to stay in their present accommodation in the community.

Table 7.3 Do you want to stay here? (111 respondents)

	Like to stay in present community placement? (6 months after discharge)			
Like to stay in hospital? (before discharge)	Yes	No	Don't know	Total (%)
Yes	25	5	1	31 (28%)
No	43	22	4	69 (62%)
Don't know	11	0	0	11 (10%)
Total (%)	79 (71%)	27 (24%)	5 (5%)	111 (100%)

This proportion included 11 people who had been unsure about whether or not they wanted to move to the community and 25 people who had previously stated that they wanted to stay in hospital. It would appear, therefore, that the experience of living outside hospital positively influenced the views of people who had indicated before discharge that they did not wish to move to the community.

Around 25% (27/111) did not want to stay in their present community placement and a further 5% (5/111) were unsure. Each interviewee was asked about their preferred place of residence. The interviewer gave each person a drawing and accompanied this with a brief description of each of five accommodation options to inform interviewees and to help them make a choice. Nineteen of the 27 residents (70%) who did not want to remain in their present community placement expressed a preference for independent living.

Table 7.4 Participation in activities (111 respondents)

	In hospital before discharge		After 6 months in community	
Activities	Percentage	(Number)	Percentage	(Number)
Occupational therapy	59	(65)	26	(29)
Industrial therapy	32	(36)	18	(20)
Housework	61	(68)	73	(81)
Shopping	58	(64)	76	(84)
Cooking	53	(59)	60	(67)
Club	50	(55)	44	(49)
Music	15	(17)	7	(8)
Gardening	11	(12)	11	(13)
Art	8	(9)	8	(9)
Drama	3	(3)	1	(1)

All except two of these people were living in highly staffed accommodation. Only one person indicated that he wanted to return to hospital. One person who expressed a preference for independent living was already doing so – but in a caravan on a farm where he worked as a labourer. His preference was for a permanent home.

The most frequently reported dislikes about community placements were related to the environment (e.g. high levels of noise), lack of independence or the freedom to do as one liked, loneliness and, more generally, insufficient money. Some residents reported that there was nothing wrong with the place where they lived, but that they would still like to move to other accommodation.

Daytime activities

This section of the interview began by asking people whether or not they participated in a specified list of activities. In addition, they were asked if they liked or disliked each activity. Only two people had paid jobs other than industrial therapy. One man worked as a farm labourer and one woman was employed as a typist in a solicitor's office. Unfortunately, the interview questions did not elicit client views about the perceived status of activities such as industrial therapy. It is unclear whether or not industrial therapy was perceived as a 'real' job. In hospital, approximately 60% (65/111) of people engaged in occupational therapy and 32% (36/111) attended industrial therapy (Table 7.4).

However, 6 months later these proportions had decreased significantly to 26% (29/111) and 18% (18/111), respectively, for each type of daytime occupation. Participation in certain activities associated with normal living, such as housework and shopping, was significantly more common in the community than in hospital. Only a few people expressed negative views about the activities in which they engaged. In answer to the open-ended question 'What do you like most about the things you do during the day?', the biggest number of people in hospital ($n = 7$) and in the community ($n = 19$) replied, 'being active or occupied'. At each time, the majority of people (approximately 80%) reported that they had enough to do, were satisfied with their daily routine of activities and, where applicable, expressed positive views about the people with whom they worked.

Although few people expressed negative feelings about daytime activities, 34% in hospital and 41% in the community reported that they did not get the chance or opportunity to do certain things which they would have liked to do, such as individual hobbies, outings, a job and shopping. In addition, similar proportions of people at both times reported in a later section of the interview that they had sometimes (44–47%) or often (5–7%) felt bored in the past month. This seeming contrast of views is discussed below.

Table 7.5 Frequency of contact with friends and relatives (111 respondents)

Interview question	In hospital		In community	
	%	(*n*)	%	(*n*)
Frequency of contact with close friends in place of residence				
No named close friends	39	(43)	47	(52)
Daily	55	(61)	48	(53)
Weekly to monthly	6	(7)	5	(6)
Frequency of contact with close friends outside place of residence				
No named close friends	76	(84)	67	(74)
Daily	5	(5)	11	(12)
Weekly to monthly	11	(12)	17	(19)
Less than 6 monthly	6	(7)	2	(2)
Yearly or rarely	2	(3)	3	(4)
Frequency of contact with relations				
No named relations	6	(7)	16	(18)
Daily	7	(8)	11	(12)
Weekly to monthly	60	(66)	51	(57)
Less than 6 monthly	12	(13)	11	(12)
Yearly or rarely	15	(17)	11	(12)
Is there anyone you could go to if you were upset or wanted help? (% of positive responses)	80	(89)	79	(88)
Staff in place of residence	55	(61)	34	(38)
Named keyworker	13	(14)	16	(18)
Family member	6	(7)	11	(12)
General practitioner	1	(1)	9	(10)
Friend	4	(5)	8	(9)
Other	1	(1)	1	(1)

Friends and relatives

The number, type and frequency of a person's contacts with friends and relatives provides an indication of the degree of isolation they may be experiencing. Approximately 40% (43/111) of people in hospital did not have a close friend there, while 76% (84/111) did not have contacts with people outside the hospital where they were resident. However, only 6% (7/111) of people in hospital did not report a named relative and 80% (89/111) indicated that there was someone they felt they could go to if they were upset or wanted help, usually a member of staff.

Table 7.5 indicates that compared to hospital more people in the community reported not having any friends within their place of residence, while more people reported having at least one friend outside.

In addition, there was a significant reduction in the number of people living in the community who reported having any contact with their relatives. However, between 60% and 70% of people at both times were visited by relatives at least once per month. Although a similar proportion of people in the community reported that they had someone to whom they could turn if they were upset, more people in the community reported that this was a family member (12%), a GP (10%), or a friend (9%) than in hospital.

Morale and life satisfaction

The morale and life satisfaction of residents were measured using three standard scales. There was no significant difference in mean scores on Cantril's Ladder (4.1 versus 4.4). Figure 7.1 illustrates that approximately similar proportions of people reported being satisfied with their lives before (72%) and 6 months after (82%) leaving hospital.

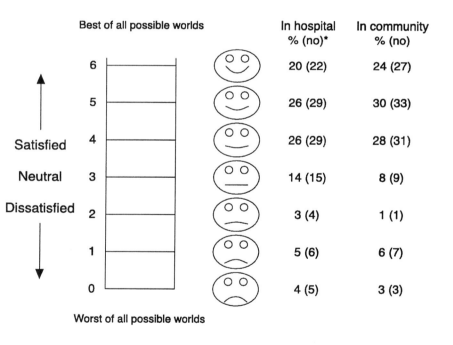

		Best of all possible worlds	In hospital % (no)*	In community % (no)
	6	☺	20 (22)	24 (27)
	5	☺	26 (29)	30 (33)
Satisfied	4	☺	26 (29)	28 (31)
Neutral	3	☺	14 (15)	8 (9)
Dissatisfied	2	☹	3 (4)	1 (1)
	1	☹	5 (6)	6 (7)
	0	☹	4 (5)	3 (3)

Worst of all possible worlds

* Information is missing for one interviewee

Figure 7.1 Cantril's Ladder of satisfaction before and after leaving hospital (111 respondents).

A second measure of subjective well-being comprised two subscales of the PFI. One subscale, consisting of seven items, measured positive affect or the frequency of pleasant emotions on a three-point scale (never, sometimes and often). The second subscale, consisting of 10 items, measured negative affect, i.e. the frequency of unpleasant emotions such as sadness, anger and fear. The two subscales were combined to provide a composite (17 item) indicator of general subjective well-being with a potential range of scores from 17 (low morale) to 51 (high morale). The ranges of scores were from 25 to 49 in hospital and from 19 to 46 in the community. There was no significant difference in subjective well-being as measured by the PFI between hospital and the 6 month follow-up interview in the community (37.7 versus 38.4).

The potential range of scores on the severity measure of depressive illness is from 0 to 36 with high scores indicating a more depressed state or prolonged sadness. At both times, the full range of possible scores was recorded. Similar mean scores were recorded before and after leaving hospital (12.1 versus 12.9). A score of 14 or 15 has been suggested as a cut-off point for indicating depression. Approximately 28% of people in hospital and 32% in the community scored above 15 on this scale.

DISCUSSION

The policy of community care in Northern Ireland is set out in *People First* (DHSS(NI), 1990) which mirrors the English policy document *Caring for People* (Cm 849, 1989). A key aspect of community care policy noted in *People First* is the requirement for purchasers and providers to involve users in the development and design of services. In practice, users are only beginning to participate in local service design and development (Northern Ireland Association for Mental Health, 1993).

The evidence from this analysis of residents' views before and after leaving long-stay hospital indicates a high degree of satisfaction with their surroundings, both in hospital and when living in the community. This is commonplace in studies of patient satisfaction with health care. It is also important to note that the majority of long-stay residents in this study had been selected for discharge and had successfully completed a programme of preparation for community living before their first interview. It is likely that they represented some of the more cooperative and capable residents of long-stay psychiatric hospitals in Northern Ireland. In this case, the frequent endorsement of positive satisfaction ratings may also reflect the effects of institutionalization since many of the people in the study had spent a long period of time in hospital. This may have led to passivity and a reduction of critical awareness. As Knapp *et al.* (1992) have reported, people who have spent a considerable time in a rule-bound institutional setting may be reluctant to voice negative opinions about their environment or their care and their responses may not always reflect their personal views. People with mental health problems appeared to have low expectations regarding the quality of their lives. For example, 74% of people in hospital reported that they were satisfied with the degree of privacy afforded them, yet many of them did not have a room of their own in hospital and a few reported that they had to go outside the building in order to be alone. Surveys of users' views should therefore incorporate an attempt to obtain data on their knowledge of alternatives and their expectations of future services as well as their views on what they have experienced. Users of community care may have a limited perspective if not all possible options are known or understood. Nonetheless, the results do demonstrate a significant increase in levels of satisfaction with aspects of their lives in the community, despite the high level of satisfaction expressed before discharge from the hospital.

The inclusion of several open-ended questions required clients to give more than preset responses, thereby counteracting the tendency towards providing a positive answer to every question. However, some clients appeared to have difficulty responding to questions without specified options. It seemed that responses to open-ended questions tended to be provided by people with better communication skills, whereas most closed questions were answered by all users. Interviewees appeared to find it easier to understand and to respond to those questions with the least number of possible answers (yes, no or don't know) than those with more options or with possible answers (such as never, sometimes, or often).

Raphael (1972) compared three methods of obtaining the views of residents of psychiatric hospitals and found a high level of agreement between the answers to two different self-completion questionnaires and an interview. Both questionnaires had only two possible answers, yes and no, for most questions. Both questionnaires covered the same topics, but in one the questions were phrased so that half the favourable answers would be no, thereby controlling the tendency to answer yes to every question. The interview method gave the fullest data, but was far more time-consuming and needed trained interviewers.

The use of pictures and drawings contributed towards obtaining informed responses to the RI. This was evident in the responses to questions about preferred accommodation. Despite the respondents' apparently high degree of satisfaction with each place, when asked to express a preference, former long-stay hospital residents who now had experience of living in each setting voted overwhelmingly in favour of staying in community accommodation. Yet most of the community accommodation was not very different from the hospital in terms of being highly staffed. Wills et al. (1990) reported a similar significant change in former long-stay psychiatric hospital residents' attitudes towards wanting to stay in the community. Even when some patients in the community in the current study expressed a desire not to remain where they were, this was an indication of a wish to move to a different type of community accommodation usually with lower staffing and not, with one exception, a wish to return to hospital. Bearing in mind that many of the community care settings were large and highly staffed, it would seem that even a small change in living environment may lead to improved satisfaction, but that this experience may, in turn, raise expectations and may even lead to subsequent reductions in satisfaction with new aspects of life (e.g. money).

The desire to move to less supervised environments may be due to a certain degree of ignorance about the implications of receiving less support. There is a tension evident in the philosophy of consumerism as applied to health and social services. Consumerism stresses the qualities of autonomy, choice and freedom. However, the individual user is often vulnerable, disadvantaged and dependent. Service providers may find it difficult to balance the tension between providing the appropriate level of support and fostering independence for some clients who can benefit. In addition, the range of types of accommodation available at present in Northern Ireland is still fairly limited. Although difficult to achieve in practice, it may be that users need more time and opportunity to explore the suitability of, and their potential to benefit from, a range of community accommodation requiring different levels of ability. At the very least, the process of working towards a balanced care package should include an attempt to obtain information about users' views.

It is a concern that the move to community care appears to have been accompanied by a reduction in the number of people who are in any contact with friends and, in particular, relatives. It will be important to examine this area of users' lives over a longer period in order to ascertain whether or not this is a transitory feature of the process of moving home. This point indicates the need to give careful consideration to the most appropriate time to canvas the views of users of long-term care. When is it a fair test of a new service? In addition, 20% of clients did not recognize any supportive figure in hospital or the community to whom they could turn when they were in trouble. Relationships are central to the lives of people with mental health problems, as they are for other people. It is clear that the move from hospital to community care on its own does not transform the social lives of people who have spent long periods in institutions. It would appear that more attention needs to be given to the conditions necessary for developing friendships, in particular through befriending schemes.

Although the majority of individuals reported that they had enough to do and were satisfied with their daily routine of activities, there was a significant reduction in the proportion of users participating in structured activities such as industrial therapy and occupational therapy. This may indicate that service planners need to give further consideration to ways in which these hospital-based resources may be redeployed to develop new forms of community-based daytime services. The inadequacy of personal finances caused concern and dissatisfaction for a significant proportion of residents in both hospital and community. The need for additional money and improved instruction, help or training in the management of income should be considered if dissatisfaction about it is to be minimized.

It is important to note that the decisions as to what should be included in the Residents' Interview and how it should be measured were made by researchers, not by users. The data also reflect users' responses to the format of formal questions. The meanings and degree of importance which users give to their own experiences and behaviour, and the ways in which these influence their actions, are not covered by the research approach described here. For example, the majority of people reported that they had enough to do, and were satisfied with their activities yet almost half in another section of the interview reported being bored sometimes. Qualitative research methods may be required in order to gain a better understanding and interpretation of these apparently contradictory responses and to establish the relative importance which users attach to various activities such as industrial therapy. However, these are time-consuming and require skilled researchers. Structured questionnaires have other strengths. 'What must be remembered is that quantitative measures rarely precisely mirror the social or personal reality they seek to describe, but are valuable in providing a broad consumer view and in offering points of comparison' (Knapp *et al.*, 1992). Comparisons may be made between studies, client groups, care settings and over time. In addition, the RI is easy to administer and requires very little interviewer training. If the experience of this study can be generalized, interviewers need not have any formal academic qualifications. An important quality of the good interviewer is the ability to put people at ease so that they will communicate freely. The ease and length of the proposed questionnaire, the amount and type of training required, and the costs are important practical considerations when planning ways of obtaining users' views. In this case, the study objective required the collection of comparable longitudinal data on a large number of clients discharged to a large number of different community care settings.

The longer term follow-up at 12 and 24 months will show whether or not the positive views at 6 months of users of mental health services in the community who have been long-stay residents in psychiatric hospitals will change.

ACKNOWLEDGEMENT

The authors would like to acknowledge funding from the Department of Health and Social Services (Northern Ireland).

REFERENCES

Beiser, M. (1973) Components and correlation of mental well-being. *Journal of Health and Social Behaviour*, **15**, 320–332.

Bradburn, M. (1970) *The Structure of Psychological Well-being*, Aldine, Chicago.

Cantril, H. (1965) *The Pattern of Human Concerns*, Rutgers University Press, New Brunswick/New Jersey.

Cm 849 (1989) *Caring for People: Community Care in the Next Decade and Beyond*, HMSO, London.

(DHSS(NI)) (1986) *A Regional Strategy for the Northern Ireland Health and Personal Social Services, 1987–1992*, Department of Health and Social Services (NI), Belfast.

(DHSS(NI)) (1990) *People First: Community Care in Northern Ireland for the 1990s*, Department of Health and Social Services (NI), Belfast.

(DHSS(NI)) (1991) *A Regional Strategy for the Northern Ireland Health and Personal Social Services, 1992–1997*, Department of Health and Social Services (NI), Belfast.

Feragne, M., Longabaugh, R. and Stevenson, J. (1983) The psychosocial functioning inventory. *Evaluation and the Health Professionals*, **6**, 25–48.

Henderson, S., Duncan-Jones, P. and Byrne, D. G. (1980) Measuring social relationships: the interview schedule for social interaction. *Psychological Medicine*, **10**, 723–734.

Knapp, M. R. J., Cambridge, P., Thomason, C., Beecham, J. K., Allen, C. and Darton, R. A. (1992) *Care in the Community: Challenge and Demonstration*, Ashgate/Personal Social Services Research Unit, Aldershot.

Lebow, J. (1982) Consumer satisfaction with mental health treatment. *Psychological Bulletin*, **91**, 244–259.

Northern Ireland Association for Mental Health (1993) *Mental Health Matters* (The Magazine of the association for Mental Health), University Street, Belfast.

Prior, L. (1991) *The Social Worlds of Psychiatric and Ex-psychiatric Patients in Belfast*, Health and Health Care Research Unit, The Queen's University of Belfast.

Raphael, W. (1972) *Psychiatric Hospitals Viewed by Their Patients*, King's Fund, London.

Renshaw, J., Hampson, R., Thomason, C., Darton, R., Judge, K. and Knapp, M. (1980) *Care in the Community: The First Steps*, Gower, Aldershot.

Seltzer, G. and Seltzer, M. (1988) *Satisfaction Questionnaire*, American Association of Mental Deficiency Annual Meeting on Residential Satisfaction and Community Adjustment, 1983.

Simons, K., Booth, T. and Booth, W. (1988) *Speaking Out: User Studies of People with Learning Difficulties*, Kirklees Relocation Project Report, University of Sheffield.

Snaith, A. R. P., Ahmed, S. N., Mehta, S. and Hamilton, M. (1971) Assessment of the severity of primary depressive illness. *Psychological Medicine*, **1**, 143–149.

Wills, W., Dayson, D. and Gooch, C. (1990). Patients attitudes before and after discharge, in *Better Out than In?*, Team for the Assessment of Psychiatric Services (TAPS), North East Thames Regional Health Authority, London.

Wykes, T. (1982) A hostel-ward for 'new' long-stay patients: an evaluative study of a 'ward in a house', in *Long Term Community Care in a London Borough*, (ed. J. K. Wing), Psychological Medicine, Monograph Supplement, 57–97.

Elderly patients' satisfaction with a community nursing service

8

Rachel Reed and Chris Gilleard

It is well known that elderly service users are unwilling to complain about their services, but the extent of their tolerance is very hard to measure. In the present case Reed and Gilleard were able to sample users before and after large cuts in a district nursing service. Overall satisfaction scores did not alter. The authors go on to show how careful attention to the components of satisfaction can unravel some of the important details, which were hidden by a simple interpretation of their psychometric measures. They also recorded users' comments on the district nursing service. In their analysis they were able to highlight some user attitudes and perceptions in ways that further illustrate their quantitative data.

INTRODUCTION: IMPORTANCE OF OUTCOME MEASURES TO HEALTH CARE REFORMS

The development of consumerism over the last 20 years has left no public sector service untouched. The last decade of change within the NHS has had at its core the issues of competition, choice, cost efficiency, effectiveness, quality control and quality assurance. These buzz-words of consumerism have infiltrated the NHS so deeply that we now talk unquestioningly of customers and clients. Their satisfaction has become one of the main indicators of quality and of service success and acceptability. The first Griffiths report in 1983 stated that managers should use market research techniques to 'ascertain how well the service is being delivered at a local level by obtaining the experience and perceptions of patients and the community' (Griffiths, 1983). Many managers now have quality assurance and control built into their job descriptions. Concepts such as total quality management feature heavily in management thinking.

PROBLEMS WITH PATIENT SATISFACTION MEASURES

Some of the earliest work on issues of quality and patient satisfaction originated with Donabedian (1966) who suggested that 'patient satisfaction is ... the ultimate validator of the quality of care'. The great number of patient satisfaction studies conducted subsequently have, however, tended to ignore the numerous methodological and theoretical problems inherent in the measurement of satisfaction itself. A number of critical reviews on the subject (Ware *et al.*, 1978; Locker and Dunt, 1978; French, 1981) summarize these problems as follows:

1. Lack of adequate definition of the concept of satisfaction. Definitions tend to reflect the researcher's point of view, to be academic and rarely to elicit what a patient may understand by the term (e.g. Stimson and Webb, 1975; Linder-Pelz, 1982). Oberst (1984) suggests that any tool designed to measure patient satisfaction based on such academic definitions, rather than on the patient's experience and understanding of the concept of satisfaction, must be of suspect validity.
2. Insufficient understanding of the process by which people make decisions about their level of satisfaction (Locker and Dunt, 1978). As Haire (1991) asks 'What does the patient mean when he or she states that they are satisfied with their care?'
3. Whereas studies have repeatedly demonstrated the multidimensional nature of patient satisfaction (e.g. Ware *et al.*, 1978; Risser, 1975; La Monica *et al.*, 1986), there is no clear understanding of how these dimensions may interrelate, or whether a hierarchy of satisfaction exists, with patients' differing needs dictating their levels of satisfaction with any one particular facet of care, at any one time. For example, an acutely ill patient may rate the 'technical quality and art of care' that saves her life far more highly than the personal supportive care or physical care environment (Oberst, 1984). Hence, patients' constantly changing needs will affect their satisfaction levels and may make it impossible for any measure to remain stable over time. Others suggest that patients are not capable of judging certain aspects of their care, especially the more technical ones (Tagliacozzo and Mauksch, 1972). Tessler and Mechanic (1975) suggest that it is not acceptable to expect people to make judgements about their care when in a state

of dependency as it is 'uncomfortable to accept that one's care may be less than adequate' (Oberst, 1984).

Such theoretical and methodological issues are further discussed in Chapter 2. Most patients report that they are very satisfied with their care. This positive response bias appears particularly evident in studies where elderly people have been the consumers (Linn and Greenfield, 1982; Carmel, 1985).

Age is the only socio-demographic variable found across studies to be consistently predictive of satisfaction. Studies which include all age groups repeatedly demonstrate that age is consistently associated with higher levels of satisfaction (Tessler and Mechanic, 1975; Carmel, 1985). Various explanations have been offered for this phenomenon. It has been suggested that people become more passive and less critical as they become older (Klein, 1979). He also offers a **generational effect** in that older people who remember the way things were before the NHS are inclined to consider only its positive attributes and ignore its shortcomings. Another suggestion is that older adults tend to be more in awe of uniformed health care professionals and have a greater respect for their authority and assume automatically that doctor or nurse knows best. It has also been hypothesized that older adults have lower expectations of health care and are grateful for every service they receive, irrespective of its quality (Haire, 1991; Fitzpatrick, 1984). One comparative study of a wide age range of hospital patients demonstrated not only that older patients were more universally satisfied, but that they also tend to have lower expectations, supply socially desirable responses, express more gratitude and are more fearful of complaining than younger groups (Breemhaar et al., 1990).

All these factors complicate the issue of accurately monitoring consumer satisfaction within an elderly population. They must be taken into account in the current NHS climate of cuts and threats to services. There remains a tendency to view elderly consumers of health care, only in terms of how much they use the NHS (and the inherent expense), rather than what they think of it (Cornwell, 1989). In spite of these many intractable problems, the lack of information about older peoples' views of their health care cannot be excused. Given their increasing numbers and the large segment of the health care budget this speciality consumes, it is irresponsible not to utilize consumer satisfaction methodologies to try and establish what the needs of elderly health care consumers are. It is important to determine how well these needs are being met by monitoring users' perceptions of the quality of care they feel they are receiving. For those in long-term care, Locker and Dunt (1978) have suggested that satisfaction with care becomes an integral component of satisfaction with life and that quality of care becomes virtually synonymous with the quality of life (see also Oberst, 1984). Health care planners, purchasers, providers and professionals should therefore be monitoring the levels of satisfaction with care amongst their elderly clients.

The present inquiry was driven by academic and professional interest in the concept and construct of consumer satisfaction and the related methodological issues (e.g. reliability and validity of the instruments used). Although the study predates the NHS and Community Care Act 1990, the issues raised have taken on greater significance in the new reformed market economy of the NHS, where all too frequently the results of consumer satisfaction surveys are used as a means of justifying the continuation, cutting or improvement of health care services. One of the main aims of the NHS reforms is to ensure high-quality personal services to the consumer, yet this aim is diluted by other more pressing objectives. For example, the purchasers have a responsibility to demonstrate value for money; the providers have a responsibility to satisfy their customers; and professionals now have an increased responsibility to determine good practice. In this context each group can interpret the results of consumer satisfaction studies to suit their own needs. Care is therefore needed in utilizing data and results from such studies.

This preamble is necessary so that the study can be seen in all its fragility. The concept of measuring consumer satisfaction, particularly among an older population, is highly complex and needs to be addressed from the broadest possible perspective. As with all service evaluation research, it can never be conducted in a vacuum, and in the context of the ever-changing NHS, scientific methods cannot be used because continual changes make it impossible to maintain experimental conditions. As the following discussion of the research findings demonstrates, by considering the results from both a qualitative and a quantitative approach, it was possible to learn more about the needs, expectations and levels of satisfaction with the Community Nursing Service than might otherwise have been gained. For example, the basic analysis demonstrated that the majority of the old people questioned were highly satisfied with their community nursing service.

HOUSEBOUND ELDERLY PROJECT – RESEARCH METHODS

As part of a broader research programme, the satisfaction levels of the housebound elderly clientele of the Community Nursing Service in an inner-city London Health Authority were measured. Following the Cumberlege report in the mid-1980s, this health authority had been the first area to reorganize its community nursing service (CNS) into decentralized localities, which were further divided into smaller neighbourhood teams. Each of the original nine neighbourhoods (reduced to seven, half-way through the research) was staffed by a team of community nurses led by a qualified district nurse (DN), who held responsibility for a caseload of patients. Caseload size varied from 72 to 244 clients.

The caseloads of every DN team leader were reviewed in order to identify patients meeting the following research criteria:

- aged 65+;
- living alone;
- housebound, i.e. unable to leave their homes without the physical assistance of another person.

A total of 404 elderly people formed the main sampling frame. From this group, complete interviews were obtained from 125. One of the main reasons for this large discrepancy was that over 30% were misidentified by the DN in that they were not housebound, or not living alone when the interviewer contacted them. Other reasons included a high refusal rate (23%); frequent sudden admission to hospital or residential care; and confusion, measured by their failure to complete an abbreviated version of the Mini-Mental Status Examination (MMSE; Folstein et al., 1975).

The interview schedule included the administration of a depression scale (Gilleard et al., 1981); a life satisfaction scale (Bigot, 1974) and a patient satisfaction with nursing care (PSNC) scale to measure their satisfaction with the CNS. This scale was adapted from the La Monica patient satisfaction instrument (La Monica et al., 1986) for use in a community setting and compared with another PSNC scale (Risser, 1975) in the pilot study. The first scale was found to be more reliable, more easily generalized to other groups of patients (external validity), and more easily understood by elderly clients, possibly because the statements were shorter (Reed and Gilleard, 1992). Examples of the statements are given in Appendix 8A. Also asked about were the degree of contact these elderly clients had with family, friends, neighbours and the statutory or voluntary services; their general health status; their views concerning the adequacy of their living arrangements; and their relationship with, and expectations of the CNS. These questions tended to produce comments which were recorded, as far as possible verbatim, by the interviewers. The comments seemed to yield much useful information about their views of the service, and clarified, or in some cases contradicted, their yes/no or agree/disagree responses to the preset structured questions of the PSNC. Finally, as mentioned earlier, a modified version of the MMSE (Folstein et al., 1975) was used to exclude those with moderate to severe dementia or confusion. All the questions and response choices were printed on cards, and read out by the interviewers, to overcome the problems of poor eyesight and hearing that seemed quite common in the sample.

The interviews were repeated 9 months later when it was possible to monitor the effects of significant changes that had occurred during the course of the research. These included:

- a 40% cut in the community nursing service budget;
- the reduction of services, particularly the bathing service (the stopping of so-called social baths);
- the introduction of mandatory charging for social care and home help services by the local authority;

- the closing of caseloads and the introduction of a waiting list for community nursing care.

SUMMARY OF RESULTS

Quantitative data

As expected from the numerous known methodological problems inherent in the measurement of patient satisfaction amongst older people, it was difficult to get this client group to express dissatisfaction with the CNS. The responses to the PSNC scale were highly positively skewed and, taken at face value, demonstrated a very highly satisfied group of customers at both time periods and irrespective of the cuts imposed on the service (Figure 8.1).

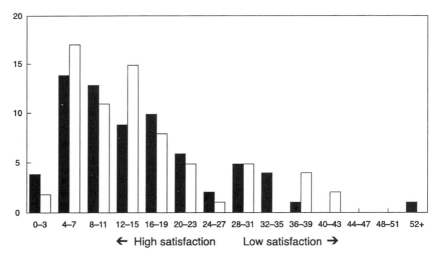

Figure 8.1 Satisfaction with nursing care: initial (black) and follow-up (white) scores; initial mean = 15.21; follow-up mean = 15.22.

High satisfaction scores are normal when satisfaction is assumed to be a homogeneous construct (Chapter 2). One of the first concerns in examining the results was therefore to establish the factor structure of the scale. (Factors, or the components of satisfaction scales, are described as dimensions in Chapter 2). Although the sample size of 125 was rather small for reliably eliciting a stable factor structure, the questionnaire included standardized questions from the La Monica patient satisfaction scale which has been demonstrated to measure multidimensionality (Risser, 1975; La Monica et al., 1986; Harrison and Novak, 1988). It was therefore possible to anticipate an expected structure.

Seven factors emerged as significant. They accounted for approximately two-thirds of the covariance matrix and seemed to represent an interpretable structure. The factors are listed in Table 8.1, and examples of items or statements making up the factors are given in Appendix 8A and Table 8.2.

Table 8.1 Means, standard deviations and skewness indices of factors making up user satisfaction

Factor	Items	Mean	SD	Skew
1 Communication	6	4.0	3.4	0.6
2 Caring approach	9	2.9	3.7	1.9
3 Uncaring behaviour	9	2.1	2.7	2.5
4 Unprofessional behaviour	6	1.6	2.1	2.0
5 Empathy	5	2.1	2.4	1.0
6 Reliability	5	4.4	2.7	–0.0
7 Neglect	6	3.2	2.6	0.9

Table 8.2 Individual factor subscales and their reliability

Factor name	No. of items	Reliability
1 Communication	6	0.7886
2 Caring approach	9	0.8071
3 Uncaring behaviour	9	0.7385
4 Unprofessional behaviour	6	0.6385
5 Empathy	5	0.7018
6 Reliability	5	0.6406
7 Neglect	6	0.6322

All the items making up each factor were scored so that a score of 2 represented dissatisfaction and 0 satisfaction. An average score corresponding to the number of items in each factor would therefore represent a neutral stance, showing that people did not express strong opinions either for or against an aspect of the service. For example factor 6, reliability, was made up of five items. The average score for this factor was 4.4 suggesting that users expressed more dissatisfaction (more scores of 2 and fewer of 0) with reliability than for other aspects of the service, although their overall rating was still positive rather than negative.

These factor scores showed that no aspects of community nursing care were rated neutrally by the elderly people interviewed, while other aspects tended consistently to be positively rated, as if criticisms on these points were either less often experienced or less easily expressed. While clients seemed to feel relatively free to comment critically on the reliability of the service, the limitations in communication and sharing information and the lack of consultation, they seemed less ready to comment critically on the caring approach, pleasant manner, empathy and professional standards shown by the nurses visiting them. These distinctions support the existence of separate dimensions of satisfaction which are perceived in different ways and which may be more or less easily expressed when replying to a questionnaire.

The next area of concern in analysing the quantitative data was to identify some aspects of consumer satisfaction that seemed to reflect variations in service, rather than variations in the characteristics of the users. One possible correlation that emerged from the pilot study was the degree of personal knowledge the older person felt they had about the nurses visiting them. This was interpreted as an indicator of a more individualized nurse–patient relationship. The index of personal knowledge was made up of answers indicating (a) knowledge of the nurse's name; (b) knowledge of something of the nurse's home life (e.g. family, etc.); (c) knowledge of where the nurse lived; and (d) knowledge of the health centre where the nurses were based. As had been hoped, there did appear to be a systematic relationship between elderly people's knowledge about the community nurses who visited them and patient satisfaction. Increased knowledge was associated with a greater sense of expressed satisfaction with the CNS. It was felt that this finding goes some way to demonstrate that the scale is sensitive to variations in levels of satisfaction within an elderly population, particularly when the analyses show that increased personal knowledge of the nurse does not seem to occur simply as a function of the frequency of visits, nor is it related to whether the same nurse(s) always visit, as neither of these influenced satisfaction levels.

In view of the cuts and changes to the CNS that had occurred over the duration of the research it was of interest if, and to what extent, the CNS was seen by the elderly people as being under pressure. To try to ascertain this, during the second stage interviews all spontaneous comments about the nurses seeming more busy or having less time were recorded. Also, users were asked specifically whether they felt they were receiving less contact from the CNS than before. Out of the spontaneous comments was created a variable termed DNPROBS which was scored as 0 or 1 depending on whether the users commented on staff shortages, or increased work demands, or other staff limitations that were not specific to the personal or professional style of any individual nurse. Changes in patient satisfaction were analysed according to whether the elderly person had or had not reported (and therefore presumably noticed and been affected by) staff pressures and limitations. It was found that the elderly people's perceptions of changes in the CNS were not related to their scores on the outcome measure of satisfaction, since there were no significant differences between those who were later to report and comment on such changes and those who did not. This was important to establish since it makes it less likely that the dissatisfied clients were specifically more attuned to problems and thus more likely to notice and comment on staffing problems. However, further analyses provided evidence of an overall and specific change in satisfaction scores relating to the experience of the service. It seemed that those people who experienced and recognized organizational difficulties in the

CNS were adversely affected and expressed a greater dissatisfaction with the service than those not experiencing or recording concerns.

This area of the results provides a good illustration of the need within the area of satisfaction research to combine quantitative and qualitative methods, in order to produce the most balanced approach to monitoring and measuring the construct of satisfaction. By recording users' spontaneous comments verbatim, it was possible to use their views to formulate a quantitative test to clarify a further aspect of service satisfaction. Such integration of qualitative and quantitative methods is essential to avoid misleading results, which can always arise if psychometric data are used alone.

The concluding part of this chapter examines some of the verbatim comments in order to illustrate the importance of monitoring satisfaction from a more qualitative perspective. It was felt this enabled the picking up of more information about the attitudes, views and frameworks within which the CNS is seen by their customer patients than was given by the use of the PSNC scale alone.

QUALITATIVE DATA

Timing and reliability of service

Typically, dissatisfaction was expressed about not knowing when the nurses would visit and the length of time nurses were able to spend with patients. Although the quantitative data was sensitive to this in that the factor termed reliability clearly elicited more dissatisfaction on the point score than any of the other facets of satisfaction (Table 8.1), much of this was lost when the results are considered overall. The agree/disagree responses to the questionnaire items do little justice to the strength and negativity of feeling expressed by some of the old people, as the following quotes and comments show:

'I prefer to know when they are coming and to have it regular to make it easier for them as I can have everything ready.'

'It's awful not knowing when they will come as some days I'm in my dressing gown and had the boiler on all day waiting for my wash and they've phoned in the afternoon to say they can't come at all.'

'They come at the wrong time when it is dinner time. I'd like them to come early so that I can get my dinner.'

'They've not got time to help – they're so pressed for time.'

'They're too quick and in a rush and they say that they have to be quick because they've parked their car outside (double yellow lines) and so they have to be in and out in 10 minutes.'

'They should stop for a few minutes and have a chat with a person.'

'They don't trouble – ain't got time if they've got three or four other patients to see – I don't blame them.'

'Often recently, they ring me up and say they can't come as all the nurses are off with flu' and do I mind if they miss me out?'

'They seem more interested in getting away to another patient.'

'One nurse can work and talk at the same time and she always makes me feel better by staying an extra 5 minutes if she can and I feel better when she has been.'

Psychological care

Another area of the study which demonstrates the advantages gained when quantitative and qualitative data are used in partnership is the issue of satisfaction with the caring and empathic style of the CNS. The questionnaire detected these as important components or dimensions of the overall construct of patient satisfaction, and the majority of respondents came out as being very satisfied with these aspects of nursing care or, alternatively, as reluctant to criticize nurses for these aspects of their behaviour. However, by reviewing some of the verbatim comments related to this area it can be seen that there is a wide variation in what elderly people expect and hope for from the CNS, and the way in which they describe the relationships they feel they have with the nurses who visit them. These descriptions ranged from close, positive, warm feelings of rapport and friendship, through to defensive statements that assert the nurses' right to be a professional with a job to do:

'They make me feel like the queen.'

'They are like friends.'

'They're decent – you feel at home with them.'

'I don't feel old when they are here – they don't make me feel like an old lady!'

'She makes me feel like one of her specials!'

'They've got a job to do – they can't be silly with people – they have to be businesslike.'

'They do their job and do what they are sent here to do.'

'They are not here long enough to know their names – can't make friends like.'

'They seem more interested in getting away to another patient.'

Such comments yield greater insights into aspects of the CNS individual clients find important than can be gleaned from the agree/disagree boxes ticked on a PS questionnaire. Yet this kind of qualitative data, taken alone, is less useful than if it is combined with quantitative results which can show, for example, how these views are distributed statistically so that, if necessary, the service can be changed or improved to meet the needs and expectations of the majority.

This point, and the overall review of the research, illustrates how patient satisfaction studies would be at their most informative and beneficial if they were approached from the joint perspective of both quantitative and qualitative methods. As Donabedian (1966) has pointed out, consumer satisfaction is 'so diverse in nature that neither a unifying construct, nor a single, empirical measure could be developed'. By acknowledging this and stressing the need for a partnership between quantitative and qualitative methodology, it is hoped that the dangers of giving too much emphasis to psychometric indices of patient satisfaction can be avoided. This is important because they can, and do in today's NHS, so easily become management tools, used to rationalize resources and streamline care into price-tagged, task-dominated packages, while still supposedly demonstrating high levels of customer satisfaction. The particular insensitivities of single-index, multiple-item satisfaction questionnaires need to be acknowledged and balanced by an equivalent concern for the analysis and interpretation of spontaneous comments arising from such patient satisfaction studies.

REFERENCES

Bigot, A. (1974) The relevance of American life satisfaction indices for research on British subjects before and after retirement. *Age and Ageing*, **3**, 113–121.

Breemhaar, B., Visser, A. and Kleijen, J. G. (1990) Perceptions and behaviour among elderly hospital patients: description and explanation of age differences in satisfaction, knowledge, emotions and behaviour. *Social Science and Medicine*, **31**(12), 1377–1385.

Carmel, S. (1985) Satisfaction with hospitalization: a comparative analysis of three types of services. *Social Science and Medicine*, **21**(11), 1243–1249.

Cornwell, J. (1989) *The Consumer's View: Elderly People and Community Health Services*, Kings Fund for Health Services Development Publications, London.

Donabedian, A. (1966) Evaluation of the quality of medical care. *Milbank Memorial Fund Quarterly Bulletin*, **44**, 166.

Fitzpatrick, R. (1984) Satisfaction with health care, in *The Experience of Illness*, (eds R. Fitzpatrick, J. Hinton, S. Newman, G. Scrambler and J. Thompson), Tavistock, London.

Folstein, M. L., Folstein, S. E. and McHugh, P. R. (1975) Mini-mental state: a practical method for grading the cognitive state of patients for the clinician. *Journal of Psychiatric Research*, **12**, 189–198.

French, K. (1981) Methodological considerations in hospital patient opinion surveys. *International Journal of Nursing Studies*, **18**, 7–32.

Gilleard, C.J., Wilmott, M. and Vaddadi, K. (1981) Self report measures of mood and morale in elderly depressives. *British Journal of Psychiatry*, **138**, 230–235.

Griffiths, R. (1983) *NHS Management Enquiry*, HMSO, London.

Haire, G. (1991) Open to question. *Nursing the Elderly*, Jul/Aug, 22–24.

Harrison, L. L. and Novak, D. A. (1988) Evaluation of a gerontological nursing continuing education programme: the effect on nurses' knowledge and attitudes and on patients' perceptions and satisfaction. *Journal of Advanced Nursing*, **13**, 684–692.

Klein, R. (1979) Public opinion and the National Health Service. *British Medical Journal*, **1**, 1296–1297.

La Monica, E. L., Oberst, M. T., Madea, A. R. and Wolf, R. M. (1986) Development of a patient satisfaction scale. *Research in Nursing and Health*, **9**, 43–50.

Linder-Pelz, S. (1982) Towards a theory of patient satisfaction. *Social Science and Medicine*, **16**, 577–582.

Linn, L. S. and Greenfield, S. (1982) Patient suffering and patient satisfaction among the chronically ill. *Medical Care*, **20**, 425–431.

Locker, D. and Dunt, D. (1978) Theoretical and methodological issues in sociological studies of consumer satisfaction with medical care. *Social Science and Medicine*, **12**, 283–292.

Oberst, M. T. (1984) Patients' perceptions of care. *Cancer*, **53** (supplement), 2366–2373.

Reed, R. and Gilleard, C. J. (1992) Measuring consumer satisfaction with the community nursing service: an evaluation of two questionnaires, in *Social Policy and Elderly People*, (eds F. Lackzo and C. Victor), Avebury, Aldershot.

Risser, N. L. (1975) Development of an instrument to measure patient satisfaction with nurses and nursing care in primary care settings. *Nursing Research*, **24**, 45–51.

Stimson, G. and Webb, B. (1975) *On Going to See the Doctor*, Routledge and Kegan Paul, London.

Tagliacozzo, D. L. and Mauksch, H. O. (1972) The patient's view of the patient's role, in *Patients, Physicians and Illness*, 2nd edn, (ed. E.G. Jaco), Free Press, New York, cited in Oberst, M. (1984) Perceptions of care. *Cancer*, **53**(10), 2366–2373.

Tessler, R. and Mechanic, D. (1975) Consumer satisfaction with pre-paid group practice: a comparative study. *Journal of Health and Social Behaviour*, **16**, 95–113.

Ware, J. E., Davies-Avery, A. and Stewart, A. L. (1978) The measurement and meaning of patient satisfaction. *Health and Medical Care Services Review*, **1**, 2–15.

APPENDIX 8A

Examples of some items from the patient satisfaction questionnaire, listed under the tentative names used to label the seven factors.

Factor one – communication

The nurses tell me what to expect before they do anything to me.
The nurses always make helpful suggestions.
The nurses explain things in an understandable way.

Factor two – caring approach

The nurses are gentle in caring for me.
I can share my feelings with the nurses when I need to talk.
The nurses do things to make me more comfortable.

Factor three – uncaring behaviour

The nurses should be more thorough.
The nurses are not as friendly as they could be.
The nurses are impatient with me.

Factor four – unprofessional behaviour

The nurses seem disorganized and flustered when they visit me.
The nurses seem unwilling to give me help when I need it.
The nurses would know what to do in an emergency.

Factor five – empathy

Just talking to the nurses makes me feel better.
The nurses help me to understand the care and treatment that I need.
The nurses make me feel secure when they are giving me care.

Factor six – reliability

I always know when to expect the nurses.
The nurses never come when they say they are going to.
I usually know which nurse is going to visit me.

Factor seven – neglect

The nurses seem more interested in getting on with things than in listening to my worries.
The nurses talk down to me.
The nurses never ask me for my opinion about the care they are planning for me.

9 | Do you remember your social worker? Identification and recall problems in user surveys

Emmanuelle Tulle-Winton

The social work process may have very little importance for frail elders who are preoccupied with keeping going from day-to-day. Service delivery may matter to them, but the processes which lead up to it are unlikely to stand out as key events. Service providers, and researchers who work with providers in mind, can easily forget the difference in perspective between providers and users of care. This chapter explores the effects of a failure to consider the user view. It illustrates the way that structured questionnaires designed to get relatively brief answers can be used in situations where users are willing to cooperate in research but are not motivated to invest the emotional energy that long, interactive, unstructured interviews demand.

INTRODUCTION

Studies of the effectiveness of social work with elderly people have not always included users of services in their design. In the few instances where they have included them, it has variously been assumed either that elderly people are difficult to interview (Willcocks *et al.*, 1982), that only qualitative methods are appropriate, or that certain areas of questioning are to be avoided. Even if those assumptions are not an obstacle to research actually taking place, they are likely to have an effect on questionnaire design. This is not to deny that interviewing older people, like other groups, presents researchers with specific challenges. However, it could argued that those challenges should be re-examined, for two reasons. First, researchers must avoid carrying out work which might perpetuate and reinforce stereotypes about the very people whose widely different behaviours, attitudes and opinions they seek to understand. Not all older people have physical or mental impairments which make them highly dependent on younger people or services; and not all of them want to reminisce about their lives with the first researcher stepping across their doorsteps. In other words, older people are not a homogeneous group, with one specific set of characteristics – usually negative. The second reason, which follows from the first, is that if we posit that those assumptions affect the way research questions are formulated and made operational, then they are also intimately linked to the type of data that will be collected and to the meanings attributed to their interpretation.

This chapter is therefore an attempt to reflect on and examine the way in which a team of researchers designed their research guided by a range of assumptions, not only about the ability of users to cope with an interview situation, but also about the conclusions that would be drawn from the data collected. In other words, what is intended here is an appraisal of the hypothetical framework which guided the direction of the enquiry and the nature of the interview schedule.

ORGANIZATION AND OUTCOMES

The research was focused on the outcomes of different organizational models or philosophies of social work on service delivery and assessment patterns. The basic research question was: what difference does it make to the clients themselves whether the social work team serving them is organized on a specialist model, a generic model, or follows a community social work (CSW) approach? Would the differences in assessment patterns, collaborative work and service delivery, expected in a large dataset, be apparent in a small sample of users? If it were possible to capture profiles of distinctive practice at team level, what would this mean for the clients and how would this be assessed? The challenge was to manage the enquiry in a way which satisfied not only the initial research question but also more pragmatically in a way which would give us a picture of the quality of people's lives. The whole research project was a fully integrated and triangulated programme of enquiry, i.e. methods were mixed: a large structured data collection exercise and face-to-face interviews with a small subsample. The interview for the face-to-face interviews used within-methods triangulation (Denzin, 1978), in this case combining sets of questions variously placed on the qualitative–quantitative continuum.

The main dataset was derived from anonymized case review forms for allocated referrals of elderly people. The forms were completed by social workers in 15 area teams in Scotland and Northern England at two time periods. The first was after initial allocation to a social worker (Time 1) and, for those cases not immediately closed, either at 6 months or at closure, whichever was the earliest (Time 2). Data collection started in late 1990 and the final sample comprised around 1200 cases (findings from this exercise are reported in Fuller and Tulle-Winton (1993)). Out of this dataset was drawn a sample of cases for face-to-face interviewing.

Lists of randomly selected index numbers from four teams of contrasting organizational types (specialist, generic or CSW) were drawn up by the researchers. The lists were then sent to team seniors with a letter requesting them to check that all the numbers listed represented clients who were still alive, did not have dementia, or had not entered residential care. The rationale behind the latter's exclusion was that their experience of entry to residential care would in itself be so overwhelming as to obliterate any recollections of social work processes taking place prior to admission. People who had dementia were excluded because of doubts about the ability to collect the type of data needed from them (Bland *et al.*, 1992).

It was apparent that the variable time-lag between the episode of social work described on the case review form and the timing of the interviews might lead to recall difficulties. It was therefore planned to select first those clients who had been referred three months prior to interviewing. Recall is indeed a crucial factor influencing the reliability of responses in survey research and is not necessarily a function of age, but simply of memory attrition increasing over time. Hence in work such as this, where the main focus is on recalling specific events, it is generally recognized that time-lags should be kept as short as possible.

Eventually face-to-face valid interviews were carried out in June 1991 and January 1992 with 49 clients in Scotland and the North of England. Forty-one interviews took place in the homes of the clients. Four interviews were carried out in a day centre and another four in long-stay hospital or residential care. Of the four respondents who were interviewed in a residential setting, one was in hospital, one in a private nursing home and another two were in residential homes, one on a respite visit. Despite all precautions taken to exclude such clients from the sample, those few were found to have remained, either because they were recent admissions or because they simply had slipped through the net. All three clients in long-term care were found difficult to interview. Nevertheless, they were included in the analyses because quite a lot of data was obtained from the interviews. The researcher also had some doubts about the reliability of some of the other respondents' answers and felt that judgements about systematically excluding these three respondents, while keeping others, would be somewhat arbitrary. Furthermore, their contributions prompted some of the issues which this chapter addresses. The three people were, however, excluded from the analyses which sought to address the initial research question on which the interviews were based.

RESPONDENTS

The interview sample comprised 33 women and 16 men (proportions similar to those found in the main sample), whose ages ranged from 53 to 90 and included three women who did not know their age. There were no respondents from ethnic minorities. Half of the respondents were more than 81 years of age, marginally older than clients in the main sample. Half of the respondents lived alone and three-quarters had relatives who lived within easy travelling distance and who visited them weekly. Eight of the interviews took place with a relative present and participating in the interview. Bury and Holme (1990) refer to those helpers as proxies. However, in their case, the presence of proxies had been planned, whereas our own proxies were self-appointed. Two of the proxies were spouses, five were daughters or sons, and one was a sister. No age group was more likely to have a proxy. It was not clear whether the interviews would have been possible without them and what impact on the respondents' responses and self-assurance they had, but the interviewer was very reluctant to ask the self-appointed proxy, usually the main carer, to leave the room, in a few cases their own living room or kitchen.

All the respondents were, or had recently been, clients of social work teams. The services they received ranged from a one-off aids and adaptations assessment to more prolonged and intensive involvement, characterized by complex packages of care. Nearly half (43%) were receiving between three and five services. Home helps or home carers were the most commonly received service. Only four clients did not receive at least one service at the time of the interview. For example, one respondent had requested help with her telephone bills and had not been successful. Another had requested a shower, but had been turned down because of budget constraints. Twenty-nine out of 49 had a home help or home carer. One-third perceived those visits as combining a practical and a social element, i.e. home helps were often described as being good company. Twenty-six of the 29 reported these visits to be at least weekly, although this is a misleading statistic as the visits ranged from being daily and lasting half an hour (e.g. to get the person up) to being weekly but lasting 2 hours. Only 14 clients received meals-on-wheels. Six clients said they had discontinued, refused, or not requested them because they did not like the thought of them. Only nine respondents reported a visit by a bath nurse despite 23 reporting being unable to wash all over by themselves. Other regular visitors mentioned were chiropodists and health visitors. Furthermore, respondents who received those home-based services outnumbered those who received services outside the home: only a quarter went to a day centre and four to respite care, three respondents went to lunch clubs and a few went to see a chiropodist.

Clients varied widely in levels of disability with three of them reporting no problems of mobility but a quarter reporting significant difficulties carrying out their daily activities, including washing themselves. On the whole then, the respondents selected for interview were representative of the social work clientele. They varied widely in their communication skills. The majority of respondents were able to converse without any problems while 19 had impairments more commonly found in older service users such as deafness, slurred speech, confusion – in cases extreme – and suspected dementia. These made interviewing more challenging, although in only one instance were doubts raised as to the reliability of the respondent's answers, which made absolutely no sense. In all other situations, interviews proceeded and yielded valuable data.

METHODS

The purpose of the interviews was to get the clients' views of their most recent contact with their social worker during which an assessment for services had been carried out. The area of inquiry was very tightly specified in that it focused on that single event, and only certain aspects were of interest:

- What did clients think of the assessment that was carried out and the way social workers presented themselves and their work?
- How satisfied were they with the services they received, i.e. did they think they addressed the needs which they themselves thought they had?

The main expectation was that accurate recall of the social work process might be one indicator of effective social work: it would show that the social worker had clearly introduced themselves, had explained what social work was, and had attempted to bring their clients into the decision-making process up to service delivery and possibly beyond. Conversely, accurate recall might also indicate that the social work episode had been made memorable because of its unpleasantness. In any case it was possible that some clients might have greater difficulties remembering their initial contacts with the team, in view of the inevitable time-lag between referral and the interviews, in some cases stretching to a year.

It was decided to focus on the following areas of questioning or headings: personal details, reported health, social work process, services in place, mobility, morale and satisfaction with processes of service delivery.

The main assumption which guided schedule design concerned the respondents' ability to understand, and answer, structured questions. Some of the arguments put forward ran as follows. Old people often fail to voice critical opinions when asked directly. There seemed to be ample evidence that by asking standard satisfaction questions, we would get a high acquiescence rate, upwards of 80% (Berger, 1983; Willcocks, 1984; this book, Chapter 2). This was despite suspected latent negative feelings about certain aspects of the social work process, for instance the assessment process, arrangements for and timing of service delivery, and especially the provenance of the initial referral. As a corollary to this, it was assumed that some elderly people would prefer to tell stories, that is, to launch into perhaps lengthy reminiscences about various aspects of their lives (Chapter 5 gives some examples) or into accounts of unhappiness, loneliness and rejection. These would include any ill-feeling towards carers, who might have set in motion this social work episode without prior consultation with the respondent (Biggs, 1993), thus perhaps casting a shadow over the whole process. Some respondents were expected to be cast in the role of victim, with decisions about their lives taken without explicit consultation, perhaps by younger people – typically a middle-aged carer or a GP. Hence, in addition to the standard satisfaction questions, placed at the end of the schedule (Berger, 1983), a set of loosely structured and flexibly phrased questions was designed to chart what were believed to be the key stages of the assessment process. Respondents who needed prompting could answer questions directly asked of them, although room was left on the schedule after each question for the interviewer to jot down relevant parts of voluble respondents' unstructured stories, thus superimposing a predefined structure on those accounts. After establishing that the respondents remembered who their social worker was (names would be available), the aim was to chart the following stages in the history of the clients' contact with the social work team:

- *Stage 1: source of referral* – self or other.
- *Stage 2: opinion on plans to refer* – if referral was organized by other, had there been discussions with the elderly person and had their opinions been sought?
- *Stage 3: reasons for referral* – as understood by user.
- *Stage 4: description of first social work assessment* – whether an appointment had been made and how; whether the social worker had clearly explained who they were and the purpose of their visit; whether a clear explanation of all possible options had been given; whether the client felt they had got what they wanted out of the dialogue and what they thought of the social worker.
- *Stage 5: salience of services received* – would user manage without?
- *Stage 6: unmet needs* – were there other areas of their lives which they felt remained unaddressed?

A similar, flexibly designed set of questions to elicit clients' views of the services they received was also opted for. After establishing what those services were, they were asked whether they could comment on the frequency, timing and appropriateness of the services and what difference to their own and their carers' lives those made. The answers to questions in Stages 1–3 were precoded, although there was room for respondents' supplementary comments to be jotted down.

The Philadelphia Geriatric Center Morale (PGCM) scale and the Activities of Daily Living (ADL) scale (Bowling, 1991; Kane and Kane, 1981) were chosen to measure morale and mobility, respectively. It had been hypothesized that some responses might be more attributable to low morale or decreased mobility than to the social work process, as encapsulated in the six stages described above. Hence the standardized scales were intended to act as control variables. The PGCM contains 17 items which respondents were invited to respond to by either yes or no. However, there were misgivings about the tone of the PGCM scale due to discomfort at the prospect of asking respondents, at the front line of such concerns, direct questions pertaining to death, 'Do you sometimes feel that life isn't worth living?'; loneliness, 'Do you feel lonely much?'; and perspective on life, 'Do things keep getting worse as you get older?' or 'Do you have a lot to be sad about?'. What should be done if respondents became very upset by the questions? Would the relative youth of the interviewer limit the depth of understanding of the respondents' emotions (Oakley, 1981)? Indeed, much of the literature commenting on this and other similar scales highlights their workability and statistical attributes, skimming over their acceptability to vulnerable respondents (Challis, 1981).

DID THE STRATEGY WORK?

The above question posed itself at two stages in the research: as the interviews were carried out and at the analysis stage. The most striking impression left with the interviewer was that most of the respondents turned out to be laconic: in many instances the data that was gathered was not as rich as had been anticipated. In fact most respondents, except the more articulate and voluble, seemed keener to answer the more structured parts of the interview schedule (Chapter 7 provides a similar finding). One possible explanation might be that the interviewer had been unsuccessful in eliciting fuller accounts from less forthcoming respondents. Furthermore, the respondents may already have had initial ideas about what the interviews would entail which led them to expect, or prefer, certain types of questions rather than others.

Looking more closely at those parts of the schedule which worked better may hold some clues as to why difficulties were experienced with the more loosely structured questions. Questions relating to health and the ability to carry out normal, everyday tasks as listed in the ADL scale may have had more direct meaning to the people interviewed. The concerns underlying those questions were those which they faced in their everyday lives. This was similarly so for the questions pertaining to the frequency and timing of home-based services. Some respondents might have forgotten who their social worker was but they always knew who their home help was. A reason may be because home helps are a high profile, almost universally known, service but also because some home helps were perceived as an important part of users' lives, often the only regular visitor, without whom everyday life would be less manageable and all the lonelier. One client said that her home help 'chats as she's working'. Most home helps could make time for a quick cup of tea and some gossip. One client regretted losing her cheerful and chatty home help for another who was 'not much company'. Hence most respondents seemed positive about their home helps and the other services they received. However, significant criticisms were voiced: five people said they would like their home help hours increased and two did not think the service was appropriate for them. In these two instances, one man felt that having this service reminded him that he had lost part of his independence which disturbed him greatly; the other user, also a man, felt that the length of the visits gave the home help too little time to do anything meaningful and truly helpful. Four clients complained about the meals delivered to them because they did not like them or they were not hot enough. Over half of the respondents reported not needing any additional help, six did not know what else was available, and four were reluctant to increase their current levels of support for fear of losing their independence.

Contrary to initial expectations, the administration of the PGCM scale posed few difficulties. It worked very well with more impaired respondents who understood the rules of the exercise. Respondents would always pick out the keyword in the statements presented to them and answer them according to the instructions. Often, younger or more voluble respondents did not restrict themselves to a yes/no response but, because they were easier to communicate with, could be invited to summarize their thoughts. As far as the content and nature of the scale were concerned, respondents responded very readily to all the items and seemed unruffled by the subject matter, some even joking about the sombre content of the majority of the items. In two instances only was it felt that the topics raised by the scale were too sensitive leading, in one case, to cessation. The man in question had suffered a very serious stroke which had left him paralysed and practically unable to speak. Both he and his wife clearly had difficulties coping with the upheavals caused by this extreme level of disability. It did not seem appropriate to risk adding to the feelings of loss, grief and anger which this couple were experiencing. Even in this case though, no offence was perceptible in reaction to the scale and its subject matter. In this and the other case, however, the interviewer was uncomfortable at the prospect of leaving unwanted feelings for respondents to deal with (Duncombe and Marsden, 1993).

SOCIAL WORK PROCESS QUESTIONS

It became clear early on in the interviewing period that the questions pertaining to the social work process were not going to yield the data that had been hoped for, or would only do so in a handful of cases. It is therefore unhelpful to talk about difficulties when considering the less successful aspects of the interview schedule, because this reinforces assumptions made about respondents, i.e. the subjects of the investigation. In fact, some advantage was gained from what seemed to be data of unpromising quality: it provoked a reflection on the very process which is described in this chapter. First, few respondents seemed to be triggered into qualitative accounts of any kind, let alone the topic of interest;

secondly, few appeared to show interest in the issues presented to them. Inevitably there were problems of recall: although three-quarters of the respondents knew who the named social worker was, only a third of clients who had not referred themselves to the social work team knew who had done so. Furthermore, just under half of the respondents had no recollection of either the social worker's visit or any aspect of its content. Recall was further hampered by the fact that the social worker had visited only days prior to the interview to seek the client's consent. In a few cases the assessment had been for aids and adaptations and respondents only cared that they had got what they wanted.

Certainly it is true that some of the older respondents in the sample were less able to understand or answer some questions. However, this age effect was true of the three questions which pertained to Stages 1 and 2 of the process under consideration and so it is felt that explanations for the apparent lack of data must lie elsewhere.

So, where were those qualitative moments of reminiscence that it was hoped would be triggered, and why did the questions generate so little emotion, except in a handful of the more confident respondents? First, it seems that the importance of these concerns had been overestimated, for the sample (Chapter 2 discusses the salience of different life domains for different respondents). Secondly, because of the very nature of the sample and the way it was drawn, respondents were at different stages in their involvement with the social work team, which was itself of varying intensity. Lastly, little was found to suggest that respondents worried about who had referred them to the social work team, let alone that they felt themselves to be in a power struggle with their GPs or relatives. This is not to deny that these situations exist, and indeed two instances were found. However, if this was a more widespread phenomenon it was not articulated by the great majority of respondents. Perhaps then, the focus of the schedule was too narrow and did not focus on what really mattered to the people consulted. Clients did show what concerned them the most and they also had a fair idea of what had brought on the attention of their social worker. Their attentions seemed to be turned elsewhere: they cared about the services they received and that those should continue (Sinclair et al., 1988). Few clients had access to alternative forms of help and many (84%) could only bravely say that they would just have to manage as best they could, should their current services be withdrawn or reduced.

Hence, Simms' (1989) appeal for a more broadly based enquiry should have been followed to avoid the artificial segmentalization of not only the field but also of people's lives. In other words, the research may have failed to appreciate the importance of assessing the place of the enquiry focus within the respondents' world view, before designing the interview schedule (Peace, 1990). In summary, it was perhaps too optimistic to expect life-history-type accounts which would fit into the structure thought to underlie the process of social work, especially in a short interview.

CONCLUSION

This chapter has shown how assumptions made about potential respondents and what was salient to their everyday lives provided data that lacked the focus and richness expected of it. It is true that a few respondents were found to have lost a considerable amount of their communication skills and were therefore very difficult to interview, but this was by no means true of the majority. In spite of their difficulties, they were able to answer some parts of the schedule very competently, including structured questions pertaining to their mortality and their experiences of ageing. It has also been shown that older service users can answer structured questions and that, given the opportunity, they may like to give qualitative accounts of their experiences, but only where those are of relevance to their own world view or where they are inclined to do so. Hence, regardless of impairment or communication difficulties, respondents well remembered the services they received and, perhaps inevitably, offered a mainly positive account of them. They did show discernment, however, and expressed some criticisms, but about specific aspects of the services they received (Salvage, 1986). That some respondents felt unable to provide answers to the questions dealing with the social work process was of course a disappointment. However, this did force reflection, to learn from these attempts. This reflexive process went beyond merely pointing out the strengths and weaknesses of the research design and interview schedule. It allowed exploration of the wider issues resonant in recent debates about the relationship within the research process between the researcher, the research and the researched (Stanley, 1990; Oakley, 1981) and about what counts as new knowledge. Indeed much is already known about the services to the older users of social work or health. It is, however, more difficult to obtain accounts of how those services really match up with people's own expectations and articulation of needs and wants.

REFERENCES

Berger, M. (1983) Toward maximising the utility of consumer satisfaction as an outcome, in *The Assessment of Psychotherapy Outcome*, (eds M. J. Lambert, E. R. Christensen and S. S. DeJulio), Wiley, New York.

Biggs, S. (1993) *Understanding Ageing*, Open University Press, Milton Keynes.

Bland, R., Bland, R., Cheetham, J. *et al.* (1992) *Residential Homes for Elderly People: Their Costs and Quality*, HMSO, Edinburgh.

Bowling, A. (1991) *Measuring Health*, Open University Press, Buckingham.

Bury, M. and Holme, A. (1990) *Life After Ninety*, Routledge, London.

Challis, D. J. (1981) The measurement of outcome in social care of the elderly. *Journal of Social Policy*, **10**(2), 179–208.

Denzin, N. K. (1978) *The Research Act: A Theoretical Introduction to Sociological Methods*, McGraw-Hill, New York.

Duncombe, J. and Marsden, D. (1993) Love and intimacy: the gender division of emotion and 'emotion work', a neglected aspect of sociological discussion of heterosexual relationships. *Sociology*, **27**(2), 221–241.

Fuller, R. and Tulle-Winton, E. (1993) Specialism, genericism and others: does it make a difference? A study of social work services to elderly people. *Caring for the Elderly in the Community*, Conference Paper, April 1993, Plymouth.

Kane, R. A. and Kane, R. L. (1981) *Assessing the Elderly: A Practical Guide to Measurement*, Lexington Books, Lexington, Mass.

Oakley, A. (1981) Interviewing women: a contradiction in terms, in *Doing Feminist Research*, (ed H. Roberts), Routledge and Kegan Paul, London.

Peace, S. M. (1990) *Researching Social Gerontology: Concepts, Methods and Issues*, Sage, London.

Salvage, A. V. (1986) *Attitudes of the Over-75s to Health and Social Services*, Research Team for the Care of the Elderly, Cardiff.

Simms, M. (1989) Social research and the rationalisation of care, in *The Politics of Field Research - Sociology beyond Enlightenment*, (eds J. F. Gubrium and D. Silverman), Sage, London.

Sinclair, I., Crosbie, D., O'Connor, P. *et al.* (1988) *Bridging Two Worlds - Social Work and the Elderly Living Alone*, Avebury, Aldershot.

Stanley, L. (ed) (1990) *Feminist Praxis: Research, Theory and Epistemology in Feminist Sociology*, Routledge, London.

Willcocks, D. (1984) The 'Ideal Home' visual game: a method of consumer research in old people's homes. *Research, Policy and Planning*, **2**(1), 13–18.

Willcocks, D. M., Ring, J., Kellaher, L. *et al.* (1982) *The Residential Life of Old People: A Study in 100 Local Authority Homes, Volume II Appendices*, Research Report No 13, Survey Research Unit, The Polytechnic of North London, London.

PART THREE

User-Oriented Surveys

Stroke survivors' evaluations of their health care

10

Pandora Pound, Patrick Gompertz and Shah Ebrahim

Service providers have their own agendas for user surveys. They may design questionnaires which are too long for frail users and may not seem relevant to their needs. This chapter sets out a three-stage process of service evaluation which moved from a long questionnaire to one that was short enough for the great majority of patients discharged into the community after rehabilitation for stroke. The answers to service related questions do not usually pose problems for service providers because they only request information that they wish to use. Unusually in this project, having asked service related questions, the authors found that users gave them an answer that they did not regard as valid. A different, user-oriented approach to the next stage of the research showed that user perceptions of physiotherapy were different from professional beliefs. The question then arises as to what a user-oriented service should provide and in what ways. Whose views matter when professionals and users conflict?

INTRODUCTION

'Strange, I felt terrible, and this hand was going dead. And I went to phone up my daughter and I couldn't dial, I kept getting the wrong answer and a man answered the telephone, he said you've got the wrong number dear. ... I went to go to the toilet and wet meself. I had no control over me bladder. I went to go in the bedroom to get a clean pair of knickers and fell. That was the end of me.' (Mrs Greenwood – to protect the identity of the interviewees all names have been changed)

Stroke is a condition most people are familiar with. In a Western population of 100 000 people there are about 750 people who have survived a stroke and each year in the same size population about 200 people have a new stroke. Strokes are so called because they usually occur rapidly and without warning. Either a clot blocks an artery supplying blood to the brain, or there is bleeding into the brain from a burst blood vessel, with the result that part of the brain is damaged or destroyed. Some of the common effects of this damage are paralysis on one side of the body, loss of speech, problems with communication, balance, memory, vision, perception, swallowing, incontinence and depression. To some extent, unaffected parts of the brain take over the functions of the damaged parts and in most cases the person learns new ways of using their bodies and of living.

Most people who have a stroke come into medical care. The care they receive has traditionally been adequate at best and, at worst, characterized by neglect or disinterest. More recently, however, the management of stroke has aroused debate. In 1988 a panel of experts presented evidence in a public forum, noting that 'The services that are provided in hospital, primary care, and the community seem haphazard, fragmented, and poorly tailored to patients' needs, and there is a striking lack of convincing data on the effectiveness of widely used medical, psychological and specific rehabilitative treatments' (Consensus statement 1988). The conference met to try and establish appropriate responses to stroke and to set out recommendations for practice. More recently the government (Secretary of State for Health, 1991), identified stroke as a key area, with its main targets being to reduce stroke incidence and mortality (particularly in the younger age groups) and ensure the maximum quality of life for survivors.

Yet people who have strokes are seldom asked for their views on the services they receive. This may be partly due to the fact that between 32% and 48% of stroke survivors experience some sort of difficulty with speech and communication (Anderson, 1992), which makes interviewing more difficult. On the other hand it may be because the majority of people who have strokes are elderly. Elderly people are often regarded as inherently unreliable sources of information, although obviously there is no justification for this belief (Dorevitch et al., 1992). Additionally, stroke, perhaps more so than any other condition, is presented in the literature as a family illness (Editorial BMJ, 1974; Mykyta et al., 1976; Field et al., 1983; Anderson, 1987; Anderson, 1988a; Cassidy and Gray, 1991) and much of the literature, even that which claims to put the stroke survivor centre stage, tends to prioritize the disadvantage suffered by the carer. While it is obviously difficult to isolate the effects of stroke, and while carers undoubtedly suffer great disadvantage, what is striking in many of the papers is the invisibility of the person who has actually had the stroke.

However, there are signs of change. A recent study (Greveson and James, 1991) asked patients (and carers) what their priorities were and found that most wanted better post-discharge support, more information and more practical help. Another (pilot) study (McLean et al., 1991) directly asked patients and carers about their needs and concluded that families needed more information and counselling after stroke. Finally, Anderson (1992) asked people (9 months after their stroke) whether there was anything about their experience in hospital which they especially liked or disliked. He found that about two-thirds recalled a positive aspect, the most common being that nurses had been kind and encouraging, and that less than half recalled a negative aspect, usually that it was difficult to obtain help from nurses, particularly at night. Anderson did not ask patients systematically about their attitudes towards rehabilitation, but notes that several commented that they would have preferred more therapy.

When we were planning the North East Thames Stroke Outcomes Study (NETSOS) we needed a questionnaire with which to assess people's satisfaction with the care they received. Since no such questionnaire existed in the field of stroke (Seale and Davies, 1987) we had to develop our own, the details of which have been described by Pound et al. (1994). (The NETSOS register contains information on all people admitted with acute stroke to the four major hospitals in two adjacent health districts in North East Thames between January 1991 and March 1992.)

This chapter focuses firstly on the way we determined the content of the questionnaire and, secondly, on our efforts to interpret accurately the results we obtained using it. In the course of the study we move from a small number of in-depth pilot interviews to a large-scale survey and then back to in-depth interviews. In so doing, we attempted to go beyond the relatively superficial level of satisfaction questionnaires to explore the complexity of stroke survivors' evaluations of their treatment. There is increasing acceptance of the political necessity of collecting patients' opinions about their health care, but if it is **really** accepted that there is a place for both lay and medical perspectives, much more effort is needed to understand fully the context in which lay evaluations are made. What follows is an attempt to do this in the field of stroke.

PILOT STUDY

Methods and sample

We wanted to develop a questionnaire that was comprehensive and relevant, or **content valid** (Brewer and Hunter, 1989). In other words the questions would need to cover all the areas of care which patients might experience. In order to try and ensure content validity (other aspects of validity were tested, as was reliability (Pound et al., 1994)) we reviewed the literature, talked to colleagues and interviewed seven people who had recently been discharged from hospital following a stroke. Their names were taken from a stroke register which had been set up as a pilot for the outcomes study. Although 15 people, taken consecutively from the register 2–3 months after their stroke, were invited to participate, only seven agreed to be interviewed. Three did not feel well enough, two were unreachable despite repeated visits and telephone calls, and three were unwilling. Of those interviewed, all were white Caucasian and five were women. Six people rented their homes from the council, and one lived in warden-supervised accommodation.

As far as possible we wanted the interviewees to set their own agenda and describe their concerns according to their own priorities. The interviewer used a guide to ensure that each conversation covered the same general areas, but within these areas the conversation was flexible so that issues could be explored in more detail according to each individual's particular situation (Patton, 1987). Essentially the conversation began with people's description of onset of the stroke and the story was brought up to date, with the interviewer asking open-ended questions about the care and treatment received in hospital and after discharge.

A content analysis (Patton, 1987) was then conducted on the data. In the case of both the pilot interviews and the later interviews, this involved several careful and systematic readings of the transcripts in order to identify themes or patterns. Themes which recurred, for example people's descriptions of the way physiotherapy had helped them recover a particular skill, were identified and coded. Themes could emerge in two main ways; either they were patterns which materialized irrespective of (or despite) the interviewer's questions, or else they surfaced in response to a particular question posed by the interviewer. The number of times each theme occurred was then counted in order to give some indication of the prevalence of the theme across the whole body of data (Silverman, 1985). The various themes were then organized into more general categories, for example 'satisfaction with physical recovery'.

Findings

The literature had drawn attention to the poor quality of services after discharge (Isaacs et al., 1976; Mackey and Nias, 1979; Brocklehurst et al., 1981; Ebrahim and Nouri, 1986; Legh-Smith et al., 1986; Wade et al., 1986; Anderson, 1988b), in particular the provision of meals-on-wheels, home helps, district nursing, aids and adaptations, the quality of out-patient services and discharge preparation itself. Health professionals suggested that nursing care, information giving and the quality of the ambulance service might be given more consideration. However, the main concern voiced by stroke survivors themselves was survival and recovery. For example Mrs Griggs, when asked about her primary concern on going into hospital, replied:

'The major thing was always am I going to die?'

People seemed to evaluate each aspect of the service according to its perceived impact on recovery and although other areas such as the quality of the food or discomfort with mixed sex wards were mentioned, the general impression gained was that comfort could be sacrificed in exchange for a good recovery. In view of the fact that stroke is a potentially fatal condition this is not surprising. Although a certain amount of spontaneous natural recovery occurs in all people who survive a stroke, and although the contribution of rehabilitation to the recovery process has not yet been determined, people generally believed that admission to hospital had either saved their lives or brought about recovery that would not otherwise have occurred:

> Interviewer: 'What do you think would have happened if you had not gone into hospital?'
> Mr Dodd: 'I would have died.'

> 'What would I have done if I'd taken no notice and laid here? Would I have got my sight back? Would I have been able to speak?' (Mrs Horton)

Recovery of basic activities of daily living such as walking and talking was a major concern:

> 'Twelve weeks in hospital before they discharged me. But in the meantime they were able to make me walk again, and I'm being treated to learn to write again. I couldn't even write my own name. Now I can write my signature.' (Mr Dodd)

There was great satisfaction with physiotherapy and all believed that it had had an impact on their functional recovery, but there was marked dissatisfaction with the **amount** of physiotherapy available and the ease and speed with which it could be arranged. Physiotherapy, which forms one of the major components of rehabilitation after stroke, aims to encourage the restoration of movement and function, and to ensure that nothing prevents the recovery of useful movement. Anxiety about the amount of physiotherapy received was closely related to concern with recovery, and appeared to be the second most important issue for this sample:

> 'That's one thing I don't think they make long enough, I mean you are asking my opinion? ... After about 5 weeks they said she had had her quota and she couldn't go any more, because of the other people on the list ... . I still think that therapy did her leg good, right Mum?' (Mrs Ticker's daughter)

QUESTIONNAIRE DEVELOPMENT

Taking into account subject areas derived from the interviews, the literature and the consultation with colleagues, a questionnaire containing 50 questions was drafted. This was sent to a sample of 28 people who had had a stroke 6 months earlier. However, there was only a 35% response rate, many questions were unanswered and the format, which consisted of several branch questions with instructions, was obviously not easy to understand. These detailed questions were therefore replaced by 13 general statements, each with response categories of strongly agree, agree, disagree or strongly disagree. The questionnaire was divided into two sections, one on in-patient care and the other on services after discharge. This version was sent to another sample of 28 people, again 6 months after their stroke. This time, the response rate was 65%, all the questions were answered and the format appeared to be well understood and acceptable to the respondents. The questions and responses are shown below, in the order they appear on the questionnaire. The categories of agree and strongly agree are collapsed to give a general rating of satisfaction.

1. Hospital care and treatment – satisfaction
   (a) I have been treated with kindness and respect by the staff at the hospital – 94%.
   (b) The staff attended well to my personal needs while I was in hospital (for example I was able to get to the toilet whenever I needed) – 88%.
   (c) I felt able to talk to the staff about any problems I might have had – 82.5%.
   (d) I have received all the information I want about the causes and nature of my illness – 72%.
   (e) The doctors have done everything they can to make me well again – 87%.
   (f) I am happy with the amount of recovery I have made since my illness – 69%.
   (g) I am satisfied with the type of treatment the therapists have given me (e.g. physiotherapy, speech therapy, occupational therapy) – 85%.
   (h) I have had enough therapy (e.g. physiotherapy, speech therapy, occupational therapy) – 46%.

2. Discharge and after – satisfaction
   (a) I was given all the information I needed about the allowances and services (e.g. home help, district nurse, meals-on-wheels) I might need after leaving hospital – 67.5%.
   (b) Things were well prepared for my return home (i.e. aids such as stair rails or wheelchairs had been organized if necessary) – 67%.
   (c) I get all the support I need from services such as meals-on-wheels, home helps, district nursing, etc. – 68%.
   (d) I am satisfied with the out-patient services provided by the hospital (e.g. the day hospital or appointments with doctors or therapists) – 74%.
   (e) I think the ambulance service is reliable – 70%.

THE SATISFACTION SURVEY

The questionnaire was sent to all survivors (n = 219) on the NETSOS stroke register when they reached the sixth month after their stroke. People were also sent a postal version of the Barthel Activities of Daily Living Index (Mahoney and Barthel, 1965), the Nottingham Extended Activities of Daily Living Scale (Nouri and Lincoln, 1987), the Nottingham Health Profile (Hunt *et al.*, 1986), the short form of the Geriatric Depression Scale (Lum *et al.*, 1982) and the Faces Scale (Andrews and Withey, 1976). The response rate after three follow-ups was 87%. Of the 191 people who returned questionnaires, 42 were unable to complete the satisfaction questionnaire due to dysphasia or confusion. The mean age of the remaining 149 people was 71 years; 74 were women; 119 were white, 11 black Caribbean, 8 Bangladeshi, 3 black African, 3 Indian and 3 Pakistani. One person was described as other Asian and details about race were missing in one case.

The results of the satisfaction survey (above) reflected the findings from the pilot study. People were generally very satisfied with most aspects of in-patient care, but there was less satisfaction with the amount of recovery made and with most of the domiciliary services received. The most striking finding was that while 85% of people were satisfied with the *type* of therapy (physiotherapy, speech therapy and occupational therapy) they received, the highest rate of dissatisfaction recorded (54% dissatisfied) was with the *amount* of therapy received.

The informal reaction of colleagues was that people were wrong to want more therapy. This is because from a clinical point of view the benefits of continued therapy after stroke have not been demonstrated. Although a recent study (Wade *et al.*, 1992) suggests that there may be benefits late after stroke, the most that can be concluded at present is that physiotherapy at least **seems** to be associated with modest improvements (using functional and physical outcome measures) in the first few months after a stroke (Freemantle *et al.*, 1992; Tallis, 1992). We were therefore in the position of knowing that stroke survivors were very dissatisfied with the amount of rehabilitation they received, but we did not know why. While the satisfaction survey was able to indicate broad areas of dissatisfaction therefore, it was unable to give the depth of information necessary to interpret the data accurately or usefully. Ideally we needed to go back to people and ask them.

QUALITATIVE STUDY

As a separate study we had conducted 40 in-depth interviews with a subsample of people from the NETSOS register, 10 months after their stroke. The interviews covered areas such as medical treatment, rehabilitation, nursing care, support after discharge, any disadvantage experienced and whether or not stroke had changed people's lives. We analysed the data from these interviews to see if they held any clues as to why people felt they needed more therapy. For reasons of simplicity and brevity we will here consider physiotherapy only, since this is the most common form of rehabilitation after stroke. Before presenting the findings, the interview sample is briefly described.

Sample and methods

The sample comprised 21 men and 19 women. Thirty-five people were white, 3 were Bangladeshi and 2 were black Caribbean. The mean age at the time of interview was 71.5 years (range 40–87 years). Twenty-three people lived in council housing, five in warden-supervised accommodation, eight were owner occupiers, two were living in privately rented houses, one person was in bed-and-breakfast accommodation and another was staying in her daughter's home at the time of the interview.

Eighty-two people's names had been taken consecutively from the NETSOS register during a period of 9 months, and had been invited to take part in an interview. As with the pilot study the take-up rate was disappointing. Only 40 people accepted, giving a rate of 49%. However, people who had not responded to the invitation were not chased up because it was felt that they had already contributed a great deal to the outcomes study. The main reasons given for non-participation were poor health. (Those lost to follow-up in the outcomes study during the 9 month period – those who had moved out of the study area, those still in-patients at 10 months and those known to be unable to participate in an in-depth interview due to dementia ($n = 3$) or severe speech impairment ($n = 3$) – were excluded from the sampling frame. Additionally, because fewer women than men were able to participate in the interviews, mainly for reasons of ill-health, men were excluded from sampling during the last 2 months of the study period.)

The scores obtained using the outcome measures 6 months after the stroke indicated that there were no significant differences in disability, well-being or depression between those who accepted the invitation to be interviewed and those who refused. However, the same package of outcome measures was also sent 12 months after the stroke, and by this stage those who had accepted the invitation to be interviewed were found to be significantly less disabled, using the activities of daily living (ADL) scales, than those who had refused. Nevertheless, the level and range of disability amongst sample members was still fairly high. The ADL scores indicated that most of the sample were moderately dependent in basic activities such as self-care, using the toilet and mobility, while for more advanced tasks such as shopping, washing and cooking, most people needed daily support from a carer or from social services.

All interviews were conducted and tape-recorded in peoples' homes (except one which took place at hospital). The methods employed during both data collection and analysis were the same as those employed in the pilot study, described above.

Findings

First and foremost the interviews allowed a detailed view of the effects of stroke on people's lives. This contextualized the question and made it much easier to understand the value of physiotherapy from the insider's perspective. The 40 people described disadvantages in many areas of handicap:

- getting out of the house – 25
- leisure activities – 15
- housework (including shopping and cooking) – 15
- mood changes – 15
- walking – 14
- communication – 13
- washing, bathing and dressing – 12
- relationships – 10
- costs incurred and lack of money – 9
- memory and confusion – 7

The majority of people (25) were partially or totally housebound, due to a combination of mobility problems and an inaccessible environment. Several (15) felt disadvantaged because they had had to cut down on leisure activities or because of mood changes (15). A frequent cause of disadvantage to women was the inability to do housework (only two men felt disadvantaged in this area, as opposed to 13 women).

Fourteen people were unable to walk in the way they wanted to. Many people's bodies had changed suddenly and uncontrollably as a result of their stroke. The after-effects of stroke and the feelings of alienation from one's own body could continue for many months. Mr Higgins had lost all feeling and movement in his left hand. During the course of the interview he slapped it several times with his right hand as if it was an impediment hanging from the rest of his body that did not belong to him. Several people described their arms, legs and toes as dead. Ms Mansell had given her arm the name of Dodo, suggesting that it was both extinct and apart from the rest of herself.

The common perception of stroke summons up images of people who are paralysed, immobile and dependent. Given this popular imagery, and in many cases the reality of stroke, it soon became more clear why physiotherapy, one of the few treatments available after the event, and one which is active, physical and aims to restore movement and abilities, was so appreciated by stroke survivors.

Appreciation of physiotherapy

Twenty-four people had received physiotherapy. Using average scores on the two activities of daily living scales, people who had physiotherapy were slightly more disabled than those who had not had physiotherapy. Nineteen of the people who had received physiotherapy were positive about it, one person was negative and four were indifferent. Although the following discussion draws on data from all 40 interviews, the focus is on those who received physiotherapy.

The most common reason for wanting more physiotherapy was because people believed it would bring about further recovery. Over half the people (13) who had physiotherapy believed that it had been instrumental in regaining the use of their limbs or specific abilities and many also suggested that it had been crucial to their recovery. Because physiotherapy was perceived to have brought about recovery in the first place, people seemed to believe that the more they had, the better they would get. At the time of the interview (10 months after the stroke) several people felt that therapy could benefit them further. As Mr Moore's wife said:

'He went down to the gym, yes, cos I went there a couple of times to see what they did with him. It was very helpful, but um, ... I said to the physio, "Will it [continue]?" and she said, "No". So, no more, no more physio, so, she said, "There is a limit to what you can do." So I said, "Well what about his hand?" I said, "He can't do anything with his hand'', so she said, "No, it's just been allowed to get that way." But I don't know ... .'

Whether in fact it is true that continued therapy would directly bring about further physical recovery is not known. However, if morale and self-esteem have any connection with recovery then it would seem that physiotherapists are playing an important role and one for which they were much appreciated. Seven people, most of whom had given up believing that they would ever again regain their former abilities, described the ways in which physiotherapists had restored their faith in their bodies, for example Mr McCarthy:

'He [physiotherapist] said, "You can walk." I said – this was after so long, you know, 2 months or something like that, 6 weeks maybe – he said, "You can walk." I walked behind him, I just walked, I thought I was Jesus! [Laughs] I couldn't believe it, you know! I just felt like Jesus walking on water!'

Similarly, people who already had determination and willpower seemed to draw upon the therapists as a resource to help them in their struggle for recovery, as Mrs Patten suggests when asked if she had had any physiotherapy:

'Oh yes, I had – and I said, I'm going to walk with this frame you know, I thought, no, I was so determined ... she took me walking up and down into the ward, oh, and then she brought me scrap paper and pencil for writing, you know. And I thought, no, no, I'm not going to do this, and she said, you will, perhaps you'll do it better when you get home. I sent all my Easter cards out!'

However, while people were overwhelmingly concerned with the outcome of their treatment, the interviews suggested that they also gained a great deal from its **process** and this was illustrated in their appreciation of exercise. Exercise is one of the components of physiotherapy and it may be that in the context of stroke, exercise takes on particular meaning. We noted above that stroke connotes paralysis and immobility and that many people described their limbs as heavy, numb or dead. Exercise is all about moving the body and in some cases there was the suggestion that without it, the body might completely seize up. People variously referred to the benefits of exercise as it 'keeps you moving', 'keeps you going' or 'keeps you busy'. An extract from Mr Higgins' interview illustrates many themes common to this sample:

'[He is on the floor demonstrating his exercises] Yes, I do that now, I'm not so bad, like I used to. I hold that like that – it all helps, see? Keeps you busy. And of course this lot – like the army used to say, I want your knees touching your chin, like that – yeah! [Laughs – another exercise.] That's what I do, you see, to keep meself moving. And it all helps, the muscle in your leg. ... When you're getting on, the old bones ain't moving about like they used to be. I think it's what you try and make it yourself. You could either let yourself go, and that's it, say, well I've had enough, and not bother, or, like as I am with this, I could sit down and not do nothing. But I don't do it like that, I don't work like that. I might get away with it and I might not. So, I go and exercise on me own.'

People were particularly appreciative where they had been given a programme of exercises to follow after discharge. As was the case with many people, Mrs Hughes now depended upon someone else to carry out even the most basic activities. She was unable to fulfil roles she had previously enjoyed and was only able to exert autonomy in a restricted number of areas. However, exercise was one of these areas. Her partner describes the value of her programme:

'It was helpful, because er, she [physiotherapist] explained to her what to do with her legs sitting down. And putting her heel down, stretching her toes out, so it gives her exercises she can do whether I'm here or not. [Mrs Hughes: "I keep exercising me arm."] So if she's got a spare 10 minutes and she gets a bit bored with herself, she can move her arm 'cos she taught her how to do it. Do you understand me?'

DISCUSSION

Issues arising from the research

Both at the pilot stage and in the later qualitative study the acceptance rate for the interviews was low. While overexposure to the project might explain some of the reluctance to participate in the later interviews, it does not help explain the poor response at the pilot stage. Health problems, particularly the effects of the stroke, seemed to be the most common reason given for refusal at both stages. This raises the question of bias in the sample, particularly with regards to people with speech impairments. While the sample included people with milder speech difficulties, with carers interpreting where necessary, it is likely that the concerns of people with **severe** speech problems were not adequately represented. Similarly in the satisfaction survey, 22% of people were unable to complete the questionnaire due to speech problems or confusion. This is a significant problem and there is a need to develop more imaginative ways of conducting research in this area.

The various effects of the stroke presented difficulties for the interviewer. While some people had speech impairments, others were confused and a small number had emotionalism. The latter is one of the rarer effects of stroke: a tendency to laugh or cry at what are considered to be inappropriate moments. One woman, in addition to having a fairly serious speech impairment, burst into short floods of tears every few minutes during her interview. All these factors contributed to making the interviews hard work and the interviewer was constantly worried about asking too much of people.

Although there is a growing body of literature on researching sensitive topics (Lee, 1993; Renzetti and Lee, 1992), there is less on research which is conducted in stressful situations, such as when the interviewee is in poor health (e.g. Cannon, 1989). When the interview appears to demand a lot of the interviewer, it is understandable that the interviewer may feel guilt and/or want to reciprocate in some way. One of the ways in which the interviewer dealt with this was to provide practical help when this was asked for. In total, this was provided in 14 cases and mainly involved help with organizing welfare benefits and the provision of aids and adaptations.

Importance of patients' views

The stroke survivors interviewed for this study demonstrated that they are critically concerned with recovery and the outcome of their treatment. However in patient satisfaction research people are less frequently asked for their views on the outcome of their treatment and what it means to them than they are for their opinions on the hotel aspects of health care or the personal qualities of staff (Cleary and McNeil, 1988; Fitzpatrick, 1984; Hall and Dornan, 1988; Wiles, 1993). This study suggests that the personal qualities of therapists were of lesser importance to patients compared with their main priority which was to get as much treatment as possible and to get better.

However, an increase in the amount of physiotherapy given to stroke survivors, while possibly resulting in greater satisfaction with the service, might not bring about a concomitant reduction in disability. Because of (apparent) paradoxes such as this, and studies suggesting that patients may be satisfied with care which is not considered beneficial from a clinical point of view (Orth-Gomer et al., 1979; Ross Woolley et al., 1978) there is caution about the use of patient-centred outcome measures (Sensky and Catalan, 1992). This is largely due to the dominance of medical perspectives in defining standards for the quality of care. However, there are many ways of defining quality (Donabedian, 1988). Patients and clinicians each have their own priorities; sometimes these coincide, but when they do not, the conclusion should not automatically be that the patient is wrong. While the clinical benefits of continued physiotherapy after stroke have yet to be established, we have attempted to argue that stroke survivors have many good reasons for wanting physiotherapy to continue.

Although the people in this sample were primarily concerned with physical outcome (and in this they are in agreement with their doctors), they also demonstrated that physiotherapy had an effect on several other levels. In other words, the treatment provided benefits over and above those it was specifically designed to produce. This underlines the need for more appropriate outcome measures in trials of rehabilitation. Traditional measures focus almost exclusively on functional outcomes and fail to reflect the other benefits which may be gained from physiotherapy such as an increased feeling of well-being or a sense of self-worth.

CONCLUSION

This study has demonstrated some of the benefits of combining qualitative and quantitative research methods in the evaluation of health care. Qualitative methods are capable of providing insights into patients' priorities and predicaments, which should bring about a deeper understanding of the way in which patients evaluate their health care (Williams, 1994). In our study, the interviews drew attention to the possibility that the condition which brings people into contact with medical care will have an impact on the way they evaluate it. In this case, the nature of stroke itself seemed to be a significant factor in determining people's response to physiotherapy, and exercise in particular.

The qualitative work conducted during the pilot stage helped to increase the content validity of the questionnaire. Stroke survivors' concern with the quantity and outcome of their treatment was an issue which emerged from neither the literature search nor discussion with colleagues. The patient satisfaction survey was important because it was able to verify the findings from the pilot study and provide evidence of people's dissatisfaction on a larger scale. However, it was one thing to know that people were dissatisfied with the amount of physiotherapy they had, and another thing to know **why** that was. Further qualitative work was able to suggest some answers and begin to provide the insight necessary to bring about sensitive change.

REFERENCES

Anderson, R. (1987) The unremitting burden on carers. *British Medical Journal*, **294**, 73.

Anderson, R. (1988a) The contribution of informal care to the management of stroke. *International Disability Studies*, **10**, 107–137.

Anderson, R. (1988b) The quality of life of stroke patients and their carers, in *Living with Chronic Illness: The Experience of Patients and Their Families*, (eds R. Anderson and M. Bury), Unwin Hyman, London.

Anderson, R. (1992) *The Aftermath of Stroke: The Experience of Patients and Their Families*, Cambridge University Press, Cambridge.

Andrews, F. M. and Withey, S. B. (1976) *Social Indicators of Well Being: Americans' Perceptions of Life Quality*. Plenum, New York.

Brewer, J. and Hunter, A. (1989) *Multi-method Research: A Synthesis of Styles*, Sage, Newbury Park.

Brocklehurst, J. C., Morris, P., Andrews, K., *et al.* (1981) Social effects of stroke. *Social Science and Medicine*, **15a**, 35–39.

Cannon, S. (1989) Social research in stressful settings: difficulties for the sociologist studying the treatment of breast cancer. *Sociology of Health and Illness*, **11**(1), 63–67.

Cassidy, T. P. and Gray, C. S. (1991) Stroke and the carer. *British Journal of General Practice*, **41**, 267–268.

Cleary, P. D. and McNeil, B. J. (1988) Patient satisfaction as an indicator of quality care. *Inquiry*, **25**, 25–36.

Consensus statement (1988) Treatment of stroke. *British Medical Journal*, **297**, 126–128.

Donabedian, A. (1988) The quality of care. How can it be assessed? *Journal of the American Medical Association*, **260**, 1743–1748.

Dorevitch, M. I., Cossar, R. M., Bailey, F. J. *et al.* (1992) The accuracy of self and informant ratings of physical functional capacity in the elderly. *Journal of Clinical Epidemiology*, **45**(7), 791–798.

Ebrahim, S. and Nouri, F. (1986) Caring for stroke patients at home. *International Rehabilitation Medicine*, **8**, 171–173.

Editorial (1974) Stroke and the family. *British Medical Journal*, October 19, 122.

Field, D., Cordle, C. J. and Bowman, G. S. (1983) Coping with stroke at home. *International Rehabilitation Medicine*, **5**, 96–100.

Fitzpatrick, R. (1984) Satisfaction with health care, in *The Experience of Illness*, (eds R. Fitzpatrick *et al.*), Tavistock, London.

Freemantle, N., Pollock, C., Sheldon, T. A., *et al.* (1992) Formal rehabilitation after stroke. *Quality in Health Care*, **1**, 134–137.

Greveson, G. and James, O. (1991) Improving long-term outcome after stroke – the views of patients and carers. *Health Trends*, **23**, 161–162.

Hall, J. A. and Dornan, M. C. (1988) What patients like about their medical care and how often they are asked: a meta-analysis of the satisfaction literature. *Social Science and Medicine*, **27**(9), 935–939.

Hunt, S. M., McEwen, J. and McKenna, S. P. (1986) *Measuring Health Status*, Croom Helm, London.

Isaacs, B., Neville, Y. and Rushford, I. (1976) The stricken: the social consequences of stroke. *Age and Ageing*, **5**, 188–192.

Lee, R. (1993) *Doing Research on Sensitive Topics*, Sage, London.

Legh-Smith, J., Wade, D. T. and Langton-Hewer, R. (1986) Services for stroke patients one year after stroke. *Journal of Epidemiology and Community Health*, **40**, 161–165.

Lum, O., Brink, T. L., Yesavage, J. A., *et al.* (1982) Screening tests for geriatric depression. *Clinical Gerontology*, **1**, 37–43.

Mackey, A. and Nias, B. (1979) Stroke in the young and middle aged: consequences to family and society. *Journal of the Royal College of Physicians of London*, **13**(2), 106–112.

Mahoney, F. I., Barthel, D. W., *et al.* (1965) Functional evaluation: the Barthel Index. *Maryland State Medical Journal*, **14**, 61–65.

McLean, J., Roper-Hall, A., Mayer, P., *et al.* (1991) Service needs of stroke survivors and their informal carers: a pilot study. *Journal of Advanced Nursing*, **16**, 559–564.

Mykyta, L. J., Bowling, J. H., Nelson, D. A., *et al.* (1976) Caring for relatives of stroke patients. *Age and Ageing*, **5**, 87–90.

Nouri, F. M. and Lincoln, N. B. (1987) An extended activities of daily living index for stroke patients. *Clinical Rehabilitation*, **1**, 301–305.

Orth-Gomer, K., Britton, M. and Rehnqvist, N. (1979) Quality of care in an outpatient department: the patient's view. *Social Science and Medicine*, **13a**, 347–350.

Patton, M. Q. (1987) *How to Use Qualitative Methods in Evaluation*, Sage, London.

Pound, P., Gompertz, P. and Ebrahim, S. (1994) Patients' satisfaction with stroke services. *Clinical Rehabilitation*, **8**, 7–17.

Renzetti, C. and Lee, R. (eds) (1992) *Researching Sensitive Topics*, Sage, London.

Ross Woolley, F., Kane, R. L., Hughes, C. C., *et al.* (1978) The effects of doctor-patient communication on satisfaction and outcome of care. *Social Science and Medicine*, **12**, 123–128.

Seale, C. and Davies, P. (1987) Outcome measurement in stroke rehabilitation research. *International Disability Studies*, **9**, 155–160.

Secretary of State for Health. (1991) *The Health of the Nation*, HMSO, London.

Sensky, T. and Catalan, J. (1992) Asking patients about their treatment. *British Medical Journal*, **305**, 1109–1110.

Silverman, D. (1985) *Qualitative Methodology and Sociology: Describing the Social World*, Gower, Aldershot.

Tallis, R. (1992) Rehabilitation of the elderly in the 21st century. *Journal of the Royal College of Physicians of London*, **26**(4), 413–422.

Wade, D. T., Legh-Smith, J. and Langton-Hewer, R. (1986) Effects of living with and looking after survivors of a stroke. *British Medical Journal*, **293**, 418–420.

Wade, D. T., Collen, M. C., Robb, G. F., *et al.* (1992) Physiotherapy intervention late after stroke and mobility. *British Medical Journal*, **304**, 609–613.

Wiles, R. (1993) Consumer involvement in outcomes measurement – what are the barriers? *Critical Public Health*, **4**(4), 35–40.

Williams, B. (1994) Patient satisfaction: a valid concept? *Social Science and Medicine*, **38**(4), 509–516.

11

Leaving home: a real choice for people with learning disabilities?

Andrew Jahoda and Martin Cattermole

Yes/No questionnaires which concentrate on skills of daily living are often administered to people with learning disabilities. The type of response achieved tends to reinforce the belief that people with learning disabilities are incapable of coping with anything more complicated. This chapter discusses alternative research methods of participant observation, the importance of getting to know individuals so that the context of their lives informs the research, and the need for semistructured interviewing. The authors show that adults with learning disabilities who are leaving the parental home have a wide range of expectations and experiences which they are able to discuss. Staff concentration on domestic and other basic living skills can obscure the importance of wider emotional and practical experiences which provide a better quality of life and more successful outcome to independent living.

The last 25 years have been a period of slow revolution in services for people with learning disabilities in the UK as well as many other countries. Before the 1970s the main alternative to living in the family home was hospital care. The 1971 government White Paper *Better Services for the Mentally Handicapped* (DHSS, 1971) led to local authorities developing both living accommodation, mostly in the form of 20–30 place hostels, and day services based in adult training centres.

During the 1980s the emphasis in residential services changed towards the development of smaller, staffed group homes using ordinary housing in the community. The availability of relatively high state benefits to people in private and voluntary residential homes led to a large increase in this provision. Between 1976 and 1990 the number of places available in local authority and private and voluntary residential accommodation almost tripled. However, this growth was matched by a fall in people living in hospital, meaning that the overall level of service has remained virtually static (MENCAP, 1994).

Public and professional attention has tended to focus on the movement of people from hospital to the community, obscuring the reality that over half the adults with learning disabilities in Britain live with their families (MENCAP, 1994). Unlike most other adults, few people with learning disabilities get the opportunity to leave home as part of a step to achieving adult status. Most continue to live with parents, and often an alternative is only sought when parents can no longer provide support.

The 1989 White Paper *Caring for People* (Cm 849, 1989) and the resulting NHS and Community Care Act (1990) have set a new framework for services for elderly and disabled people in the UK. The new legislation gives local authorities a lead role in assessing the needs of individuals and arranging packages of care. One of the objectives of the White Paper was to reduce the need for residential care, and instead:

'... to promote the development of domiciliary (care at home), day and respite services to enable people to live in their own homes wherever feasible and sensible' (Cm 849, 1989).

The meaning of this objective is ambiguous in the case of people with learning disabilities, the overwhelming majority of whom do not have a home of their own. This problem reflects a wider neglect of the housing dimension to community care (Arnold *et al.*, 1993), as the emphasis of the new legislation has been on elderly people, most of whom do have somewhere to live. For people with learning disabilities the effect of the act may well be to keep them living in the family home for as long as possible, particularly as funding limits are likely to force local authorities to target help on people whose caring arrangements are breaking down.

Among the forces shaping these changes in service provision and legislation, the views of people with learning disabilities themselves have only recently begun to play a part. First, an active self-advocacy movement has begun to assert their perspective, which is a separate viewpoint from that of their informal carers. Secondly, there has been, to at least some extent, a greater readiness by agencies to consult with service users directly, and this is now formally required of local authorities as part of the production of a community care plan. In addition, there has been increasing research interest in finding ways of seeking the views and perspectives of people with learning disabilities (Brechin and Swain, 1987).

This chapter considers a number of methods used to tap the views of people with learning disabilities. Particular attention is paid to the pioneering participant observational work of Edgerton (1984). Then a brief account is given of our own research looking at the move from family home to a more independent setting in the community. The results presented focus on the issue of choice. This is followed by a short discussion of the results and critical reflection on the short-comings of the method used. Finally, a number of practical suggestions are made about the use of participant observation to obtain the views of service users in everyday settings.

GETTING TO KNOW YOU: GAINING INSIGHT INTO PEOPLE'S LIVES AND VIEW OF THE WORLD

Edgerton (1984) pioneered an anthropological approach to study the lives of people with a learning disability. His classic work *The Cloak of Competence* (Edgerton, 1967) used participant observation to examine the experience of people who were discharged from a long-stay hospital in California to live more independently in the community. The method is labour intensive and time consuming. However it has considerable rewards, providing insight into the respondent's point of view, allowing them to talk about issues which are important to them, when they want to talk about them. The method requires 'long-term immersion into the lives of the people being studied'. Nevertheless Edgerton (1984) is careful to point out that it '... requires a disciplined detachment ... an objective or outsider's assessment of what these people actually do and how well what they say they do fits with what they actually do'.

The additional aim of gathering background knowledge is not merely to check the veracity of the respondent's statements, but rather to understand the wider context of a person's life. This insight cannot be gained at arm's length but involves engaging with and getting to know an individual. For example, the observer might accompany someone to family gatherings, or on shopping outings, and speak to friends, relatives and professionals she has contact with (An alternative is for the researcher to be a practitioner, Chapter 13.)

In addition to focusing on the views of people with learning disabilities, Edgerton's greatest contribution has been to reveal the complexity of their lives. In a book of case studies, examining how old age was experienced by individuals who had been followed up since they left hospital in the 1960s, Edgerton and Ward (1990) provide an account of one man's optimism in the face of awful odds. Richard coped with life-threatening physical problems, debt and poverty. A lack of personal hygiene and domestic skills meant he lived in filthy conditions. Perhaps even more distressing was that he was taken advantage of by people who regarded him as low and incompetent.

'... he has no one to care for him, only a "girlfriend" who exploits him to the best of her ability. Given these circumstances, one would expect Richard to be depressed, anxious, worried, or at the very least discouraged with his plight. He has little reason to be happy with the way things are, but nonetheless, he is happy with things exactly the way they are.'

This contrasts with the mechanistic view, which describes actions of people with learning disabilities as though they were simply driven by simple external forces. How often is the motivation for a person's action described as attention seeking or a person's comment as a mere repetition of what they have heard someone else say? There are still those who simply believe that people with learning disabilities cannot describe their feelings or report reliably about features of their environment. An example of plain prejudice masquerading as informed opinion was produced by Strongman (1985), when describing how difficult it was to study the feelings of people with learning disabilities:

'To analyse what, if anything, a person of IQ 40 is feeling is as difficult as it is to evaluate what, if anything, an animal is feeling. It might even be more difficult since the animal is probably better adapted to its environment than is the mentally retarded person.'

Given such beliefs, it is of little surprise that until recently researchers asked parents and carers to answer on behalf of people with learning disabilities. Despite evidence that they can report accurately about features of their environment, negative attitudes continue to obstruct informed debate about the most effective ways of obtaining their views.

Questionnaires

Questionnaires are probably the most commonly used method to ascertain the views of people with learning disabilities, covering areas as diverse as self-concept and life satisfaction to sexual attitudes (Benson and Ivins, 1992; Flynn and Saleem, 1986; Flynn and Hirst, 1992; Lindsay et al., 1992). However, there remains considerable controversy about the use of questionnaires with this population. Two of the key factors are problems of comprehension and a tendency to produce socially desirable responses.

Comprehension

The rationale of a questionnaire format is to use the same line of questioning with each respondent. This ensures that answers are not contaminated by subtle differences in the style or content of the questioning. However, if the person with learning disabilities has difficulty comprehending the question in the first place, then the answer is likely to be meaningless. There are particular dangers where forced-choice yes or no responses are sought. Zetlin et al. (1985) carried out an important study examining the problems which adults with learning disabilities had in responding to an adapted version of the Piers-Harris Self-Concept Scale and the Coopersmith Self-Esteem Inventory. They used probe questions to get the participants to qualify their initial yes or no responses. Zetlin *et al.* found that difficulty with comprehension, having a personal agenda, or seeing the statements in terms of particular personal issues were three of the factors that made 39% of the qualified responses problematic. There was no simple relationship between IQ and the type of qualifiers used by the subjects. Therefore, a rigid questionnaire format may provide the researcher with a false sense of scientific certainty. The approach may highlight problems of comprehension rather than facilitate the expression of service users' opinions.

It is commonly believed that pictures provide an easier medium for people with poor expressive verbal abilities to indicate their views. For example, Flynn and Hirst (1992) carried out a national survey of adults with learning disabilities and used a Lickert-type scale of five faces from sad through to happy (Chapter 7). The faces were meant to correspond to degrees of satisfaction from very dissatisfied through to very satisfied, and the respondents were asked to point to a face which showed how they felt. However, Gray *et al.* (1983) found that the greater the similarity of facial effect, the more confusion those with learning disabilities experienced. Therefore using simple choices, such as a happy and a sad face, might provide a more robust measure of people's feelings.

Avoiding a sense of failure

Using questionnaires can also lead to problems of social desirability (Orne, 1962). In other words, respondents can have a tendency to present themselves in the best possible light or to give the answers which they believe the interviewer is looking for. Although this is widespread in social science, people with learning disabilities are thought to be more likely to produce socially desirable responses than their non-handicapped counterparts (Zetlin *et al.*, 1985). Unfortunately such observations are made without providing reasons why this is the case, leaving the tacit assumption that it is somehow due to their learning disability. However, it seems possible that heightened social sensitivity may lead interviewees to take account of the questioner's feelings, rather than any cognitive deficit.

An interview is a social situation and does not take place *in vacuo* but in the wider framework of people's lives (Farr, 1982). A questionnaire most closely corresponds to a test situation, which most respondents will have experienced in the past. Zigler and Burack (1989) pointed out how repeated failure sensitizes children with learning disabilities to test situations. Further support for this observation comes from Wishart's (1991) work with school children. She described how negative experience makes a very early impact:

'Whereas a normal 4-year-old child may enjoy showing off their skills, experience indicates that the 8-year-old with Down's syndrome is far more likely to view any IQ-type test as yet another test aimed at finding out what they cannot do.'

Not only do children with learning disabilities develop a fear of failure, but as they grow into adulthood their views are not afforded the same respect or status as their non-handicapped peers. They come to the interview setting as part of a stigmatized and relatively disempowered group (Croker and Major, 1989; Jahoda et al., 1988; Ryan and Thomas, 1987), not as people who are used to being taken seriously. Hence it comes as little surprise that they may wish to present themselves in the best possible light to the interviewer. The purpose of the open-ended interviewing approach is to break down the barriers of power imbalance (Chapter 12) and promote greater comprehension.

MOVING HOME: THE MOVER'S VIEW

The longitudinal research project we carried out (Markova et al., 1988) looked at the lives of four groups of people moving from home and long-stay hospital to live more independently. This chapter focuses on those moving from their family home to live in accommodation provided by a Scottish housing association. Twelve people with a learning disability and, where possible, parents and staff from their new homes took part in the study. The aim of the research was to follow the tenants' move from their family home to the housing association. The principal methods used were extensive open-ended interviews, covering a range of issues about the nature of their lives and the move to live more independently. These were carried out immediately after the person left home and repeated 6 months later. Time was also spent with the tenants in order to gain insight into their lives at home, and their daytime and leisure activities. Parents and staff were interviewed to provide a fuller picture, and to compare their view of events with the service users' view.

INTERVIEWING: REACHING A COMMON UNDERSTANDING

The interviews were semistructured. This meant that the interviewer had check-lists of areas she wished to cover, combined with particular questions or strategies to open up a dialogue on a certain subject (Chapter 3). The goal was to establish a common agenda and make the questioning as comprehensible as possible to the participants while avoiding asking leading questions.

Spending time with the tenants prior to starting the interviews allowed the interviewers to develop a rapport. This helped to break down barriers, and base the interviews on a relationship of trust and mutual respect. Crucially, it also

gave the researchers insight into the characters and events which the interviewees referred to, facilitating greater mutual understanding and promoting
dialogue. When the tenants were talking about matters of interest to them they
talked fluently and clearly about their lives, and had the opportunity to raise
issues which were important to them. The spirit of the interview was made clear
to the tenants at the outset: they were the experts and the researcher was the
novice coming to learn from them.

Between 2 and 5 hours of interviews were carried out with each person,
which produced a vast amount of data. It is beyond the scope of this chapter to
present even a synopsis and discussion of the results. Instead, several findings
relating to choice are presented and illustrated with case material. These demonstrate the kind of insights which can be obtained from using a more open-ended
approach.

STUDY FINDINGS

Playing an active role

The circumstances leading to a change of abode, and people's motivations for
leaving their family home, may provide a link with their ultimate feelings of
satisfaction or dissatisfaction. All this presupposes the tenants did in fact play
an active role in their move to live more independently. To examine whether
they felt they had played an active or passive role in their move from the family
home, their responses were categorized as follows:

- *Active* – the tenants had played a central role in the process of moving from
  home. They felt that the decisions taken had been their own and talked as if
  what happened to them was under their own control.
- *Passive* – the process of moving out had been brought about by others. The
  tenants may have consented, but they had played little part in the process.
  They talked as if what happened to them was in the hands of others.

The following quotes illustrate the basis for these categories:

- Man aged 45 years categorized as active:

  'Then this place came up, that it was ready. I had to get an application and
  come to see it. I came down one day to see it. I says, "I'm coming in here,
  I'd like to come in here".'

- Woman aged 24 categorized as active:

  'I actually came down and got an application form, and filled it and sent it
  away when I was at college. And I got word back 23rd August. I had to
  talk with my parents before the letter came back.'

- Man aged 22 years categorized as passive:

'That's the reason I was sent here. My mum and dad thought I was leaving everything to them. They felt I needed to get away for a wee while. My dad found out about this place. I wasn't forced to go, he just asked if I was interested. My mum and dad have done a lot for me. If it hadn't been for them, then I wouldn't be in this place, probably.'

● Woman aged 26 years categorized as passive:

'My mum wasnae too great, and she wanted to see me settled down. But she didn't want me to go to the one place in [her home town], because there's no supervision there or something. So she put me into key housing.'

The majority, eight out of the 12 tenants, felt they had played an active part in the move from their family home. However, in all cases the choice was between moving to the hostel or staying at home; no-one was able to choose between a range of alternatives.

A dream come true or a real choice

The move from their family home was the culmination of years of struggle for a number of the tenants. Two such women were Ms Johnson and Ms McDonald. Although they both wanted to leave home, their knowledge of the possibilities and realities were vastly different.

Ms Johnson, aged 40, had led an isolated existence at her parents' home. She did not attend day services, but had met her boyfriend at a club for people with learning disabilities some 20 years previously. They had been engaged for most of this time, meeting under the close supervision of Ms Johnson's parents once a week at her house. She constantly pressed her mother to allow her to marry and leave home. However, it was only after the timely intervention of her boyfriend's father, who was terminally ill, that her parents relented.

Ms Johnson was an agent of change, her parents acknowledged that her constant pressure influenced their decision to allow her to marry and leave home. Her move from home was not a sudden decision but the fulfilment of an aspiration which had been held for most of her adult life. But her sheltered home life resulted in a lack of knowledge about alternative living situations. She was motivated by a romantic view of married life and being a housewife. Hence, arranged visits and several overnight stays were not a sufficient basis on which to make an informed choice about a new abode. The problem did not relate to domestic proficiency, as her mother had given her daily tasks to do when she lived at home. Rather, housework was not sufficient to fill her days. Her husband attended the adult training centre and Ms Johnson became even more isolated than she had been when living with her parents. Being a housewife was not as intrinsically rewarding as she had imagined, and she did not have an alternative vision or network of support to fill the vacuum.

Consequently she became depressed, and her very elderly parents moved to a house nearby in order to provide additional support.

Ms Johnson's biography contrasts with the experience of Ms McDonald, aged 39, a woman who struggled over a 5 year period to achieve independence and leave home. In her case change was more gradual, resulting in a transformation of the relationship with her mother. She had proved an extremely demanding child, and an accident left her with a limp. She was not allowed to travel unaccompanied, apparently requiring help to get on and off buses. However, she began to see people from her adult training centre leaving home to live independently, eventually visiting friends in supported tenancies. Her aspirations grew and she began to assert her wish to leave home. Eventually her mother came to respect her daughter's wishes and fostered her move to live independently. In turn, she began to branch out, staying weekends at her boyfriend's flat and obtaining a job with several others from her centre, selling the first editions of daily newspapers late at night at a city-centre railway station. In this instance she not only played an active part in the move to live more independently, but was also able to make an informed choice about where she wanted to live with clear expectations about the life she wished to lead.

These case studies powerfully demonstrate how background experience, and relationships with significant others, influenced these women's ability to make choices. Ms Johnson remained extremely socially isolated, never escaping the jurisdiction of her loving but protective parents. Hence her longing to marry her boyfriend, and make him a good wife remained an aspiration for some 20 years. She lacked the opportunity to observe or talk with other married couples about the reality of their lives, and her parents had always been careful to ensure that she and her boyfriend would never be allowed to behave like an ordinary couple. Leaving home and marriage were ends in themselves and she was unable to imagine the wider ramifications. In contrast to Ms Johnson, Ms McDonald had built up sufficient knowledge and experience to allow her to challenge the status quo. Despite her main social contacts being other people with learning disabilities, she became aware of the possibilities for living more independently. Moreover, she realized that she could play a part in achieving her goal. Through seeking greater independence she obtained insight into the realities of living in supported accommodation, and enlightened her mother about the housing opportunities for people with learning disabilities.

Moving home: a chance to live or a chance to learn

The concept of independence, for many carers and professionals, is bound up with the notion of domestic competence. When Ms McDonald described her interview with the housing association, she recalled being asked 'stupid' questions focusing on self-help skills:

'And I says, "It's something I've always wanted to do is live on my own." They asked me if I could do this and do that – cook and this sort of thing. Say – but it does nae matter, you always get help with that anyway – I says "Oh aye, I can do certain things, certain things I can't do." That was the day of the meeting.'

Ms McDonald did appreciate the intrinsic value of acquiring household skills, but contrary to the view of most of the staff we interviewed, this was not her priority. In common with other tenants she had led a fairly restricted home life, and was largely cut off in a 'handicapped' world, not of her making. Daily activity was provided by adult training centres and her social life revolved round specially organized activities for people with learning disabilities (Jahoda *et al.*, 1990). Her main reasons for leaving home were greater freedom and a chance to explore new horizons. When asked what she enjoyed about living in the housing association she replied:

'Well you can come in and out when you want. Do anything you want. Nobody bothers. Never got that sort of freedom at home. If I went out anywhere and I came in late – "where have you been?" She [mother] treats me like a wain [child] doesn't she?'

When staff emphasized their role as trainers and overlooked the tenant's aspirations, the result was conflict. Staff members would view the tenant as irresponsible and in turn the tenants regarded the staff as authoritarian. This finding emphasizes the interpersonal nature of choice and decision making. Without taking seriously and attempting to understand the views of service users, it was impossible for staff to reach a shared agenda and negotiate common goals.

IMPLICATIONS FOR PRACTICE

These findings demonstrate that people with a learning disability can participate in a real sense in major decisions about their lives if given the opportunity. This is not always realized or put into practice. Two of the people interviewed had succeeded in bringing about the move in face of opposition from their parents, and even those who played a relatively passive role felt, with one exception, that the staff of the housing association had sought and taken into account their wishes. The case studies also underline an important point about choice-making made by Mittler (1984). People with a learning disability cannot be expected to participate actively in decisions of this kind if they have had such limited experience of the world that they do not have a realistic idea of what they are being asked to choose between. Their difficulties stem not from the disability itself, but from having led a sheltered or 'handicapped' life (Cattermole *et al.*, 1988). A practical implication for both parents and staff working in services is that people with learning disabilities should be helped to lead less segregated lives.

Unfortunately the study showed that staff often continue to place too great an emphasis on training skills as a path to independence, while people with learning disabilities may emphasize other issues such as greater freedom or an improved social life (Cattermole *et al.*, 1990).

There is growing recognition that people with learning disabilities should participate in major decisions which are made about their lives. For example, shared action planning (SAP) (Brechin and Swain, 1987) is a form of goal planning which places the individual with a learning disability at the centre of the process. However, the authors acknowledge that major decisions are made in the context of relationships with significant others (Brechin and Swain, 1988). A parent's views about her son's future living arrangements may conflict with his own aspirations, while a keyworker or advocate's perspective may differ again. To prevent the aspirations of the person with learning disabilities being ignored, SAP takes account of the different perspectives and then asks the participants to negotiate common goals. Inevitably this demands compromise, but at least there is a greater chance of the individual with learning disabilities being taken seriously.

Moving from home is a time of significant change in the life of people with learning disabilities. As the above findings demonstrate, people's past experience greatly influences their expectations and aspirations for living more independently. Edgerton's (1967) classic study of people being discharged from a long-stay hospital in California powerfully demonstrated the importance of the past in shaping our future. He described how those who had left the hospital with few if any personal possessions bought various items such as old photograph albums, china and even old letters in order to give the impression of having a personal history. It was a real attempt to buy a history which had been lost through institutionalization. To obtain a sense of belonging or to have foundations on which to build a future is also a concern of people who have spent their childhood in care. If professionals want to have a real dialogue and promote choice, then it is necessary to gain insight into the person's background and view of the world. In essence, they have to get to know the person.

Methods have been developed from ethnographic work which can provide insight into the perspective of people with learning disabilities, and might be helpful in identifying where they would like to live. For example, **neighbourhood walks**, developed by Drewett *et al.* (1993), are a simple but effective idea. The assessor or researcher asks people with learning disabilities to take her on a guided walk to particular facilities in the area where they live. During the walk individuals can demonstrate knowledge of their local area and identify features which have most salience for them.

Unfortunately, assessments of deficits still predominate. Under the NHS and Community Care Act (1990), people with learning disabilities are legally entitled to have an assessment of their care needs. While service users' views may be sought as part of this process, the greatest concern is with personal competencies or difficulties. As an expert, the assessor may feel no need to tap the individual's aspirations, feelings and past experiences to determine their care needs. Intelligence tests are increasingly used as a means of deciding who will gain access to services.

If people with learning disabilities are seen as simply a sum of their competencies and deficiencies, then a simple score may be sufficient to determine a future residential placement. But they have likes and dislikes, hopes and fears like everyone else. Therefore, care managers should be wary about ignoring their world view. For example, what happens if a man in his sixties, who regards himself as youthful and treasures his freedom, is placed in an old people's residence? In another instance, a woman may be assessed as extremely competent and be housed in a flat of her own with minimal support. Her care needs may be met, but her life may be emotionally barren if she is socially isolated and craves for friendship, or just someone to talk to once the housework is done.

FUTURE RESEARCH

Open-ended interviews used in the research allowed people to provide meaningful answers and express their feelings. Nevertheless, there are considerable problems with this method. In particular, collecting and dealing with the data is time consuming and complex. This is an important consideration in terms of time and resources. While it is possible to generate qualitative and quantitative data using this method (Cattermole *et al.*, 1990), it is not likely to be as reliable or easy to replicate as with a psychometrically robust questionnaire.

Choice and the move to independent living remains a rich vein for future research. The novel idea of supported living initiatives offers people with learning disabilities ordinary tenancies which are separate from support services. This is an exciting development which could offer real choice in terms of housing. Supported living initiatives will also create a new relationship between service users and providers, requiring greater mutual understanding. Future research should not merely attempt to find out what people wish for in terms of housing, but examine the communication between service users and professionals. It is time to focus on the complex and little-valued skill of listening.

REFERENCES

Arnold, R., Bochel, H., Brodhurst, S. and Page, D. (1993) *Community Care: The Housing Dimension*, Joseph Rowntree Foundation, York.
Benson, B. A. and Ivins, J. (1992) Anger, depression and self-concept in adults with mental retardation. *Journal of Intellectual Disability Research*, **36**, 169–175.
Brechin, A. and Swain, J. (1987) *Changing Relationships: Shared Action Planning with People with a Mental Handicap*, Harper and Row, London.

Brechin, A. and Swain, J. (1988) Professional/client relationships: creating a working alliance with people with learning difficulties. *Disability Handicap and Society*, **3**, 213–216.

Cattermole, M., Jahoda, A. and Markova, I. (1988) Leaving home: the experience of people with a mental handicap. *Journal of Mental Deficiency Research*, **32**, 47–57.

Cattermole, M., Jahoda, A. and Markova, I. (1990) Quality of life for people with learning difficulties moving to community homes. *Disability, Handicap and Society*, **5**, 137–152.

Cm 849 (1989) *Caring for People: Community Care in the Next Decade and Beyond*, HMSO, London.

Croker, J. and Major, B. (1989) Social stigma and self-esteem: the self protective properties of stigma. *Psychological Review*, **96**, 608–630.

DHSS (1971) *Better Services for the Mentally Handicapped*, Cmnd 4683, HMSO, London.

Drewett, R., Dagnan, D., Tonner, J. and Maychell, C. (1993) Neighbourhood walks: a semi-quantitative method for assessing the access people with a learning difficulty have to resources in their community. *Mental Handicap Research*, **6**, 142–154.

Edgerton, R. B. (1967) *The Cloak of Competence*, University of California Press, Berkley.

Edgerton, R. B. (1984) The participant-observer approach to research in mental retardation. *American Journal of Mental Deficiency*, **88**, 498–505.

Edgerton, R. B. and Ward T. W. (1990) I gotta put my foot down, in *I've Seen It All!: Lives of Older Persons with Mental Retardation in the Community*, (eds R. B. Edgerton and M. A. Gaston), Brookes, London.

Farr, R. (1982) Interviewing: the social psychology of the interview, in *Psychology for Occupational Therapists*, (ed. F. Fransella), The British Psychological Society and the Macmillan Press, Exeter.

Flynn, M. and Hirst, M. (1992). *This Year, Next Year, Sometime ...? Learning Disability and Adulthood*, Social Policy Research Unit, York.

Flynn, M. C. and Saleem, J. K. (1986). Adults who are mentally handicapped and living with their parents: satisfaction and perceptions regarding their lives and circumstances. *Journal of Mental Deficiency Research*, **30**, 379–387.

Gray, J. M., Fraser, W. L. and Leudar, I. (1983) Recognition of emotion from facial expression in mental handicap. *British Journal of Psychiatry*, **142**, 566–571.

Jahoda, A., Cattermole, M. and Markova, I. (1990) Moving out: an opportunity for friendship and broadening social horizons? *Journal of Mental Deficiency Research*, **34**, 127–139.

Jahoda, A., Markova, I. and Cattermole, M. (1988) Stigma and the self-concept of people with a mild mental handicap. *Journal of Mental Deficiency Research*, **32**, 103–115.

Lindsay, W. R., Bellshaw, E. Cullross, G., Staines, C. and Michie, A. (1992) Increases in knowledge following a course of sex education for people with intellectual disabilities. *Journal of Intellectual Disabilities Research*, **36**, 531–539.

Markova, I., Jahoda, A. and Cattermole, M. (1988) The meaning of independent living for people with a mild mental handicap. *Health Bulletin*, **46**(4), 246–253.

MENCAP (1994) *Mencap Strategic Review*, Royal Society for Mentally Handicapped Children and Adults, London.

Mittler, P. (1984) Quality of life and services for people with disabilities. *Bulletin of the British Psychological Society*, **37**, 218–225.

National Health Service and Community Care Act (1990) HMSO, London.

Orne, M. T. (1962) On the social psychology of the psychological experiment with particular reference to the demand characteristics and their implications. *American Psychologist*, **17**, 776–783.

Strongman, K. T. (1985) Emotion in mentally retarded people. *Australia and New Zealand Journal of Developmental Disabilities*, **10**, 201–213.

Ryan, J. and Thomas, F. (1987) *The Politics of Mental Handicap*, Free Association Books, London.

Wishart, J. G. (1991) Motivational deficits and their relation to learning difficulties in young children with Down's syndrome, in *Innovatory Practice and Severe Learning Difficulties*, (eds G. Lloyd and J. Watson), Moray House Publications, Edinburgh.

Zetlin, A. L., Heriot, M. J. and Turner, J. L. (1985) Self-concept measurement in mentally retarded adults: a micro-analysis of responses, *Applied Research in Mental Retardation*, **6**, 113–125.

Zigler, E. and Burack, J. A. (1989) Personality development and the dually diagnosed person. *Research in Developmental Disabilities*, **10**, 225–240.

<table>
<tr><td>

12

</td><td>

People with mild learning disabilities and challenging behaviour: user input to service evaluation

</td></tr>
</table>

Julie Dockrell

Evaluation studies of service provision should, and increasingly do, incorporate the views of service users. Even if they are compulsorily detained under the Mental Health Act 1983, or a court order, users have a right to be consulted about their services. This chapter shows that even without the participant observation described in Chapter 11, good interviewing allows people with learning disabilities to talk freely about themselves. The patients who took part in the evaluation of a specialist unit for people with mild learning disabilities and challenging behaviours had views about their own problems and were able to identify weaknesses in their treatment and make suggestions for improvement. However it is easy for evaluators to collect and use information without making any change to the existing distribution of power. The researchers benefit but the users do not. Dockrell suggests that future research design should aim to empower users rather than collude with the existing power structure.

Evaluation of provision for clients with learning disabilities rarely addresses the clients' perspective, either on the services provided or the service delivery. The Griffiths report states 'the people receiving help will have a greater say in what is done to help them and a wider choice' (Griffiths, 1988) and the White Paper

Caring for People (Cm 849, 1989) sets out a new view of the client as consumer. The stated aim is to develop client-oriented services. In this chapter the views of clients with mild learning disabilities and challenging behaviour are considered. Frequently these individuals have very little control over their lives. They are often under the purview of the criminal justice system or are held under a section of the Mental Health Act. There is only one published account of consultations with clients who experience learning disabilities and challenging behaviour (Grey and Jenkins, 1994). This chapter aims to highlight the value of addressing clients' views and the limitations of the techniques used. The clients interviewed formed part of a broader evaluation of a special unit designed to cater for the needs of this specific group of people.

The White Paper on community care (Cm 849, 1989) established the right of people with learning disabilities to normal patterns of life within the community. Service users are to be treated as individuals. The exercise of choice and the importance of supporting users in the maximum possible degree of independence were emphasized. A central tenet of the White Paper was the involvement of users in care planning.

Research on community care and deinstitutionalization has placed considerable emphasis on the need for the person with a learning disability to develop self-help skills and appropriate behaviours to benefit from the opportunities afforded in the community. Service evaluations and service developments have commonly focused on the development and performance of such skills and behaviours (Chapter 11 offers a critique of this approach). The presence or absence of these behaviours are assessed on a range of standardized, objective tools such as the Adaptive Behaviour Scale. For example, Locker *et al.* (1984) concluded that small community-based hostels can help adults with mental handicap acquire the necessary skills for independent living, but research generally has ignored the context in which the person lives and, invariably, the perspectives of the individuals' themselves have been excluded. Rarely are the service users consulted when identifying either service needs or in evaluating service provision. There are several notable exceptions. Edgerton (1984) used participant observation to assess individual adaptation to community life. Zetlin (1983) highlighted the mismatch between the views of young people with learning disabilities and those of their parents (Ben-Ari and Reiter, 1982; Flynn and Saleem, 1986). Such conflict of views is particularly important since, when consultations do occur, it is predominantly the parents or keyworker who are involved. Consulting significant others highlights the carers and/or staff perspectives but this fails to address the clients' concerns and views directly. Neither standardized measures nor the views of significant others directly meet the need to establish a client-oriented service.

There are difficulties in consulting the consumer (Chapters 2 and 3). Surveys which attempt to assess consumer satisfaction in the health service usually report highly positive results and, particularly when used with disadvantaged client groups, need to be very carefully designed (Grey and Jenkins, 1994). For example, with elderly clients it is very easy to produce results that suggest that the vast majority of clients are entirely happy with whatever service they are given (Wilson, 1993), but it is difficult to get a more balanced picture (Wallace and Rees, 1984).

The issue of communication is very important for people with learning disabilities. It is often assumed that individuals are unable to communicate their needs and wishes accurately. Preliminary evidence suggests that the ability to recall information is poorer among groups of individuals with learning disabilities (Clare and Gudjonsson, 1993). Moreover, people with learning disabilities are more susceptible to leading questions and more acquiescent in their responses. It becomes important when interviewing individuals to allow time and flexibility in responding since they are more vulnerable to influence of the interview questions than their average-ability peers. One possible way to bypass such difficulties is to conduct unstructured interviews that allow the clients to identify their own service needs and highlight the mismatch between service needs and service provision. This approach demands an awareness of their service needs and knowledge of the range of services available. Commonly these individuals depend on professionals for both interpretation of their needs and identification of the available services. Two key questions ensue – what needs do people with learning difficulties and challenging behaviour identify for themselves, and how do they evaluate the services that they are offered?

Cattermole *et al.* (1990) considered the views of clients with learning disabilities (but no diagnosis of challenging behaviours) in an attempt to identify service needs and views of service provision. In their study individuals were interviewed before and after an initial placement in the community. They identified: a broad range of aspirations beyond community placements; the sensitivity of individuals to the context in which they were living; and an impressive ability to outline possible directions for future services. The clients in this study were outlining their service needs for the service providers. As Cattermole *et al.* argue, if research is to be of any value to staff working in services, it must provide a guide to what they can do, in their everyday work, to improve the quality of life for people with learning disabilities. Thus, this study highlights the value of interviewing clients with learning disabilities in devising appropriate service provision.

BACKGROUND TO THE EVALUATION

The closure of long-stay mental handicap hospitals resulted in a range of new resettlement initiatives for clients with learning difficulties (King's Fund, 1980). The Mental Impairment Evaluation and Treatment Service (MIETS) was one such initiative. Heralded as a centre of excellence, MIETS was located in a refurbished ward at a large psychiatric hospital and was established in 1987. Its rôle was to prepare clients with mild learning disabilities and challenging behaviours for community placements. The clients' challenging behaviours, such as physical violence, arson and sexual abuse, were so severe as to make direct transfer to the community a risk. MIETS, staffed by a multidisciplinary team, provided services for 15 district health authorities (Dockrell *et al.,* 1993).

The evaluation design of MIETS built on several interrelated perspectives: views of service users and providers, e.g. health authority managers and senior clinicians, direct care staff and the clients (Dockrell *et al.*, 1993); changes in the behaviour of clients and subsequent placements (Gaskell *et al.*, in press); and an economic analysis of the service (Dockrell *et al.*, in press). In this chapter the findings of the more traditional evaluation format are reviewed briefly to set a context for considering the clients' views.

OVERVIEW OF EVALUATION FINDINGS

In 1990 a survey completed by managers in the 15 districts identified 218 people in the region with mild learning disabilities and challenging behaviour (5.9 per 100 000 of the population). MIETS, with 13 beds, could only offer a service to a minority of these identified cases. A complementary survey of direct care staff and professionals in the health authorities led to a distinction between challenging behaviours that are **dangerous** and those that are **problems**. Problem behaviours were quite frequent but posed few difficulties to staff. Dangerous behaviours, such as serious physical violence and arson, were less common but posed considerable difficulties. Seventy per cent of the clients of MIETS were referred for behaviours in the dangerous category.

Thirty-four clients formed the central focus of the evaluation. The clients were typically male, displaying some form of dangerous behaviour, on medication, and admitted from hospitals or prison. In MIETS all the clients were assessed for mental illness, intellectual functioning and future placement needs. In addition there were a variety of individually tailored assessments. Sixty-five per cent of the clients were assessed as mentally ill. The interventions included stabilizing medication, behavioural programmes directed at specific problems, and skills training. There was also extensive social work involvement. MIETS was established to provide intensive assessment and treatment. However, a detailed observational study of eight clients showed that for much of the day they were on their own in an unstructured environment. Most of clients' time (56%) between 8 am and 4 pm was spent either not actively engaged or in their bedroom.

The Adaptive Behaviour Scale (part 2) was used to assess changes in the behaviour of clients from preadmission to predischarge from MIETS and from preadmission to 6 months post-discharge. A general trend of statistically significant decreases in maladaptive behaviour was observed (Gaskell *et al.*, in press). It was concluded that, for most clients, a period in MIETS was associated with reductions in dangerous behaviours, but not in their eradication. Following a period in MIETS the clients' problems were better understood, dangerous behaviours were reduced and strategies for their management were devised.

This brief review of some of the results of the evaluation indicates that a specialist unit of the MIETS type can provide a valuable service, and meet the objectives of providing a careful assessment of clients and assisting in the managements of specific behavioural problems. The results are consistent with the results of a questionnaire study, which found that professionals and direct care staff in the health authorities held generally favourable views about MIETS.

The effectiveness of MIETS in terms of helping to achieve community placements depends, in part, on the ability and willingness of the health authorities to provide appropriate facilities. A stated objective of MIETS is to help district teams enable a client to participate as fully as possible in daily life. For 32 out of 34 clients (94%) MIETS recommended a high service intensity community placement, detailing medication requirements and management programmes. All clients remained the responsibility of the relevant district health authority and the implementation of these recommendations and the resulting quality of life opportunities for the clients depended on the health authority's priorities, skills and the available facilities.

Seven of the 14 clients who were discharged into institutional placements went to destinations that were not recommended by MIETS. Four clients went to NHS or to private hospitals because their health authority was unable to provide suitable community placements, and three cases, all in one health authority, went to a hospital home. However, the view was expressed by some health authority managers that the placement recommendations by MIETS were unrealistic, particularly in the early years. Sometimes the placement specified was not available; in others the community care programmes devised in MIETS were too difficult to implement. However, if all the health authorities had been able to make available the recommended community placements, 80% of MIETS clients would have moved into community settings. Given that MIETS caters for clients that are too difficult for many local teams to manage, this is a significant achievement, and may counter some of the general criticism of special units (Hoefkens and Allen, 1990).

This chapter is concerned with the views of the MIETS residents of their problems, placements and futures. In parallel with other clients experiencing learning difficulties and challenging behaviours, clients in the MIETS had very little direct control over their lives. Fifty-two per cent of the clients were admitted under the Mental Health Act and 79% were on some form of medication. At the time of referral 38% of the clients were in NHS hospitals, 26% in private or special hospitals, 21% in prison and 15% in the community. Four specific questions guided the design of this section of the MIETS evaluation:

- To what extent were the clients themselves aware of their problems and the extent to which their problems restricted their access to ordinary lifestyles?

- What benefits and problems did they identify with the MIETS provision?
- To what extent did they feel that their stay at MIETS had provided them with new skills and assisted in their move to more appropriate provision?
- To what extent did the clients' perspectives of the MIETS provision concur with the standardized data collected in the other phases of the study?

METHOD

In-depth interviews were carried out with clients at five preset data collection times. The interviews were semistructured, the researcher having a list of questions and issues to cover, while encouraging the interviewee to talk freely and raise issues that they considered important. Questions were phrased in a general way and there was an attempt to cover different perspectives. Clients were encouraged to outline both positive and negative aspects of the service and their own situation. Where necessary, probes were used to elicit specific examples to support general statements.

The interviewer was a member of the evaluation team and was not based in the unit. Although this should have increased clients' confidence in the anonymity of their responses there is little doubt that the closed nature of the ward and the imbalance in power between staff and clients resulted in a degree of reticence.

The interview was voluntary and clients were assured of confidentiality. A few clients either refused to be interviewed or were not available for interview. Using the responses as a guideline it seemed that all the clients who consented to the interview understood the questions asked and all except two provided extensive and detailed information. Two clients found the interview demanding and generally restricted their response to a simple yes or no.

The numbers of clients interviewed at each point were:

- preadmission – 12
- 3 months post-admission – 16
- predischarge – 15
- first follow-up – 9
- second follow-up – 12

All interviews were transcribed and coded using the computer package Textbase Alpha for the analysis of qualitative data. A coding frame was devised, based on both the clients' comments and the aims and objectives of the MIETS unit. Eight central domains were identified: views about MIETS; views about MIETS following discharge; clients' views about their own problems; insight into their problem and treatment strategies; views on significant others; views on current placement; views on past placements; hopes for the future.

The clients interviewed were admitted for a range of problems, including aggression, arson and sexual difficulties. Their ages ranged from 17 years to 44 years. Seventy-five per cent of the interviewees were male. This reflects the sex distribution of the MIETS clients. Forty per cent of those interviewed had been diagnosed as mentally ill. Interviews took place in a range of establishments including prisons, special hospitals and community homes and therefore reflected the range of establishments that serve this client population. Not surprisingly most of the interviews took place in MIETS ($n = 31$). This was due to the ease of accessing clients, the implicit encouragement to comply and the study design.

CLIENTS' AWARENESS OF THEIR PROBLEMS

In this section the focus is the clients' opinions of MIETS, highlighting both the strengths and limitations of the unit from the user's perspective. Details of how the clients view their own problems and their service needs are presented initially. A deliberate decision was made to include extensive quotes so the clients could speak for themselves in their own words. Where appropriate the numbers of clients supporting a particular view are included.

The clients interviewed displayed a marked awareness of their problems and a stated wish to alter the situation. Moreover, many clients had specific views of the aetiology of their problem behaviour. Addressing the clients' views of the cause of their problems may prove important in the success or otherwise of treatments and placements.

Prior to entering MIETS, nine of the 12 clients interviewed outlined the types of problems that caused them difficulty.

'Drinking, sex and fire setting. Those are my main problems and suicide.'

'My bad temper.'
'You think that's a problem, do you?'
'Yes.'
'Are you going to do something about it?'
'I'd like to, yes.'
'So, that's your problem temper, drink, anything else?'
'Setting fires and that. I'd like to stop that. Don't want to keep doing it all my life.'

'Basically I have problems in saying no to other men. Before I came here I was staying with a chap and we had a long relationship and that spilt up when I came here. So I told the staff what happened ... so I had a blood test – HIV blood test – which came up er pos er negative which I've got to go and have another one in 3 months' time.'

The majority focused on their lack of temper control and this mirrors the concerns that are raised in the original referrals to the unit.

'I tend to lose my temper too quick. I'm like my dad ... very very quick tempered. Me dad was quick tempered and so am I.'

'I keep losing me temper all the time. Haven't lost me temper here since I've been here.'
'Does it get you into trouble?'
'Yea.'
'Would you like to do something about it?'
'Yes.'
'What would you like to do about it?'
'Stop it.'
'Why?'
'Well it don't get me anywhere.'

'Well I've had it all my life, on and off. These outbursts. I mean it's because that's the way you are – everybody's different – everybody's got different tempers, different effects you know.'

Thus clients are aware of their difficulties and see these difficulties as problems. However, the severity of the problems is not always addressed. These tempers are serious, they are either very dangerous or are compounded by additional problems:

'I think I had a lot of bad feelings at home and also I think, I don't know, I used to see my Mum and Dad fight and argue and it used to scare me, not actually scare me, I think it frightened me and in the end I was just taking on anybody. I took anybody on who actually stared at me in the street. Say you was out in the street now and I didn't know you. I didn't know anybody, and somebody actually came past me and stared at me like you were, I say what you f...ing staring at? You wanna a picture? And that's how I'd go, and after that I'd flip and have fights. I'd pick fights with knives and things. If you wanna know, I did knife someone once and it wasn't a very pretty sight. If it had gone deep, she could be paralysed.'

The level of understanding of these behaviours varies considerably. One client states that a reason she set a fire was for 'for attention' because 'I knew if I did I'd get away from that place, I'd be put on better tablets and I'd be able to sleep and I did'. Another links his own fire setting to depression:

'Usually when I'm depressed like yesterday I felt like setting an alarm off here. Then the night before I felt like catching my bed alight but I had no matches.'

Some clients have worked out in some detail the basis of their problems:

'I think it's because I've had a lot of my body damaged at birth so I haven't got a full self-control ability on me so I can't not hit all the time because I haven't got full control over my body. It's a bit like putting water and electricity together that it explodes. Because the electricity can't control the elements of the water. Same with me I get pressure to hit people I can't control the pressure ... I've been with different people most of my life, I've been with people that are weird ... I've seen people who are quite difficult and disturbed and distraught ... I have less self-control than they do.'

Despite these assertions that he was damaged at birth this client does not believe he has always had these problems:

'No all my life. But what I have has developed out of some bizarre
mystery of life at the age of 16 I've had it since then.'
'Did you not have it before?'
'No. It's one of the bizarre mysteries of life.'
'There must have been something that started it off?'
'No there was nothing apparent that started it off.'
'What do you feel like when you hit someone?'
'It's not very pleasant but I just get a compulsion. It's all very compul-
sional to me.'
'Is there anybody you wouldn't hit?'
'I don't know. I honestly don't know. Another thing if I'm with other
people at a table I find I throw a lot less then if I am on my own. If it's not
breakable I throw a lot less because I feel a lot less compulsion.'

But equally there are clients who have an unsophisticated understanding of their problem behaviour, certainly not consistent with what have often been long-standing difficulties.

'They started swearing at me ... I got a bit angry about it a bit upset about it ... so I lit a fire, lit up the toilet roll.'

'A bit of counselling might help. Even seeing a film seeing how bad it is might put me off that sort of thing. Or actually joining the fire brigade. I don't think that's a very good idea ... Join the fire brigade for a day and see how dangerous it can be.'

'Well I only get upset with people I only hit people if they hit me first. If someone hits you first you hit them back. I punch them straight in the face. My mum told me to do it ... well if they hit me first I have to hit them back don't I?'

In a minority of cases there is a marked psychotic element.

'Why did you do that?'
'Cos I kept hearing voices. They were saying I'd like to go over there and
light a fire.'

For a number of clients there are other pressing problems in addition to their index problem:

'I have problems yes with money ... Not so much counting, but if I was in a shop and a lady bought some stuff and that, I might find it difficult to count the change out. [Interviewer asks if any help is being given] Not here, but I would like help with that.'

For some there is the hope that MIETS will solve their problems. Prior to entering the unit 66% of clients believe that MIETS will be of help.

'Well while I'm here they're going to look after me –they're going to help me so I won't do that again – 'cause they're going to give me tablets so when I come out of here I'm going to be cheerful.'

Many clients are aware that they have a serious problem that requires help. Half the clients believe their problem to be a result of some internal factor, whereas the remainder believe their behaviour is a result of the situations and circumstances in which they find themselves. A minority of the clients ($n = 4$) believe that their problem is permanent and cannot be solved.

'I have had it for so long that's it is very similar in a way to a drug addict. They're hooked on it and they can't get off it. Very similar to the drug addict I'm hooked on it for such a long time that I can't stop it. It's like a drug addict that is addicted to a drug they get addicted to that and they can't get stop it because they see a compulsive mechanism in it. It's the same with me hitting people and throwing things and all the other things I do I can't stop it easily because I can feel the compulsive mechanisms in it ... .'

He is not alone:

'I'm 38 now – I'm 39 next year. It would be too late for me to change – it's best for me to change to start out and I can't. I'll be honest with you – I'll be in and out of this place for the rest of my life I think. I don't want to – I wish I could stay away and get on with my life, but I can't – I don't know why. It's because I think I'm more secure in hospitals than I am outside. I think that could be the reason why.'

In marked contrast to their keyworkers' perceptions, few of the clients believe that they cannot control their behaviour. However, prior to attending MIETS, clients do not mention any ways of overcoming their problems. In fact for some clients MIETS plays an important role in addressing their problems.

'I used to run away and not face them, right, so this is when MIETS has actually trained me that its the best way to say it, actually trained me, cause now, if I'm actually going to lose control or I'm actually gonna do something stupid, I know the consequences. I feel the consequences, I know I'm actually going to get told the consequences, right, when I was in ... [community home] I used to go wild. I never used to be able to face the consequences.'

These interviews establish that individuals are aware of their problems, have views about the origins of these difficulties and are on the whole optimistic that they can be helped.

CLIENTS' VIEWS OF MIETS

In the first part of this section the clients' views about the unit before and during their stay at MIETS are considered. In the second part the clients' retrospective analysis of their time at the unit is outlined. Before admissions most clients (75%) knew why they were being admitted to the unit. The remainder did not understand the reasons for the move to the unit and this caused considerable distress and uncertainty about their future.

During their stay in the unit interviewees rarely offered spontaneous positive comments about MIETS itself. However, 5 clients did so:

'I do like it here.'

'Yes actually I'm glad I came here. Cos I wanted to get some help and that. Sort my problems out.'
'Do you think you are doing that?'
'Yes. cos if I weren't here. I'd be doing two and a half years in prison.'

'They teach me and I learn [talking about the unit]. That's what you come across here for – to learn, to help you. That's what the nurses are here ... to help the people.'

'Last time I talked to you you didn't like it. I was ill and I just wanted to get out. All I wanted before was to try and kill myself all the time. Now I've improved cause of me tablets. It is a good place ... I'd come back if I was ill.'

Despite the sparseness of positive comments about the unit at the predischarge interview two-thirds of the clients felt that MIETS had helped them.

'No I'm getting a lot more help here that I was at Moss Side. They help me a lot.'

'They've helped me a lot with my temper ... help me behave myself.'

'They seem to talk to you here and they try and see what the problem is and if they can actually help you with the problem, they'll help you, but if they can't they say they can't help ya.'

In addition there were many comments highlighting the helpfulness of the MIETS staff.

'They're as helpful as they can be.'

'The staff help me. They help me a bit more when I came here.'

'Oh yeah [the staff] are very helpful.'

Such comments were made by 50% of the clients at some point during the interviews carried out in the unit. Clients also commented on the value of some of the treatment methods.

'It just helps me to have sex education all the time – learn about sex and the ways you can do it in privacy and all that lot ... No I haven't [heard about these issues] that's why they're teaching me, then I won't do it with boys again.'

Six clients stated specifically that the unit had helped them control their behaviour. However, the extent to which the interventions practised in MIETS would generalize to the community is not clear. Some tactics mentioned by the clients themselves would not be easy to carry out in the community, although this insight is not explicitly mentioned by the clients themselves. For example:

'Let's go back to your fire setting. Is there any help that you'd like that you aren't getting?'
'Not that I can think of. They've taken my matches off me and that's good enough.'

'There are a couple here [patients] who are always poking their nose in or being mouthy to you, and that's when you feel like smacking them in the mouth, but you know that you can't, cos you'll end up either in the seclusion room or all medicated.'

The criticisms directed towards the unit tended to focus on the physical and social situation rather than the assessments and interventions. There was a general view for many clients that residency at MIETS brought with it new and unnecessary restrictions. At the time of the final interview within the unit 80% of the clients were complaining of the restrictions.

'Can you walk out of here?'
'No.'
'Would you like to be able to go out?'
'Yes.'
'What would you like to do?'
'Go and walk in the park. I like parks.'

'What do you do here most of the time?'
'Nothing.'

'I don't like the doors being locked because I think they should be open all the time ... I think if people run away they should be put on a different ward more secured like.'

Many of the clients expressed negative views about the seclusion tactics room. Clients were placed in a bare seclusion room (the green room to the clients) when their behaviour was felt to be unmanageable. Many of the clients' dislike of the green room stemmed from direct experience:

'The green room smells a lot ... . Don't like being locked up. Tell you what if they keep me locked up too much longer, I'll kick the door down and break out.'
'Do you think the staff could have done something else rather than put you in the side room?'
'Yeh could have brought us into our bedroom.'
'Could you have calmed down?'
'Yeh.'

'It's not very nice. Especially when you've been in there a couple of hours.'
'What does it feel like? Describe it to me.'
'It's boring, depressing, very depressing. When you get put in there you're OK for a little bit, then once the minutes go past you just sit staring at the four walls and you've got nothing to do. You're not out with your mates. It upsets you sometimes. I don't like them stripping off my clothes all naked. I don't think it's right, I don't want them to do that.'

'Is it useful?'
'No, I feel bad. Every time I go in there I end up banging my head anyway. Almost cracked my head.'

There was a general dissatisfaction with the activities on offer. Thirty-two per cent of the clients raised specific concerns, in addition to the general restrictions, about the daytime activities on offer:

'Well it's better than being in prison, and you've got nice grounds, but apart from that that's all there is to it. I mean they help you where they can.'

'Play a game of pool, we do art, we do my life book – babyish things.'

'I don't mind doing OT now and then but I get bored with it – it's the same thing all the time.'

Two clients noted the learning possibilities from the activities on offer:

'What do you do in OT?'

'Living skills, stress management, sex education. But I'm not going cause I feel a bit drowsy still.'

'Have you learnt anything in OT?'

'Yea. I like computers the best. I'm going to computers tomorrow.'

Several clients had ideas which they felt might improve the situation.

' I think they could sort of hold a few more discos here. You know I think a few discos. And I think one of the things I would like to see done is a holiday for patients, you know.'

'Well one thing I think should improve is the dinners. Put some decorations up in the kitchens so that it feels more homely and that.'

A fuller and more structured programme based on consultations with clients would represent a better use of the resources of a highly staffed service.

POST-MIETS INTERVIEWS

Clients interviewed after leaving the unit were consistently positive about the role the unit had played for them in rehabilitation. This was not at all true of other placements that the clients had experienced. There was only one client on discharge that felt that MIETS had not helped him. However, most of the clients had criticisms of the unit, again focusing on the lack of opportunities and the internal restrictions. At 6 month follow-up 59% of the clients remembered the therapeutic strategies that had been developed for them at MIETS but only 33% said that they were actually using the strategies in their daily activities.

MATCH AND MISMATCH IN SERVICE EVALUATION

Let us return to the four questions that informed the design and analysis of this section of the evaluation. The client interviews extend the preliminary conclusions drawn by Cattermole *et al.* (1990) and Grey and Jenkins (1994). Clients with challenging behaviours and mild learning disabilities can comment on their problems and the services they experience. On the whole the MIETS clients were aware of their problems and were sensitive to the context in which they lived. They articulated clearly both the strengths and limitations of the MIETS provision. They were generally positive about the service but identified gaps in provision. For example, the fact that 25% of the clients reported that they did not know they were to become resident in the unit reflects the lack of communication found in some instances between MIETS and the districts and clients. This caused the clients unnecessary distress.

To a large degree the gaps identified by the MIETS clients match those identified by other aspects of the evaluation and significantly question the notion that people with learning disabilities are inherently unreliable sources of information. This view is also supported by Grey and Jenkins who conclude that 'responses were in agreement with the responses of families and referrers, although some issues were raised by clients which were not raised by the other two types of consumer'. The MIETS clients directed their comments towards the physical and social situation in the unit rather than the assessments and interventions. There was a general view from many clients that residency at MIETS brought with it new and unnecessary restrictions. The more formal aspects of the evaluation also identified the limited opportunities in the unit and the restrictions afforded by a hospital ward but had not acknowledged the impact of these constraints on the clients' lives and attitudes. Thus, when the limitations of the MIETS unit are addressed, both data sets highlight the restrictive nature of the facilities, the lack of purposeful activity time and the potential difficulties in generalizing therapeutic techniques to the community. Moreover, the positive comments about the unit focused on similar aspects of the service provision. Both clients and the rest of the evaluation highlight the detailed assessments and interventions carried out in the unit and the extra support provided. Both sets of data note that MIETS meets a gap in service provision. In addition the clients introduce an element missed in the technical report, that is the importance of the staff's approach. Over 50% of the clients attest to the helpfulness of the staff. The client interviews thus serve as a valuable addition to the other aspects of the evaluation and serve to strengthen the overall conclusions.

Service evaluations of the kind carried out with respect to MIETS rarely occur. They are costly both in time and money. Nevertheless every service should consider the impact of the planned interventions and the extent to which the service is acceptable to the users. The MIETS evaluation suggests that when we are concerned with the users' experiences we should ask the users. They contribute reliable and valid information. If service providers are to rise to the challenge they should consult their users. Monitoring interventions and considering cost/benefit analyses can be dealt with by others.

LIMITATIONS OF THE PRESENT APPROACH

The results presented here indicate that service users with mild learning disabilities and challenging behaviour can and should be consulted. However, they also raise serious questions about the methods and the context in which this is done. There are two specific questions that need to be considered:

- What did the clients gain by participating in the interviews?
- What did the evaluation gain by interviewing the clients?

The answer to the first question must be very little. Clearly these clients felt able to address some service limitations but despite the open-ended format the agenda was set by the researchers not the clients or the service providers. The focus of the enquiry should have been the respondents' world view. By maintaining an overriding ideology of objective measurement we failed to consider the clients' wider views about their difficulties and their lives. There are important gaps in the interviews. They did not address the emotional needs of the clients or their hopes for the future but focused on their experiences in MIETS.

As researchers we listened but we did not act. MIETS clients have not received details of the evaluation, they were not involved in group discussions. In general we colluded with the power imbalance. In many respects the purpose of the evaluation overrode the process. Despite our best intentions the clients maintained the position of objects of study. Their views were peripheral to the academic exercise. This need not occur when the users are asked for their views in the context of service delivery. The dangers of reducing the client perspective and further disempowering them should nonetheless be considered in any similar situation.

In marked contrast, the evaluation gained from the client interviews in several ways. The conclusions of the more structured aspects of the evaluation were corroborated by the individuals actually using the service. Moreover, the clients' views provided important insights about developing service provision for this group. It would be perfectly feasible to involve individuals in running the service to a greater extent, to develop a users forum and to develop user-based criteria to evaluate the service. Moreover, the clients' views contribute to the debate about the types of units that should exist. At present there is still not sufficient data to allow conclusions to be drawn about the most successful service model for these clients but the service users object to features that can and should be changed. Emerson et al. (1994) argue that to provide high-quality services 'it is crucial to take a systemic view of the inputs, processes, outputs and outcomes of the services for people with challenging behaviour.' A central ingredient of this systemic approach must be the users' views.

ACKNOWLEDGEMENT

The research reported in this chapter was funded by the Nuffield Foundation.

REFERENCES

Ben-Ari, A. and Reiter, S. (1982) The emotional dynamics in the family as perceived by the retarded adult. *Journal of Practical Approaches to Developmental Handicaps*, **6**, 3–5.

Cattermole, M., Jahoda, A. and Markova, I. (1990) Quality of life for people with learning difficulties moving to community homes. *Disability, Handicap and Society*, **5**, 137–152.

Cm 849 (1989) *Caring for People: Community Care in the Next Decade and Beyond*, HMSO, London.

Clare, I. C. H. and Gudjonsson, G. H. (1993) Interrogative suggestibility, confabulation and acquiescence in people with mild learning disabilities (mental handicap): implications for reliability during police interrogations. *British Journal of Clinical Psychology*, **32**, 295–301.

Dockrell, J. E., Gaskell, G., Normand, C. and Rehman, H. (1993) Service provision for people with mild learning difficulty and challenging behaviour: the MIETS evaluation, in *Research to Practice? Implications of Research on the Challenging Behaviour of People with Learning Disabilities*, (ed. C. Kiernan), BIMH.

Dockrell, J. E., Gaskell, G., Normand, C. and Rehman, H. (in press) An economic analysis of the resettlement of people with mild learning disabilities and challenging behaviour. *Social Science and Medicine*.

Edgerton, R. B. (1984) The participant–observer approach to research in mental retardation. *American Journal of Mental Deficiency*, **5**, 498–505.

Emerson, E., McGill, P. and Mansell, J. (1994) *Severe Learning Disabilities and Challenging Behaviour*, Chapman and Hall, London.

Flynn, M. C. and Saleem, J. K. (1986) Adults who are mentally handicapped and living with their parents: satisfactions and perceptions regarding their lives and circumstances. *Journal of Mental Deficiency*, **30**, 379–387.

Gaskell, G., Dockrell, J. E. and Rehman, H. (in press) Community care for people with challenging behaviours and mild learning disability: an evaluation of an assessment and treatment unit. *British Journal of Clinical Psychology*.

Grey, L. M. and Jenkins, J. (1994) Investigating service satisfaction among people with learning disabilities. *Clinical Psychology Forum*, **67**, 20–22.

Griffiths, Sir R. (1988) *Community Care: Agenda for Action*, HMSO, London.

Hoefkens, A. and Allen, D. (1980) Evaluation of a special behaviour unit for people with mental handicaps and challenging behaviour. *Journal of Mental Deficiency Research*, **34**, 213–228.

King's Fund Centre (1980) *An Ordinary Life: Comprehensive Locally Based Residential Services for Mentally Handicapped People*, (Project Paper 24), King Edward's Hospital Fund for London, London.

Wallace, A. and Rees, S. (1984) The priority of client evaluations, in *Evaluation Research Highlights in Social Work 8*, (ed. J. Lishman), Jessica Kingsley Publishers, London.

Wilson, G. (1993) Users and providers: perspectives on community care services. *Journal of Social Policy*, **22**(4), 507–526.

Zetlin, A. (1983) Self-perspectives on being handicapped: stigma and adjustment, *107th Annual Meeting of the American Association on Mental Deficiency*, Dallas, Texas.

User involvement in hostel accommodation: overcoming apathy

13

Richard Shaw

As funds decrease, staff working in community care services may increasingly find themselves doing research on user views, rather than paying for outside consultants. The practitioner–researcher has the advantage of knowing the research area well, and the disadvantage of possibly being seen as biased. Users may be even less willing to risk giving offence than they already are with outside interviewers. This chapter uses a theoretical model of service provision to criticize the simplistic approach to resident participation which relies on formal consultation. Shaw points out that not all users welcome keyworking, often promoted as a less formal route to resident participation. The construction of an attitude survey may show more clearly what staff already suspect: that residents' views on consultation and participation are very different from those of senior management and the Housing Corporation. As long as all goes well residents expect staff to run their service.

INTRODUCTION

The purpose of this chapter is to look at the differing ways in which residents can participate in the running of a residential project. It is based on work in one hostel for elderly/frail men with some history of homelessness where I was a member of staff.

According to Robson (1993) 'the practitioner–researcher is someone who holds down a job in some particular area and at the same time carries out systematic enquiry which is of relevance to the job'. As he says in his discussion, there are advantages and disadvantages in this. To find out what service users think, it seems sensible to interview them. If an interviewer works with the residents every day then this could be seen as an advantageous situation. A friendly relationship already exists so residents can engage in uninhibited discourse and freely state their views. 'The interviewer needs interpersonal skills of a high order' (Oppenheim, 1992) but a rapport has already been created in the above situation. However, to a resident, the production of a socially ingratiating experience may become the aim and they may engage in 'elaborate displays of friendship and hospitality' hence downgrading the validity of the information offered. This is an unavoidable hazard in practitioner research.

Participation can be broadly defined for my purposes as any channel of communication between residents and staff in which a clear view or preference regarding conditions within the project is stated by a resident. Members of staff are (theoretically) supposed to be responsive to such expressions of view. The drawbacks of different channels of communication are discussed below, as well as client reservations on speaking out. The chapter initially looks at the characteristics of the client group (who will be termed users, clients or residents) and then moves on to the service package envisaged. It incorporates a review of the ways in which users can influence the nature of this service package. The chapter ends with a report of a satisfaction survey designed to produce an accurate outline of residents' feelings on the standard of the services they received. In my conclusion I record the results of the survey, the adequacy of existing methods of communication within the project, and make some recommendations for improvements.

CLIENT GROUP

The operational policy of the hostel states the admission criteria as 'people from the age of 21 years who are homeless and require on-going support and care for alcohol problems'. Added to this, each successful referral should have some level of physical frailty. Hence, most residents are aged or appear so because of poverty or self-neglect.

At the time of the survey all 18 residents came from one of three sources. First, the outreach service, run by the national charity which owned the hostel, provided a contact point for those sleeping on the street or in their own makeshift accommodation (i.e. in the various cardboard cities of inner London). Usually, such people are placed in larger generalist hostels which cater for clients with varying needs, but those considered physically frail were brought to the project directly. Secondly, the charity's resettlement agency, which aimed to place those living in generalist hostels in more appropriate accommodation, had provided five residents. Those persons referred from outreach and resettlement were the least successful in adapting to life in their new home. The third and final group of people to take up residence consisted of eight residents transferred from another home owned by the same charity. The transfer was arranged because of plans to convert their existing home into a project for those with mental health problems. They had all been given the choice of moving but had had no say in the decision to change the nature of their current home. As one resident said, they had to move or face living in a 'mental institution'.

WHY DID SOME REFERRALS FAIL?

If users did not want to stay in their new home, and instead chose to move back (even if this meant to the street), then for them the levels of satisfaction were not high. Four people left shortly after the project opened. One rough-sleeper disappeared shortly after moving in, to be found in an intoxicated state in the underground car park where he had initially been contacted. He gave no explanation for his disappearance, although other residents commented that he had not been happy where he was. It is probable that he had become accustomed to his existence of sleeping rough and had many friends on the street outside. This is an extreme example of a referral gone wrong: the person concerned may not have seen himself as suitable for hostel life so he opted to continue his chosen lifestyle. As one prospective resident brought in by outreach said 'It's a nice place, but I prefer my independence right now'. Choice plays its part in homelessness.

Three other referrals failed. One was resettled from a large first-stage hostel. Such projects have reputations for noise, sometimes violence, drink abuse and theft – in varying degrees. Unsurprisingly, a move out of such a place for a physically frail person into a brand new, purpose built home was seen as a good idea. However this overlooks the fact that some individuals enjoy the large social networks and the adrenalin pumping incidents which occur. One man complained that he was not happy in his new home. There was no 'crack' (fun) and he resented being in an 'old folks home'. Boredom and loneliness were his companions among the relatively sedate resident group. 'Why did they bring me here?' was an often repeated question. Of the other two, one returned to his old large hostel and another simply handed his keys in.

The above examples are important because they show that what is perceived as good for a client does not necessarily relate to what the client himself feels is important. A quality service for these people was about meeting psychological needs, such as providing compatible company, rather than improved physical conditions.

A theoretical formulation of service quality has been developed by Normann (1991). He distinguished between core and peripheral elements of the service and between tangible and intangible benefits to the user. In the above example the core, as perceived by the providers, is physical (shelter), whereas the service users see the core as social. For a group as varied in their needs as the homeless a simple formulation is not meaningful. For example, a core service for an able bodied person could mean better material conditions but for someone who is disabled it must include better physical adaptations.

A service concept, practically applied, leads to a service package. The first part of the package consists of **facilitating goods** (Normann, 1991), which at the project could be identified as single rooms and communal areas containing a TV in one living room and a hi-fi in another. There were snack-making facilities and a catering firm provided main meals at fixed times. Specialized equipment such as lifts, wide doorways, rails and medicare bathing facilities existed for disabled residents.

The second part of the package is made up of **explicit intangibles**, i.e. the physical benefits which arise. In practical terms this meant a high staff to resident ratio (seven staff to 18 residents) which influenced the amount of care which could be given. Links could be provided with outside agencies such as physiotherapists and contacts made with external carers in day centres or, for example, alcohol recovery schemes. Lastly **implicit intangibles**, i.e. psychological benefits, rely on the production of beneficial social relationships as an output of the service; for example, supportive relationships with staff, or the writing of jointly produced care plans. Such things will not be appreciated by all residents. They may be dismissed as patronizing and unnecessary. These categories overlap, since physical benefits can induce psychological benefit.

The first step in assessing the attitudes of a set of clients toward the quality of the services they receive is the definition of a service concept and the service package on offer. A good service, as defined by an organization, will not always correspond to the users' views. Alternatively, a client might make demands of a service which are not in his best interests (for example opting out of an agreed care plan which specifies a cutback in excessive alcohol intake), or are not in the interests of other users. The idea that the customer is always right is mistaken (Normann, 1991).

Service packages might be deemed to be of high quality by their designers but, with the exception of care plans, they rarely offered the client group any say in what constitutes quality. For example, no potential users were asked to participate in the initial stages of development of the hostel project, although up to ten had been identified and so were available for comment when service specifications were decided. Services contracted out, such as catering arrangements, were specified by purchasers and providers only. The experience of managers was relied upon when designing services to meet the requirements of future residents. A care audit produced by managers was strongly influenced by *Homes Are For Living In* (DHSS, 1989), with its list of quality of life indicators. The plan was to leave subsequent monitoring to inspection units and client/staff interactions. In one sense choice existed: clients were not forced to move in.

There was, however, a policy on tenant's consultation. This was produced by the Housing Corporation and the guidelines were outlined in *The Tenant's Guarantee* (Housing Corporation, 1989). This document requires that residents understand the overall aims of the scheme in which they are living, that participation is encouraged and that 'associations should review regularly and consult the residents about the running of schemes'. If residents' views cannot be accepted they should be given reasons, and 'Housing associations should also inform the residents in simple terms of policies and procedures'.

The charity's own draft policy on tenant consultation and participation was perhaps produced to ensure future financial support from the Housing Corporation. It stated that the organization was 'committed to encourage resident involvement in the affairs and management of the association' in order to ensure a more responsive service. The charity claimed to be committed to consultation with residents before arriving at final decisions in areas of 'housing management which affect them substantially', such as alterations to the physical environment, rules and the extent of services.

The existence of such policies on paper might in reality mean nothing more than a policy of communication, i.e. users will be informed but have no power of veto. Crucially, without a client group which is motivated to participate in decision making, such policies may be little more in practice than 'we (staff) speak out, and they (residents) listen'. However, it is possible for a culture to exist where staff are concerned with the production of social relationships and this may lead to frank exchanges between staff and residents. The flip side of this is that residents may be unwilling to endanger such relationships by criticism.

The salient feature of residents' participation was the periodic residents' meeting. Initially, in the hostel, attendance was close to zero; however, later attendances increased to almost 50% of residents. However, as I will argue, success cannot be measured in terms of numbers alone. At residents' meetings, the most vocal contributions came from those who had previously held some position of authority or who had lived in charity accommodation for a long time. They may perhaps have known senior figures in the organization for many years and even have been employed by it in the past and may by their actions (i.e. performing small tasks around the home and jealously guarding them) indicate that they would like to enjoy some special status with the staff. Such people, along with more dominant personalities, were limited in number, but accounted for most of what was said. Domineering personality traits may exist in individuals who have not always expressed a great deal of respect for the resident group, which calls into question the representativeness of their utterances. While the main speakers were hogging the limelight, most other residents said nothing or occasionally chipped in with very minor points. Attempts by a chairperson to elicit responses invariably failed because the recipient of such attention clammed up immediately.

Such unwillingness to become good 'prosumers' (Flynn, 1993) was reflected in the fact that the agenda for residents' meetings was normally written by the staff. The 'any other business' item was an opportunity for the more confident residents to lambast other people's behaviour. True, the issues on the agenda could be tedious and trivial, and may not have captured the users' imaginations, especially if individuals had been conditioned to believe that it was the staff's job to provide solutions (and why not? many users would say).

In contrast to the formality of a residents' meeting, keyworking was seen by many as the main way for one member of staff to facilitate freedom of choice by choosing a programme of care jointly with a resident. Keyworking and care planning were seen as important by the charity; residents' views on this are examined below.

INTERVIEWS AND ATTITUDE STATEMENTS

Residents draw on their own experience when judging what they see around them and what they receive (Chapter 2). If they have been accustomed to an efficient supportive service before they arrive, they will hardly comment on the maintenance of such standards. The opposite is true if standards fall short of expectations. Likewise, those who have lived in poor physical conditions, or where the staff were not able to provide support, will be more positive in their responses. Even so, residents were not always as forthcoming as might have been hoped.

I decided I would opt for an exploratory method of interviewing, asking general questions about the service. Unless a person veered off the subject, I would do little talking myself. Some respondents waxed lyrical on certain issues, notably the disruptive behaviour of others, the dictatorial nature of some staff members, and one person made unfavourable comparisons between his new home and his last hostel. Interestingly, a couple of residents stated that management appeared to be in a world of their own. Overall, most people were favourable in their assessments. Comments such as 'nothing beats this gaff' or eulogies to certain staff members ensued. I wanted to make questions open and hope for reflective answers. However, short positive responses were the norm (Chapters 7 and 9 register similar experiences). I decided to put such positiveness to the test by an anonymous survey of resident satisfaction.

After reviewing my collected material, I converted the opinions expressed into attitude statements. These have been defined as 'a single statement that expresses a point of view, a belief, a preference, an emotional feeling, a position for or against something' (Oppenheim, 1992). It was noticeable that certain negative attitudes which were not expressed in interviews had been stated at other times and these were added to the pool of statements. If a particular issue had not been touched on, material from *Homes Are for Living In* (DHSS, 1989) was used (e.g. statements 4 and 23 on aspects of privacy, as shown in Appendix

13A). Although such attitudinal dispositions can be criticized on the ground that they are not always formed rationally, they have the advantage of giving all residents the chance of weighing up pros and cons without letting the more dominant personalities affect the outcome (Oppenheim, 1992).

I decided that such statements should form the basis of an attitude scaling survey. After all, I was attempting to discover feelings about the service offered, not to gauge rationality. The set of statements used in the end may look meaningless in places but since they were based on the views of residents, it was hoped that respondents would invest their own meaning in them, and feel strongly enough about them to indicate a high or low level of agreement, rather than uncertainty. The attitude scaling model recognizes that 'attitudes are usually dormant and only expressed when the object of the attitude is perceived' (Oppenheim, 1992). A survey covering a wide range of service areas should, hopefully, provoke this type of reaction. On the final page of the survey, there was a section asking the residents to rate eight different areas within the hostel on a scale of 1–5 according to their perceived importance, and providing an opportunity for them to invent new categories and rate them (no-one did, which either means that I had covered all the categories the users regarded as significant or they could not be bothered to respond).

RESULTS

The method involved grouping together statements and weighting the responses to produce numerical scores which could be used to measure satisfaction. Twelve out of 18 residents responded and generally most responses were positive. High scores were recorded for statements which indicated a degree of loneliness and depression (statements 49 and 53 in Appendix 13A) and statements which expressed a link between the incidence of disruptive behaviour and an unwillingness to venture into communal areas (statements 28 and 32).

The much vaunted keyworking and care planning systems seemed not to be valued by some, as responses to statement 43 show that seven did not know who their keyworker was while nine didn't care! (statement 44). Five did not want care plans (and some asked what they were) (statement 19) but 12 felt that they could talk to staff when they needed to (statement 14). Perhaps this indicates that allocated keyworkers are not that important, but the informality of feeling able to approach someone may be. Importantly, all but two respondents preferred living in their new home when compared to their old one.

In all cases the highest proportion of responses were in the 'very important' category, except for the question on participation which elicited a less enthusiastic response. This may indicate a lack of relevance to the client group. The responses to statements about the residents' meeting were generally positive with very little indication that residents should have more say (statements 9, 16, 21, 40 and 54). A high proportion of residents believed that meetings were relevant and interesting but they were also satisfied with the existing situation and believed that it was basically the staff's job to run things (statements 5, 22, 40 and 50).

The statements were grouped into five areas: food; living environment; care planning and keyworking; quality of staff; satisfaction with resident participation; and desire for more resident participation. The scores for each statement were calculated by multiplying each reply by the relevant weighting on the 1–5 scale (strongly agree to strongly disagree; Appendix 13A). Positive statements were weighted five for strongly agree to one for strongly disagree. Negative statements reversed the weightings so that strongly disagree became five. The method has the disadvantage that weightings are standardized rather than being based on the respondents' own views of the importance of the different components (Chapter 8 gives a factor analysis). On the other hand the results produced (Table 13.1) were entirely credible in this case.

Table 13.1 Residents' attitudes to different aspects of daily life

Aspect	Max possible score	Score (value)	Score (%)
Living arrangements	840	660	79
Food	480	368	77
Quality of staff	540	356	66
Care planning	360	213	59
Participation (satisfaction with)	240	135	56
Participation (desire for more)	300	130	43

The table shows high satisfaction with physical arrangements but rather less with other aspects. Satisfaction with current arrangements for participation was not high (56% positive replies) but the low score in favour of more participation suggested that participation was, like care planning and keyworking, not very highly valued by the residents.

Apart from these relatively low scores, the highly positive nature of these responses could have been confidently predicted simply by interacting with residents on an everyday basis, and this might indicate that existing methods of communication were quite adequate. There did appear to be an overall confidence in the staff's ability to sort out difficulties (except when responding to disruptive persons – statement 32). Grievances and conflicts were expressed in the usual way for people living in shared accommodation, through flare-ups between residents or complaints to higher bodies (i.e. the staff).

In other words, formally instituted residents' meetings were not the normal way of sorting things out (even taking into account the residents' appreciation of them). Most of us share our home with others, but we do not have minuted meetings in order to sort things out. We rely on one to one communication, which was the practice within the group discussed. One interpretation of the results is that the staff group had failed to motivate the resident group to participate actively in the structure of user participation (e.g. committees, representatives, etc.). However, this is simply another way of saying that they have failed to mould the residents into what the advocates of such resident participation want, rather than what the residents themselves want to be. Perhaps it is not so much a question of overcoming apathy, but of recognizing that participation can take unstructured forms: the substance of many users lives revolved around such things as the TV or meals and it is disruption to these routines which provoked the most noticeable reactions, which were usually expressed by directly approaching staff. The long tradition of independence, isolation and individuality of many homeless people also militates against formal collective methods of expressing views.

Finally, if it is accepted that the survey succeeded in uncovering user views, I could shed a cynical light on the findings by speculating that some of the positive responses recorded were perhaps just another attempt by residents to avoid giving offence to staff (even anonymously), or that residents may hold lingering suspicions that the staff were somehow able to decipher who put which response down on paper. This is always a risk faced by the practitioner researcher. Perhaps then, the only way to ensure accurate expressions of residents' views is to employ independent facilitators at their meetings (where no staff would be present) or by employing independent advocates in order to represent individuals to the staff teams concerned with them.

REFERENCES

DHSS (1989) *Homes are for Living In*, Department of Health & Social Services Inspectorate, HMSO, London.

Flynn, N. (1993) *Public Sector Management*, Harvester Wheatsheaf, Hemel Hempstead.

Housing Corporation (1989) *The Tenants' Guarantee – Guidance by Registered Housing Associations*, Housing Corporation, London.

Normann, R. (1991) *Service Management*, Wiley, Chichester.

Oppenheim, A. N. (1992) *Questionnaire Design, Interviewing and Attitude Measurement*, Pinter Publishers, London.

Robson, C. (1993) *Real World Research*, Blackwells, Oxford.

APPENDIX 13A: RESIDENT ATTITUDE SURVEY

Statement	Strongly agree	Agree	Uncertain	Disagree	Strongly disagree
1. Most of the time there's a relaxed atmosphere here	3	7	1	1	0
2. The staff here don't show much interest in me	0	0	2	4	5
3. The food here is excellent value for money	3	7	1	1	0
4. Staff should ask residents before they show people around our home	'They do' written 4 times	4	0	2	0
5. Residents should have a say in which new people come to live here	0	2	5	4	1
6. The meals here are usually greasy and unhealthy	0	1	4	4	2
7. I keep myself to myself and that's how I like it	2	3	4	2	1
8. Drinking alcohol should be allowed in the TV and activity room	2	0	0	2	7
9. Residents meetings give us real power over what goes on round here	2	3	0	2	0
10. I don't feel at ease in the company of staff	0	2	0	4	6
11. Staff are never patronizing to me	0	3	0	3	2
12. At least this place is usually clean	6	6	0	0	0
13. The food we get is mostly too cold	0	1	1	7	3
14. If I need someone to talk to, the staff are always willing to listen	6	5	1	0	0
15. The design of this building makes it hard for me to get round in it	0	0	0	7	5
16. The problem with residents meetings is that they are always dominated by people with big mouths	2	2	0	6	0

Statement	Strongly agree	Agree	Uncertain	Disagree	Strongly disagree
17. Usually, the dinners are of a very high quality	2	6	2	2	0
18. Living here makes me feel cut off from the rest of the world	0	1	1	7	3
19. I don't want a care plan, I prefer to sort things out myself	1	4	0	5	2
20. More railings and hand grips would make it easier for me to move around here	1	4	0	5	1
21. Nothing ever changes after residents meetings	2	0	1	7	0
22. The staff should consult us more often about changes in this hostel	0	3	0	3	1
23. Staff always respect my privacy by knocking on my door before coming in	4	7	0	0	0
24. There is no point in asking the staff about anything, because they're in a world of their own	0	2	0	7	3
25. Having staff on duty all the time makes this place secure from intruders	1	10	0	1	0
26. On balance I prefer living here to my last home	2	7	1	1	0
27. Eating is boring here because it is the same type of stuff every day	0	2	0	9	1
28. I don't come downstairs sometimes as it's too noisy down there	0	3	0	5	4
29. Some of the furniture around here is pretty grotty, really	0	2	0	6	4
30. Peace and quiet is what I like about here	4	6	0	1	1
31. Chatting to staff can be a good way of passing time	3	6	1	2	0
32. If someone's a nuisance, nothing effective is done about it by the workers here	0	3	4	5	0

Statement	Strongly agree	Agree	Uncertain	Disagree	Strongly disagree
33. Having other people around to talk to is a good thing about living here	4	4	2	2	0
34. I prefer to eat traditional British food	3	9	0	0	0
35. Considering the food we get here I'd prefer to cook myself	0	1	0	4	7
36. My care plan has helped me solve a lot of my health problems	2	4	0	0	0
37. I don't really need the help of the staff with much	0	3	2	4	2
38. In future, residents should be allowed to choose the furniture and carpeting for their own home	0	0	2	7	2
39. If you want action to be taken about someone, the best person to see is the manager	0	8	0	4	0
40. Residents meetings should give us power over the way things are run here	0	3	0	5	0
41. I now regret moving into this hostel	0	1	0	6	5
42. If I need an outside specialist, the staff will find one for me	1	11	0	0	0
43. I don't know who my keyworker is	0	7	0	3	2
44. I don't care who my keyworker is	2	7	0	2	1
45. Sometimes the workers here treat you like they're not interested	0	0	1	7	3
46. I don't care about hostel policies, they are nothing to do with me!	1	2	1	5	3
47. On balance, there's enough choice on the menu here	0	8	2	2	0
48. We only get 'starvation' rations to eat at dinner times	1	0	0	4	7
49. This is a lonely, depressing place to live in	1	2	0	4	5

Statement	Strongly agree	Agree	Uncertain	Disagree	Strongly disagree
50. It's the staff's job to run the hostel, not mine	1	6	1	3	0
51. The design of the building is spacious and homely	1	9	1	0	0
52. My bedroom is furnished and decorated to my liking	3	8	1	0	0
53. Living here is so boring	0	3	0	7	1
54. I find residents meetings both stimulating and relevant	0	5	3	3	0
55. I can't stand speaking in front of groups of people	0	5	0	0	3

Finally, could you tell me if before you lived here you were

1. Living in a large hostel
2. Of no fixed abode
3. Living in another care home.

Please circle which one.
Thank you for your help!
Finally, could you rate on a scale of 1–5 the importance to you of the following things. Do this by marking your chosen number (1 can be taken to mean not important at all whilst 5 can be taken to mean very important).

Item	Not Important				Very Important
Quality of food	0	0	0	2	9
Type of furniture, carpets, decorations etc.	1	1	1	2	5
Privacy	0	0	0	0	12
The company of other residents	0	2	4	1	5
TV/Radio	0	1	1	1	6
Getting access to help if I need it	0	1	2	1	7
Peace and quiet	0	1	0	0	10
Participation in the running of the hostel	0	1	4	0	2

Please add anything else you want to and tell me how important you think it is.

<table>
<tr><td>14</td><td># Experiencing psychiatry: an example of emancipatory research</td></tr>
</table>

14 Experiencing psychiatry: an example of emancipatory research

Anne Rogers and David Pilgrim

Research which is specifically designed to alter the power balance between community care users and providers is rare and faces problems of funding and problems of design. Professionals are unwilling to see their views of users challenged. This holds across all community care user groups but the conflict is particularly strong between mental health professionals and users. Psychiatrists are very highly trained and have access to knowledge which passes as scientific. In contrast their patients are often assumed to be wholly irrational. By working with the national charity MIND and giving their services free, the authors were able to generate a large sample of former users of mental health services for a relatively small amount of money. Their findings document the gap in perceptions between the majority of mental health providers and the users.

This chapter summarizes the methodology and findings of a piece of research conducted by the authors about users' views of mental health services. We are putting this forward as an example of emancipatory research and so the current status of the latter will be outlined for the reader first. The research we conducted has been written up more extensively elsewhere (Rogers et al., 1993; Pilgrim and Rogers, 1993; Rogers and Pilgrim, 1993; Rogers and Pilgrim, 1994). Our intention in this chapter is to pull together some of the main methodological elements and themes of these publications.

EMANCIPATORY RESEARCH IN ITS RECENT SOCIAL CONTEXT

In the 1970s emancipatory research and critical theory constituted a significant contribution within the social sciences, but more recently the term has fallen out of favour. This may be partly related to some problems with its underlying assumptions. For example, the Marxist notions of false consciousness and the existence of a crisis in social conditions as the fertile ground for such research (Fay, 1993) have been superseded in social science over the last decade by post-structuralist ideas and assumptions about post-modern conditions. However, probably a more salient issue than a crisis in confidence in Marxian social science has been the question of funding. Who would fund something called 'emancipatory research' in a climate of conservative politics?

It follows that much potentially radical work has been hidden under the guise of the more neutral term 'health services research'. It is not uncommon to find radical implications insinuated into, or appended to research which, on the surface, appears to be traditionally presented and carried out. However, the very covertness of this research and the necessity for its audience to read between the lines may have limited its optimal impact. The latter is further constrained by the sources of funding for consumer research. The marketization of the public sector has meant that bottom up research is now legitimized and encouraged by NHS and social service managers. However, they often require 'quick and dirty' research, which is limited to a set of narrow, parochial expectations of improved service delivery. Typically, funded research only follows when an idea has become established. It is unlikely that general managers in the NHS will fund new areas of research focusing on theoretical innovations about the role of service users in society.

In the research reported below, we were not constrained by the purchasing power of managers in a public sector dominated by marketization. Our work was truer to the spirit of emancipatory research for this reason but consequently it had to be done very cheaply. Funding for the research reported here amounted to £2000 from MIND and £1000 from Research and Development for Psychiatry (RDP). Surveys of the scale reported here are more typically funded to the tune of £50 000 to £100 000. We gave our labour free and used the money from MIND and RDP to hire help with data collection and processing.

The research was conducted as a collaborative endeavour initiated between the then campaigns director of Britain's largest mental health charity MIND and the authors. This offered us an opportunity to act as a conduit between ordinary service users and advocacy and self-advocacy groups. It was consistent with a critical and emancipatory research framework in which those subordinated to dominant interests are given a voice (Habermas, 1987; Figlio, 1977). In line with such a framework, we were concerned to use knowledge to encourage social change and not merely to document some aspect of social reality. User self-advocacy and campaigning groups now constitute a new social movement to challenge dominant interests (Rogers and Pilgrim, 1991; this volume Chapter

11). It was our explicit intention was to inform the campaigns of this movement and be shaped by its demands. 'New' social movements can be distinguished conceptually from 'old' social movements in that they are further removed from the arena of production than the latter. Additionally, rather than seeking to defend existing social and property rights from erosion by the state, they seek to establish new agendas and conquer new territory. The new social movements (feminism, ecology, black and gay liberation, etc.) have mainly had social and cultural aims and have emphasized direct action and non-hierarchical forms of organization.

The growing collective activities of mental health users over the last two decades have been noted by a number of commentators (e.g. Chamberlin, 1988; Burstow and Weitz, 1988; Haafkens *et al.*, 1986). During the 1970s, the Dutch and US survivors' movements gained national and state recognition. For example, by 1977, 35 organizations were represented in the Netherlands (Haafkens *et al.*, 1986). Organized mental patient pressure in the US has resulted in funding for both research and mental health services to be run exclusively by patients. More recently, developments have been taking place in Britain. Users have lobbied parliamentarians. They have challenged the introduction of community treatment orders and they have campaigned against the conservative views of the organization SANE (Schizophrenia A National Emergency). The propaganda of the latter has sought to depict the mental patient as alien and violent in order to secure a return to greater coercive and institutional control.

ASSUMPTIONS ABOUT THE COGNITIVE INTERESTS OF PROFESSIONALS

In relation to 'false consciousness', one aim of the research was to raise the awareness of mental health professionals. Our starting assumption was that the contemporary discourse about users is dominated (though not exclusively) by service providers. Consequently, the preferences of professionals when intervening in the lives of others tend to limit the horizons of the public and politicians in thinking about improving mental health in society. These preferences can also limit the horizons of professionals themselves in terms of service improvements. A crucial element of critical theory is its ability to offer a critique of existing social practice and order. Part of this necessitates the eradication of false consciousness (Fay, 1993).

Given the sustained levels of dissatisfaction with professional psychiatry over the past 30 years, with its hospital-dominated practices and its impersonal treatment of its clientele, it is not surprising that users of services have developed critical views of their treatment (in its widest sense). The study reported here took place in the context of user activity directed at changing their social position. Thus the barriers in the way of change seemed to be the result of professionally defined notions of what users' interests and needs were – notions which help maintain the power, status and salaries of service providers. This is most clearly illustrated in the way professionals write about users.

Users of psychiatric services have been portrayed as objects of the 'clinical gaze' of mental health professionals. For psychiatric professionals their patients are 'the mentally ill'. This is clearly seen in the academic literature which forms the basis of most psychiatric and psychological knowledge. Clinical research in the area of mental health has tended to either exclude the views of patients or portray them as the passive objects of study. Their individual characteristics and feelings are mostly variables to be 'controlled out', in order to ensure valid results. For example, in the Medical Research Council's priorities for the funding of schizophrenia research, the emphasis is on promoting genetic and biological studies. Evaluation of services to patients is number eight out of the 10 priorities, and **user evaluation** of services and treatment is not mentioned at all. Explicitly or implicitly, 'mental patients' are portrayed in a way which emphasizes their pathology and undermines the validity of their view. Potential problem areas are seen to be:

- Views of patients which are incompatible with a professional view are disregarded.
- Patients are assumed to be continuously irrational.
- The more flattering views of service quality offered by relatives are combined with the more critical views from patients which obscures the latter.
- Criticisms by service users are reframed to provide a more palatable account which is less threatening to professional interests.

Given this tendency of professionals to suppress the voice of the service user to protect their own interests, we were concerned in our research to re-assert the legitimacy of a users' perspective.

MIXING QUALITATIVE WITH QUANTITATIVE RESEARCH

Our intention at the beginning of the project was to utilize both quantitative and qualitative methods in order to reveal and understand the overall view patients have of mental health facilities. Fixed-choice rating scales were used to give an overall assessment of whether different aspects of services were viewed as satisfactory or not. These provided a gross but important indicator of the extent to which the users in the survey viewed the service or treatment as satisfactory overall.

Thus the analysis of the quantitative data was designed to give a summary picture of the respondents' evaluations. This was supplemented by users' own words in response to open-ended questions. The purpose of the qualitative data was twofold. First, it was designed to build up a comprehensive picture of the particular aspects of treatment or services under consideration, by presenting examples of the whole range of views expressed in detail. Secondly, it was aimed at illuminating those finer details of the subjective experience of users that are obscured by, or submerged in, the more quantitative data.

In choosing this combined approach, we were conscious of the shortcomings of previous research, which had taken either a purely qualitative or purely quantitative approach. Two main methodological weaknesses may be associated with qualitative investigations. They are often limited to small samples and a deep but narrow approach; their emphasis may be on spontaneous reporting rather than the systematic prompting of a standard fixed choice questionnaire (Bryman, 1988). In mental health research these two vulnerabilities of qualitative investigations are reflected in the following examples. First, by concentrating on the effect of mental hospitalization on the patients, they have tended to exclude the wider views that patients had about their difficulties and their lives. Secondly, unstructured interviewing techniques fail to explore, in a systematic way, people's attitudes, focusing instead only on what was mentioned spontaneously in each separate case. This casts doubt on the representativeness of case studies of this type (although it does not invalidate their utility for other purposes). On the other hand, with quantitative methods there is the problem of inflexibility – the fixed-choice question limits the responses that are possible. The topics of the questions are set by the researcher, allowing no space for the respondents to raise their own separate concerns or opinions.

Our study used a survey method incorporating both fixed and open-ended questions in an attempt to combine the quantitative strength of breadth, and the qualitative strength of depth. (The methodological appendix in Rogers *et al.* (1993) provides a longer discussion of this justification.) We hoped that by including both qualitative and quantitative questions, tensions between the types of data might also help reveal something about ambivalent, paradoxical and contradictory views. An example of the usefulness of this tension between the approaches can be seen in relation to users' evaluation of psychiatric treatments (Rogers and Pilgrim, 1993). From the quantitative analysis, electroconvulsive therapy (ECT) was identified as the least acceptable intervention. The analysis of the evaluation of ECT by gender, age, class and number of admissions to hospital showed that older people and those with more than two admissions were less likely to find ECT helpful. Although the quantitative analysis suggested that ECT was often unacceptable to users, the picture emerging from the qualitative analysis was more complex, suggesting ambivalence and mixed feelings on the part of users. There were, as expected, a number of negative comments, for example: 'I never want ECT again'; 'I am afraid of it'; 'I don't agree with ECT'; 'I feel I have suffered permanent brain damage from it'. Overall, however, those making comments identified beneficial as well as harmful effects, or were neutral about the procedure. This was the case, at times, even for those who did not indicate a positive rating on the quantitative measure.

An example of this ambivalence is illustrated by one respondent who rated ECT as 'very harmful' and stated that she never wanted ECT again because it frightened her. At the same time, she identified the benefits of ECT as 'stopping the pain' and making her more relaxed. A reading of the tensions between qualitative and quantitative responses in our data suggested quantitative ratings contained more of the public images (or media stereotypes) about psychiatry, whereas the qualitative data reflected more about real experience. An apparent rejection of ECT at the quantitative level was tempered by a less damning picture which emerged from the open-ended questions. Thus the views about ECT may represent a clash between its frightening cultural images and its lived experience. The latter was characterized by the short-term nature of both benefits and side-effects.

Conversely, qualitative accounts of major tranquillizers were more critical than quantitative ratings. This may have been a reflection of the long-term consequences of their consumption versus the vague or absent cultural messages about this group of drugs. Whereas films and books have carried images of ECT, the effects of major tranquillizers (movement disorders, agitation, etc.) are rarely depicted.

THE SAMPLE

There are few existing criteria of methodological adequacy in relation to sampling frames for users' views of mental health services. First, there are problems of definition – who constitutes a 'user' of psychiatric services? A wide definition might incorporate at one extreme a person going to their GP for a one-off prescription for minor tranquillizers, or a pupil seen once by a mental health professional at a child guidance clinic. At the other extreme, it could include someone held indefinitely under the Mental Health Act as a mentally disordered offender. Although these people may or may not accept the label of psychiatric patient, their experiences, needs, and perceptions would clearly have a limited meaning if they were analysed as a homogeneous group.

In selecting a sample for a social survey, numbers are as important as the source of the sample. In the present study respondents from MIND local associations made up 68% of the total sample. One thousand interview schedules were distributed from the headquarters of National MIND. There were no fixed quotas as to how many were to be filled in by each association. This was left to the discretion of the regions, as it was recognized that the differing size, organization and interest of local groups would affect their ability to complete interviews. The remaining 32% of respondents were drawn from other sources. A smaller number of schedules were distributed to non-MIND contacts. These included mental health workers in the statutory sector (mainly social services), voluntary organizations and other interested individuals, some of whom were higher education students with an interest in mental health who carried out interviews with people who had previously been admitted to hospital.

In this research we were particularly anxious to avoid accusations that the views of people were not representative of those who are really 'mentally ill'. We also wanted to include those people in a position to have had fairly extensive contact with mental health services. With this in mind, a condition for inclusion in the sample was that the person being interviewed had had at least one period of treatment as a psychiatric in-patient. Where organizations had comprehensive lists of people known to fulfil this criterion, it was requested that this be used as the sampling frame and a sample selected at random. In practice, the latter randomization occurred rarely, mainly because such administrative records did not exist, but also because methodological pragmatism dictated that the sample and interviewers were volunteers. The time and effort being asked of the latter were already substantial, and so the researchers could not impose unreasonable conditions on them. Implicitly, there was a further criterion for selection – in agreeing to participate, respondents defined themselves as users of services.

Another question we addressed was the number of people we should include to obtain an adequate sample. The main methodological problem here was choosing an appropriate comparison population. There are no reliable estimates of the number of ex-users in the population. Although the figure of one person in four is often quoted as the number of people who are likely to experience mental health problems during their lifetime, the source of this information is by no means clear. Certainly, compared to the numbers of in-patients admitted to psychiatric hospitals each year, 516 people is an adequate number to meet the normal criteria of representativeness. However, only 37% ($n = 193$) of the sample had been in hospital during the 12 months prior to interview and we also wished to include those who had been in hospital at some time in their psychiatric career.

We were concerned to include views about the whole range of mental health services and to build a picture of people's perceptions that had emerged over time, rather than merely provide a 'snapshot' of views about their last admission. Thus, we did not want to limit the study to those who had been admitted recently. To date, there is apparently no other study which has used anything nearing the numbers used in this survey. This does not guarantee that our sample was representative, but it does provide a wide range of views from a large group of patients. Our sample was purposive not random.

We are aware that one possible criticism that could be made about the representativeness of the sample is that the MIND respondents might be a predominantly self-selected group who may be more critical of services than other ex-patients. In order to see whether this was the case we compared the responses of the MIND users with non-MIND respondents. Chi-squared tests showed no statistically significant differences between the two groups.

One of the criticisms that can be made of some health and social services consumer research is that views of users are elicited by professionals on hospital or other service delivery premises. This introduces the tendency towards 'yeah saying' and a bias in favour of high satisfaction rates. Users being investigated by professionals, who are also their clinicians, are clearly likely to be constrained in their critical responses. This may be accentuated in psychiatric patients who stand in a particularly powerless relationship to the health and social services, as they run the risk of losing their liberty through compulsory detention. In this context, the interviewing of users by non-mental health professionals, on non-statutory service territory, is likely to have produced more valid responses than hospital-based research conducted by NHS employees. However, in our study there is the converse danger – a possible overreporting of positive views about mental health voluntary organizations (particularly MIND). This is particularly relevant to questions in the interview on residential services and the voluntary sector. As mentioned above, cross-checking the views of the MIND sample with the non-MIND group did not reveal any statistically significant differences in terms of views of services, professionals or treatment. However, judging by the extent of qualitative comments, the MIND respondents appeared to have more to say about their experiences of voluntary organization services. Additionally, open-ended questions were designed to compare and contrast views about statutory and voluntary services. This required respondents to elaborate on the reasons for their views, rather than only using the cruder measure of precoded satisfaction rates.

In terms of the geographical spread and population concentration, there was a bias in the sample towards Wales, the South East and North East of England. This contrasts with the mainstream of mental health research which typically concentrates on the London area (reflecting the hierarchical nature of teaching hospitals and resourcing of services). However, the different geographical bias in our sample (away from London) led to an underrepresentation of black people in the sample compared to their numbers in the psychiatric system. Although attempts were made to include greater numbers of black people, by approaching organizations with access to black users, only 18 out of the 516 respondents were of Asian or Afro-Caribbean origin. The failure on the part of the research to adequately capture a black perspective illustrates the need to make separate arrangements to ensure that black mental health needs are not marginalized further than they are already. Black people are massively underrepresented in higher education. White researchers doing research on and about white people are in a structurally advantageous position to carry out research, as part of their contracts of employment, albeit in this case on a shoestring. However, adequate resources need to be made available for black researchers to be involved in designing and carrying out research. It is regrettable that when the deficiencies in this regard became apparent, MIND was unable to make a modest direct funding contribution to a second phase of research with a focus on black people as a priority.

INTERVIEWS

The main data collection took place between November 1989 and February 1990. There were 241 questions in all, 38 of which were open-ended. Piloting indicated that completing the schedule took between 2 and 3 hours (indicating the extensive views elicited from each respondent compared to most market research-type studies). The length of the schedule, together with the fact that many of the questions were open-ended and required a dialogue to elicit full and rich data, precluded the use of self-administered questionnaires. The interviews were carried out by volunteers in local MIND associations and other organizations. No formal training was given to individual interviewers, although a number of briefing sessions with regional MIND groups were held. Detailed briefing notes on selection, interviewing and probing were included with each schedule. The schedule was divided up into 12 sections which covered the following: circumstance and experience of first mental health problem; treatment from and relations with general practitioners; psychiatric treatment as a hospital in- and out-patient; experiences of day facilities, occupational therapy and industrial therapy; rehabilitation and resettlement, residential services in the community; treatment including psychotropic drugs, electroconvulsive therapy and psychological therapies; welfare benefits and financial and social background of the respondents.

Some pragmatic and ethical dilemmas arose for the interviewers in this study. Two in particular are worth noting here. First, there was a problem in sustaining the momentum of the interview. Thus, the last sections on psychological therapies, welfare benefits and background information about the respondents contained more missing responses than the earlier sections on admission to hospital and first mental health problems. Second, a problem which led to some abandoned interviews was that in recalling their experiences, some respondents became upset. This posed a dilemma for interviewers: whether and how to deal with the distress of the person there and then; whether or not to refer on to another agency; and whether it was legitimate to carry out this form of research at all.

We received a number of letters from interviewers complaining about the distress caused to them and respondents. During our piloting, we became aware of the possible distress which might ensue, for some, from a detailed recollection of painful memories, but we rejected the idea of discontinuing or modifying the research. There was an obvious interest in wanting to continue the research project we had started. Additionally, we felt that if we were to abandon or modify the project for these reasons we would not be giving people the opportunity to express the full force of their emotions about a topic which is, by its nature, emotive. The complaints of some of the interviewers also brought home the extent to which it is the feelings invoked in others (i.e. not patients) which often govern or inform decision making in conditions of uncertainty about mental distress.

However, this defence of our decision to carry on despite an ethical dilemma posed by occasional signals about distress does not mean that we were completely happy about the decision, nor that we have not learned some lessons. Our resources were inadequate to guarantee that any difficulties ensuing from the research were adequately dealt with. With hindsight we can warn future researchers that these problems of potential distress have to be anticipated and that appropriate responses need to be made available to respondents if they do become upset by the research interviews. We managed this some of the time, but it could not be guaranteed in all circumstances. Moreover, more thought needs to be given to the difficulties for both interviewer and interviewee in stopping an interview once it has started. Clearly, an agreement can be made at the beginning of an interview that it can be terminated by the respondent at any time – but the precise moment to stop may be difficult to ascertain. Neither party is likely to be aware of the impact of a certain line of enquiry and a respondent may want to continue despite expressions of distress. Equally a respondent may feel that they do not want to continue but feel unable to let the interviewer know for fear of stopping the unstoppable.

Although the use of untrained interviewers meant that the research encounters were not standardized (except by the structure of the questionnaire), there were some advantages in this arrangement. The quality of the responses suggested that, generally, a good rapport had been established between interviewer and interviewee, conducive to disclosure. This might not have happened to the same extent had the person been an anonymous interviewer, who had little contact with service users. The overall richness of data obtained, and the visibly careful note taking on the overwhelming majority of the returned schedules, sheds some doubt on advice given in methods text books. The latter tend to emphasize the need for extensive training of interviewers in social research. A major additional advantage in this research was that the absence of training was an absence of financial cost.

Inevitably, issues arose which were related to the reliability and validity of the data. The lack of information given to patients was, not surprisingly, sometimes reflected in some response inaccuracies. In reporting categories of prescribed drugs, for example, respondents were asked to recall the type of drugs that they had been prescribed (e.g. antidepressants) and the names of their drugs. A mismatch was sometimes noted in this regard – respondents would know the patent name of their drug but believe it to be, say, a minor tranquillizer when it was a major tranquillizer. When this occurred, the responses were recoded as missing values.

It was also recognized, with the benefit of hindsight, that there were some omissions in the questionnaire schedule. There was a failure to include a global rating for in-patient services. (This was not an omission for other parts of the service.) To compensate for this oversight, comparisons were made on the basis of judgements from results about specific aspects of the services (e.g. aspects of hospital staff behaviour towards patients) and by counting negative and positive responses to open-ended questions about the respondent's experience of hospitalization. In this way an aggregate global response was deduced.

DATA ANALYSIS

The 240 fixed-choice questions were analysed using the Statistical Package for the Social Sciences. At various points data about particular subgroups was used rather than the whole sample population (e.g. women or those who had been in hospital for more than one year). To an extent the quantitative material also guided the analysis of the extensive qualitative data obtained. For example, it was possible to select out those cases which had made positive or negative ratings about a particular aspect of service provision and then to go back and examine in further detail the reasons why people were dissatisfied or satisfied. At other times, open-ended questions were analysed in their entirety, themes were identified and expanded in the analysis and presentation of data. Throughout, examples of typical responses were given to illuminate how users perceive contemporary British mental health services.

MAIN FINDINGS OF THE RESEARCH

Our survey showed that what patients got from mental health services was not necessarily what they wanted. One of the main findings which kept on reappearing in different sections of the survey was that patients object to a predominately medicalized approach towards their problems, treatment and care.

In terms of their early experience of mental health problems only a tenth of users framed their problems in terms of seeing them as an illness

A whole range of other problems were identified as the main reason for service contact including marital problems, work stress, bereavement, physical illness and the stress of studying. Most respondents tended to understand their problems in idiosyncratic ways, which were bound up with the particular personal circumstances of the individual. These were cumulative over time, such as sexual abuse in childhood followed by isolation, etc. in adulthood. Given that most of these users would have been labelled by psychiatrists as having suffered from some form of mental illness, this indicates at the outset that a substantial discrepancy exists in the basic way in which professionals and users of services construe their mental health problems. Early intervention was found to be helpful by 60% of users. This points to the need to reconstruct acute services – early intervention, informal support and GPs are part of that picture.

Of the range of mental health professionals, users were most critical of psychiatrists

Although they were not dismissed out of hand, it is true to say that professionals and, in particular, psychiatrists were damned with faint praise. A number of

indicators suggested that nurses were preferred to psyc.
tioners were also deemed to have been more helpful th
appears to be a gap between cultural expectations of th
figure – asking deep and meaningful questions at length of
ing attentively – and what patients actually get in practic
recurred in this regard:

- *Contact was brief and cursory.* Less than one-third of ι
  reported interview times of more than 20 minutes. Less th.
  respondents reported meetings being held at their request. Thi.
  cent of patients reported never seeing their consultant psychι
  during their hospital stay. Patients reported seeing more of their ps.
  in a 3 month period when they were out of hospital than in.
- *Content of contact was unsatisfactory.* A large proportion of psyc.
  were deemed to be poor communicators. Only half of the sample tl.
  psychiatrists were easy to talk to, barely more than a third were satisfied
  an explanation of their condition given, and only 16.6% were satisfied ν
  information about side-effects of treatment.

Current services are hospital dominated yet users want a range of options outside of hospital

Again, the preference for non-medical settings was evident in the results for
out-patient and other services. Complaints about out-patient services centred
around inconsistency of medical staffing, inconvenience of travel to hospital
locations, waiting times and short interviews. From users' comments it was also
evident that the further services were away from hospital, the more they were
preferred. Continuation of institutionalized practices was criticized in day care
(e.g. 'the regimentation of it was what I liked least'). Poor accessibility and the
failure to provide facilities outside traditional office hours were also commented
on. A clear philosophy about the purpose of day provision was also something
that many users thought would be useful. In particular, the failure to demarcate
therapy from social activity was noted. Different users wanted different things.
Domiciliary care was almost absent. Very few had been offered home visits.
Contact with crisis intervention teams was only for assessment for compulsory
admission. (Of course by our sample criterion of in-patient experience, those
never entering hospital would not be present to offer the positive scenario of
hospital admission being prevented completely.)

Services are still experienced as being coercive despite the 1983 Mental Health Act

Many voluntary patients felt that they had been coerced and thus their voluntary
status was nominal. These would be recorded inaccurately on official statistics

s being informal patients. They often reported a lack of information on their diagnosis and treatment and its potential side-effects, suggesting that informed consent remains problematic in psychiatric practice.

Implications for good professional practice

Implicit in the respondents' objections to a highly medicalized approach is what they would have preferred as an alternative. Good practice which they identified in staff included: an informality in approach; kindliness without being patronized; flexibility; and a respect for their personal dignity. The respondents preferred the flexibility offered in the voluntary sector of care. There the demarcation between staff and client role was less clear. Users sometimes contributed as providers of care for others.

A BRIEF AFTERWORD

Was the research successful? A number of responses can be given to this question. The results have been disseminated to both academic and service user audiences, and been well received by the latter. The results of the survey fed into a set of campaigns run by National MIND about employment rights and informed consent to treatment. Users reviewing *Experiencing Psychiatry* (Rogers *et al.*, 1993) have, overall, been satisfied with its content. By contrast the review offered by a psychiatrist in the *British Journal of Psychiatry* was highly critical, stating that it was not helpful to mental health professionals in their current attempts to improve services in a more user-friendly direction. The Association of Metropolitan Authorities has incorporated the results into its policy development. In their own ways each of these endorsements and criticisms suggests that the research was successful.

Approaches have been made to use the questionnaire as a quality assurance instrument for services. Whether it will be used and how the results might feed back into service provision are currently open questions.

REFERENCES

Bryman, A. (1988) *Quantity and Quality in Social Research*, Unwin Hyman, London.

Burstow, B. and Weitz, D. (eds) (1988) *Shrink Resistant: The Struggle Against Psychiatry in Canada*, New Star, Vancouver.

Chamberlin, J. (1988) *On Our Own*, MIND, London.

Fay, B. (1993) The elements of critical social science, in *Social Research:Philosophy Politics and Practice,* (ed. M. Hammersly), Sage, London.

Figlio, K. (1977) The historiography of scientific medicine: an invitation to the human sciences. *Contemporary Studies in Social History*, **19**, 262–286.

Haafkens, J., Nijhof, F. and van der Peol, E. (1986) Mental health care and the opposition movement in the Netherlands. *Social Science and Medicine*, **22**, 185–192.

Habermas, J. (1987) *The Theory of Communicative Action*, Beacon Press, Boston.

Pilgrim, D. and Rogers (1993) Mental health service users' views of medical practitioners. *Journal of Interprofessional Care*, **7**(2), 167–176.

Rogers, A. and Pilgrim, D. (1991) Pulling down churches: accounting for the British mental health user's movement. *Sociology of Health and Illness*, **13**(2), 129–148.

Rogers, A. and Pilgrim, D. (1993) Service users' views of psychiatric treatments. *Sociology of Health and Illness*, **15**(5), 612–623.

Rogers, A. and Pilgrim, D. (1994) Mental health service users' views of nurses. *British Journal of Nursing*, **4**(2), 18–21.

Rogers, A., Pilgrim, D. and Lacey, R. (1993) *Experiencing Psychiatry: Users Views of Services*, Macmillan, London.

15	# Finding out about consumer views: an experiment in the group method

Gloria Lankshear and George Giacinto Giarchi

Consultation on new and complicated policies expressed in government jargon is not a simple matter. The exercise becomes one of education as well as consultation or involvement. In this chapter the authors report on a large research project designed to find out how consumers of care would like to be consulted about community care. Speaking to individuals and attending group meetings for users, carers and possible future users of community care services as well as providers allowed them to collect a range of views. Lack of knowledge and consultation fatigue were evident on the user side and some failure to appreciate the importance of user views was encountered among professionals. The authors conclude that the appointment of a full time community relations officer and attendance at existing groups is the best way to make sure user views are heard.

BACKGROUND

The NHS and Community Care Act 1990 has raised expectations that consumers of community care will be consulted about local authority plans, but practical methods of making this a reality have not been specified by the government. This raises problems for the various statutory agencies, voluntary agencies and others concerned. It was within this context that the University of

Plymouth's Community Research Centre (CRC) was commissioned to study how best to undertake future consultation with older (65+) and disabled people (16–64) in Cornwall. This chapter first discusses consultation and the problems involved. It then describes the method of consultation used by the CRC to study the views of those involved in community care. A number of the main research findings are introduced and finally some conclusions on consultation are drawn using the study findings.

Many recent consultations, for example those on the routes for new roads or indeed the Channel Tunnel rail link to France, have been seen by members of the public as being for cosmetic purposes only. There is a widespread perception that important decisions have already been made and, therefore, consultation is pointless. The disillusionment felt after major road planning consultations probably contributed to the poor response by the public to the hospital trust application meetings held in Devon and Cornwall. These meetings attracted very few of what may be termed ordinary members of the public. In nearly all cases the few people who attended were either district councillors or members of the Community Health Councils. Consultation, therefore, needs to be further defined. A better term to be used in relation to community care planning would be **involvement**. Indeed, when we are considering consultation about community care plans and related issues, it must be remembered that community care plans are, of necessity, long and wordy documents and cannot be approached in a superficial way. Therefore, involvement, which would allow time for discussion and reflection, would be of more value (to all concerned) than 'consultation' in the form that the public normally experiences. If consultation is perceived by the public as rubber stamping only, it serves no useful purpose and in addition deflects resources from being more usefully spent.

Where then should professionals start when considering consultation exercises? There are numerous difficulties and traps awaiting as they venture forth to organize public meetings, forums, conferences, surveys, open days, locality meetings, etc. Some of the most obvious and common difficulties are: lack of public interest and low attendance, especially at public meetings; attendance of the more vociferous type of person who is destructive rather than constructive; the high costs in both expenses and professional time in view of the low response rates; last, but not least, the professionals involved often feel that they have not achieved the level of communication for which they had hoped. Carr-Hill *et al.* (1989), in a package of four booklets, have reviewed existing 'customer relations' and given advice on methods of gaining customer opinions which is an invaluable starting point. McIver (1991) also gives a practical guide to obtaining service users' views.

We decided to try a variety of methods and to ask those concerned how they would prefer to be consulted. As community care involves mainly frail older people and their carers, and disabled people and their carers, these groups were our number-one target population. There was one central point in the CRC approach, namely that **existing** carer and user groups require to be fully included in the strategy of care. This is in contrast to setting up artificial groups to serve the interests of research strategies. Users and carers are in the 'front line' of community care. It has been customary to speak of social workers or other professional groups as the front-line workers, but we rejected this definition. The various professionals are normally the **secondary** backup for users and carers. In community care, formal care, in terms of time spent with clients and carers, is either short term or intermittent, not round the clock (Wilson, 1993).

Nevertheless, community care cannot work unless the professionals involved take on board a new ethos. They need to be prepared to involve people in decisions. In the past there has been a tradition that 'a good patient' was a passive patient – one who accepted the professional diktat. Therefore, the second important target population were the professional carers, to see how they viewed consultation and involvement of the public. Additionally, it was considered important to talk to a sample of the voluntary agencies and self–help groups, as well as other interested persons such as councillors and parish councils who were also involved in community care planning.

The traditional approach to consultation mentioned above has been to convene public meetings. The King's Fund Centre have improved on this method by convening special group meetings and holding 'search conferences'. The search conference method was pioneered at the Tavistock Institute of Human Relations in the 1960s. The method:

'Aims to encourage mutual understanding and coordinated action among different groups who share a common concern about a particular issue ... .
The "search process" enables people to work in a way which recognizes and takes account of their differences ... .' (Wertheimer, 1991)

The search conference arranged by the King's Fund Centre in 1991 took 2 days. It involved between 30 and 50 participants and cost £5000. The participants were identified by the King's Fund Centre staff, by asking professionals they knew to invite users and carers in the local area.

However, we felt that holding any special-purpose, organized meeting still misses out the majority of service users and carers, who find it more than enough effort to get out to even a single monthly meeting (many are wheelchair users who depend on scarce transport) or to a weekly Age Concern club. It is worth emphasizing that many 'ordinary' elderly people like their routine and do not want to go out to any extra activities. Additionally, many of the target population cannot afford extra outings.

Reaching the consumer is difficult in Cornwall which is a rural county with approximately 450 000 people but a low population density. Rural factors can create serious transport problems in running social and health services (Giarchi, 1990). Involvement is likely to be a problem for elderly and disabled people in other rural areas if they are expected to reach public meetings or forums.

RESEARCH DESIGN

Three main groups of concerned people and a substantial number of subgroups are involved intimately in the future of community care; they and a group of potential clients were the targets of the study. We aimed to ask people if they wanted to be consulted, and how they thought they should be consulted. We, therefore, had to reach a representative sample of all types of person: people who attend groups, but also those who do not attend groups; those already receiving services and those who were as yet too fit to receive services.

We could not at this point assume that any one method would suffice for our purpose. Three consultation methods (discussion groups, interviews and questionnaires) and a small number of variants on these were available to approach the chosen populations. The thematic content of the consultations was provided first, by the main government proposals for community care and later, by additions proposed by the respondents themselves. We decided to select and introduce points for structured discussion in a series of meetings. Six community care issues central to the consultative process, as contained within the legislation and in *Caring for People: Community Care in the Next Decade and Beyond* (Cm 849, 1989), were selected for discussion at the groups:

- consultation
- choice
- participation generally
- participation in planning for community care when leaving hospital
- complaints procedures
- service provider's liaison (between agencies, as experienced by the public, and as experienced by the professionals consulted)
- other issues.

We considered it important to give group participants time to raise any points that they wanted on community care issues. Groups were generally approached and seen once, except for the Medical Committee who were visited twice.

The full range of themes could not all be used when carrying out individual interviews with service users and non-users because of lack of time and resources. The range had to be restricted because of the complicated nature of the subject. The individually administered questionnaires therefore concentrated on views about consultation and how people would like to be consulted. The range of issues covered was greater in the discussion groups. However, in both the discussion groups and the individual interviews the respondents themselves introduced subjects (such as transport) which had not been one of the initial themes. Considerable freedom was allowed within the appropriate time constraints. Data from group discussions, interviews and questionnaires were transcribed, coded and tabulated for each user group.

An exact count of the male and female attenders at groups was not kept but it was very apparent that at least two-thirds were women. In Cornwall there are few ethnic minorities, although whenever ethnic minorities were talked about, the attenders at the meetings thought this very amusing and said that they, as the Cornish, were the ethnic minority. The groups chosen for the consultation experiment were already established (Age Concern, Pensioner's Voice, etc.)

SAMPLES

The three main relevant population groups, that is users, carers and professional carers, are made up of a large number of subgroups and these can be sampled as individuals or as groups. Group samples rarely consist of only one category of person. Actual research is often more complex than later described! In the carers' groups there were individuals who were very elderly and had physical difficulties such as arthritis or leg ulcers, which meant that they could equally well have been included in a 'users' category or a possible 'future users' category. In the user groups such as the Multiple Sclerosis Society meetings, there were also carers present. Some carers' groups have members whose initial reason for attending a group has ended because their husband/wife/mother has died, but they continue to attend meetings.

Sample 1 – Groups

Non-professional groups

Table 15.1 Non-professional group meetings attended January – July, 1992

Non-professional groups visited	Number of groups	Number of participants
Clubs for elderly people	10	310
Clubs for disabled	10	154
Informal carers	4	41
Church groups	4	23
Day centre/hospital	8	67
Voluntary groups	4	18
Interested groups	4	54
Total	44	669

Table 15.1 gives the composition of the sample. The groups were chosen initially from two main areas, Caradon and Kerrier. However some groups, although operational in these areas, actually met outside the areas for geographical convenience. For example U3A (University of the Third Age) was seen in

Truro. In some instances, for example the Parkinson's Disease Society, there was only one such group in Cornwall, so they were invited to take part. Completely random selection was impossible as small surveys of this kind are severely constrained by finance and are forced to pick areas. The sample was mainly taken from *Community Information Guides* which are published by Cornwall County Library. These list community groups of all kinds including Age Concern groups, Women's Institutes, church groups, parish councils and also individual town councillors and district councillors. The study we were undertaking was short term and exploratory in nature and therefore we did not have the time to make exhaustive searches for a perfect sampling frame. However, the random nature of the sample within the time and resource limits meant that it was representative of the types of population group which we considered should be sampled.

Professional and semiprofessional groups

Existing formal professional groups were approached because their attitudes were important. Without their commitment, consultation could be just a superficial exercise. The meetings were used to gauge attitudes to, and ideas about consumer participation at all levels of planning. Most professionals already held group meetings and doctors, nurses and social workers were all sampled. Physiotherapists and occupational therapists were also seen by arranging for small informal group meetings at the day hospitals when we saw the patients. The professional groups visited were chosen across Cornwall and the team found it best to initially telephone those concerned rather than make an official letter the first contact point (Table 15.2).

Table 15.2 Professional group meetings attended January – July, 1992

Professional and semiprofessional groups visited	Number of meetings	Number of participants
Home helps	5	44
Social workers	2	40
Mixed teams	9	112
Local medical committee	2	14
Day hospital professionals	4	12
Day centre professionals	3	9
Total	25	231

Sample 2 – service users

As this was an exploratory process, and questions were to be asked about people's preferences in relation to consultation methods, the team felt that they should also consult a sample of people who were known to use services but did not attend groups, clubs or day centres of any kind. With this in mind 100 current service users and their carers were also contacted and interviewed individually (these being people who were receiving the home help service or district nurse service). This sample of people were already taking part in another study of services received (Abbott, 1992), and questions on the merits of consultation and involvement and consumer participation were added. This was done to save money and research time. The sample was drawn from three GP practices in Cornwall. One was in Caradon district and two were in Kerrier district.

Sample 3 – non-users of services

One hundred non-users of services were also interviewed as representative of older people who were not receiving any services and not members of groups, but who were potential future clients. The sample of non-users was obtained by taking a stratified random sample of the over-65 age group from the three GP surgeries. Unfortunately, younger disabled people were not interviewed because there was no available list to provide a sample frame.

Constraints of space mean that this chapter will concentrate on the results of the group method, but a comparison of results from individual interviews showed that the views of all the non-professional samples were similar in content. All highlighted the same areas of concern and expressed similar preferences with regard to consultation. However, the individual interviews concentrated on consultation methods preferred and could not cover the range of topics possible in the group method.

GENERAL INFORMATION ABOUT THE GROUP METHOD – NON-PROFESSIONAL GROUPS

It was suspected that the study could not work at a purely fact-finding level. Information had to be given out so that people had enough knowledge to understand the background and the reasons why they should be interested and take part. We chose the qualitative method of discussion in groups in order to allow open exchange of ideas, feelings and perceptions regarding community care and consultation. It was considered that the level of knowledge and information about the Community Care Plan and proposed changes (amongst non-professionals) might be very low. Pilot discussion groups showed that, for non-professionals, this was the case.

Groups were telephoned (using the number in the *Community Information Guides*) informally first to explain the research, and to ask if they would take part by allowing a researcher to run a group discussion about consultation on community care. A formal letter was then sent confirming the meeting arranged and including the list of points for discussion.

For group discussions the preferred number is less than 15. However, because we wished to use groups who already met for their own reasons, it was not always possible to keep to this limit. In a few instances group discussion was not possible because we attended large open meetings, but an explanation of the research was given ('to find out how you wish to be consulted') and participants were invited to make comments. There was always a lively response and answers were recorded in note form. Members were also invited to fill in a questionnaire but were under no pressure to do so. The smaller groups were all tape-recorded and transcribed.

Before starting each discussion the group was asked if they had heard of the Cornwall Community Care Plan. Most people had not heard of it, or if they had, did not understand the implications. A short explanation of the changes which were due to take place was, therefore, given. Care was taken not to influence people in their responses, so the list of discussion points was based on quotes from *Caring for People: Community Care in the Next Decade and Beyond: Policy Guidance* (Department of Health, 1990). These points were rewritten for use with the informal groups to take cognisance of the fact that the average lay person is not familiar with government jargon. After piloting two meetings, it was decided that only one person would manage meetings at non-professional organizations such as Age Concern. Obviously, even one researcher present at a meeting will interfere with natural spontaneity to some extent; however, it was felt that the presence of only one researcher would be less threatening and intrusive than two. Group dynamics cannot be discussed here, but the researchers present at meetings reported a very relaxed and informal atmosphere.

We contacted at least one day centre and day hospital in each area. The nurse or manager in charge gave permission for a researcher to visit and hold a group discussion after their clients had been consulted. The day hospital patients were particularly frail, so the nurses suggested that visits on certain days would find people more able to contribute.

GENERAL INFORMATION ABOUT THE GROUP METHOD – PROFESSIONAL GROUPS

As with the non-professional groups, the list of discussion points was taken from *Caring for People: Community Care in the Next Decade and Beyond: Policy Guidance* (Department of Health, 1990). Actual quotations were used, and where possible circulated to those attending the groups a few days before the meetings. A formal letter was sent to representatives of the groups concerned and a telephone call was made shortly afterwards to give a further explanation and arrange a meeting. Many professional groups knew of the research which had been reported in internal journals and in the press. We had no refusals, although members of the local Medical Committee were rather surprised to be contacted. Most professional groups already met for other reasons (team meetings, etc.), but in the day hospital/centres the groups were informally gathered together on the day of our visit and consisted of the nurses, occupational therapists, physiotherapists present in the hospital at the time.

When attending the professional groups, two researchers were always present to take notes, record the meeting, and carry out additional observations. The professional meetings were all lively and animated, but in one meeting where a very senior person was present (who additionally had just been appointed and was new to the team), there was some reservation. There was also some initial shyness and unease in the home help meetings.

RESULTS FROM THE GROUPS – NON-PROFESSIONALS' PREFERENCES FOR CONSULTATION

In no uncertain terms the groups were ready to tell the researchers first, what they did not want, but also what they did want. This chapter deals only with the theme of **consultation** – full results are described in Lankshear and Giarchi (1992). The majority were extremely cynical about consultation in general and public meetings in particular. One group of disabled people asked what would be done with the findings of the study and, when told a report would be given to the Family Health Services Authority and to Social Services, members laughed and one said 'And what will they do with it, put it in the bin?'

The overriding impression was that people did not like public meetings as they did not think they got a fair hearing and felt at a disadvantage. Group participants spoke of a them-and-us situation. However, in spite of a cynical attitude the groups contacted were pleased to take part and to give their opinions. Interestingly, they did not link our visit to their group and our request for their opinions with 'consultation'.

Self-completion questionnaires were not popular, perhaps because of apathy and fear of recrimination, but also because form filling of all kinds was simply disliked. Incidentally, many group members were quite dismissive of the type and usefulness of information that could be gathered by the typical yes/no questionnaire. In fact some of the participants of the groups spoke so knowledgeably, they sounded like experts on certain aspects of research methods.

Members from the disabled user groups thought that they would like forums if they were invited and could attend together with others from their group (though few had experience of forums). The voluntary groups, such as St. John's Ambulance, particularly liked the idea of locality forums where liaison between voluntary groups might be encouraged. They also thought these might give them an opportunity to establish links with Social Services. Many participants from Age Concern (who undertake voluntary work when asked by Social Services) and other voluntary groups were very aware of the need, in view of the proposed changes, to establish more personal contact with Social Services staff. Some members felt that they needed extra liaison because, although they were expected to help and inform Social Services personnel, these same personnel did not always give enough information for them to carry out certain tasks.

When telling us what they wanted in the way of consultation a typical comment was 'Someone should come out, to where we are, and talk to us'. Another comment made by group participants in a day centre was 'We never see anybody, Age Concern or anything else concern; we are nobody's concern'.

We felt that the good response enjoyed by the research team resulted from visiting established groups at their prearranged meetings, where they felt comfortable and at ease. They were asked at the meetings what they thought of this method of consultation. As might be expected with the researchers present they all liked the method. However, to back-up the group meetings, questionnaires were available for group members (at non-professional meetings) to take away and fill in at their leisure and return, either to their group or to the researcher. The questionnaires were anonymous and 148 users' questionnaires were returned (some were returned too late for analysis). When the answers were analysed, individual interviews in their own homes were first choice, and the group method was second choice as a method of consultation for the majority of users (Table 15.3).

Table 15.3 The choice of most acceptable methods of consultation about community care

Method	Order of preference	Number	Percentage
Home interviews	1	106	71.6
Group discussions	2	86	58.1
Consumer representative	3	69	46.6
Day centre interviews	4	51	34.5
Postal questionnaires	5	48	32.4
Forums	6	44	30.0
Questionnaires in GP surgeries	7	43	29.1
Telephone interviews	8	20	13.5
Public meetings	9	18	12.2
Questionnaires included in rates/council tax	10	13	8.8
Hospital consumer groups etc	11	13	8.8
Phone-in radio	12	12	8.1
Street interviews	13	2	1.3

Some groups did contain members who thought that consultation was rather difficult, given the level of expertise needed to read and understand such documents as the Community Care Plan. It was also thought that deciding on priorities demanded too much background knowledge for the lay person to be able to contribute fully in an informed way. Some groups with voluntary members who were very involved in local matters did not welcome even more work which they thought should be left to professionals. Groups whose members made these points were the Red Cross, St. John's Ambulance, the Multiple Sclerosis Society, and the parish council groups.

One member of the parish council group said that their group had been sent a copy of the Cornwall Community Care Plan. They had thought it was too complicated and so handed it to a wife of one of the members (a nurse), who read the document and her comments were adopted as those of the group. They all felt very much under pressure already with the amount of voluntary work that they did and felt they could not cope with more. They also made the point that they are not paid to do the extra work which is very time consuming if done properly.

The idea of a consumer representative, who could go round and visit established representative groups and find out their views in order to present them to relevant planning committees, was discussed at group meetings and included in the optional questionnaire left at meetings. The idea was rather new and, in the group situation, not many comments were made. However, reactions appeared positive. When the questionnaires were returned consumer representative, as a method, was the third choice of the non-professional group participants.

RESULTS FROM THE GROUPS – PROFESSIONAL VIEWS ON CONSULTATION

All groups of professionals thought that consumers should be consulted but saw problems in doing this. All groups were sure that their clients would not attend public meetings for a variety of reasons. Many of the professionals had experience of doing small surveys which targeted older users, but had been disappointed by the results. Even in the Age Concern groups, where many fit elderly attend, professionals found it very difficult to persuade people to fill in and return questionnaires. It was generally agreed that there were problems getting feedback from older people because of their low expectations. Many professionals mentioned that older people belonged to an age when you used to accept things and be grateful. Many remember the workhouse and consider it stigmatizing to be helped by voluntary organizations, which they see as charity. Elders and disabled people were seen by professionals as frightened to criticize publicly in any way in case they lost the services they had.

The group meetings with professionals indicated that those involved in planning services would do well to involve their own service level staff when drawing up plans (Flynn, 1993). We are not saying that this is not done, it may well be, but those at service level did not feel involved, and would feel more valued if they were. Comments were made in the meetings, such as 'No one seems to think professionals should have a say anyway'; 'There is no point in our expressing a view because it is all decided elsewhere'. The home helps involved thought that they would be good representatives of very frail older people because they knew them well. They made the point that 'if you come in from outside and ask questions, they tend to tell you what they think you want to hear'.

Professionals were trying to adapt to changing ideas, but when talking about choice and participation, one of the professionals said in a derogatory way 'Oh, you mean like those women who come into the labour room with their birth plan?' There was much laughter at this, and comments such as 'Oh yes, those who shout loudest think they will get the best care'. This perception of the user who wishes to make choices as being troublesome and someone to be discouraged was only apparent in one of the professional meetings, but the users seemed familiar with this attitude. At some of the day centre meetings, which were attended by frail elderly people, comments were made such as 'It's best if you keep quiet, they don't like it if you ask, you get treated better if you just keep quiet'.

Much of the information from professionals was most illuminating. One said 'We have tried to involve consumers but ill people cannot cope, and well people do not appear to be interested'. Another said 'The problem is that the articulate middle class do not think that they will ever need the services so do not want to be bothered'. One very important point was raised: 'There are so many organizations that are never brought together and no-one knows what the others are doing. At one time we had a yearly meeting of voluntary bodies – but not now. We don't know who is doing what. It would be so useful to get everyone together.'

Some professionals made additional off-the-record comments or, by raised eyebrow and facial expression, showed some cynicism about consultation. They felt that they, as professionals, were not involved enough in consultation. Their opinions were not sought. They considered this was wasteful because they were already involved with users and carers and therefore were in an ideal position to contribute by way of observation and experience both of current and past practice.

DISADVANTAGES OF GROUP CONSULTATION

The strengths of the group method are many but there are a few disadvantages. Some individuals will not contribute in group situations, but the researchers found that those who were silent but wanted to contribute would approach them after the meeting, the car park being a useful setting for further private interviews. More personal topics may not be raised by some individuals in group meetings, so the topic for consultation has to be matched to the method. For very frail users in day hospitals and day centres who were suffering from hearing loss and from speech impairments because of strokes, the group method was difficult. However, some were able to participate in smaller groups. In the professional meetings the more junior staff were seen to feel restrained if management-level professionals were present. The keys to success were seen as good chairmanship of the meetings and discussion or consultation questions in simple language and of interest to the groups approached.

ADVANTAGES OF GROUP CONSULTATION

The Cornish study found that one of the main problems of consumer involvement is that people are expected to respond to questions asked in isolation, without additional information or time for reflection, discussion or reconsideration. One of the strengths of the use of group meetings, backed up by questionnaires, was the opportunity for further reflection and discussion of unfamiliar subjects, so that snap decisions were not made. In addition the method allowed participants to bring up entirely different points of concern and so the pitfall of not asking the right questions could be avoided. People felt free, and had the opportunity to raise their own concerns rather than only answer those of the service provider. The method allows complex issues to be explained and discussed. By visiting established groups a large number of users, carers and volunteers can be sampled in a way that is both cost conscious and acceptable to them. 'We' attended 'their' meetings, in their familiar surroundings, and so they were comfortable and felt confident to speak out. This removed stress or shyness due to being in unfamiliar territory.

REASONS FOR NON-PARTICIPATION BY ELDERLY NON-USERS OF COMMUNITY CARE

The back-up questionnaires for the non-users of community care (the fitter elders from the three GP surgeries) highlighted and confirmed one of the problems of consultation. When this group of fit elders were asked (in individual face-to-face interviews) if they would be prepared to participate actively in consultation about community care, three-quarters said they would not. Some said they were too old or had sat on enough committees in the past. The quarter who did agree, said they would be prepared to take part but only with reluctance. Only a quarter of the sample had heard of the Community Care Plan. Reasons for not wanting to help with planning or having a say in how community care money was spent ranged from 'Leave it to the professionals' to 'I'm not old enough for that yet' (from a 70-year-old) and 'I don't take interest in elderly people' (from a 79-year-old). So many older people are not interested if they are not personally in need, but when they are in need they are not well enough – a point also made by a professional.

CONCLUSIONS

Consultation is costly. It takes time and money. We saw 900 people in groups and 200 individual patients from GP practices, together with 44 carers. We also saw 22 other people in key positions, such as councillors, directors of Age Concern, etc. It is difficult to give a precise cost of our research because we had the benefit of a person between jobs who assisted in the work. There was also the added complication that the study was linked with another (Abbott, 1992). However, as a very rough guide, the whole exercise took two people 8 months to carry out the fieldwork. This type of study cannot, therefore, be undertaken very often.

The majority of this cross-section of users, non-users, and formal and informal carers across Cornwall were opposed to the use of public meetings for consultation. Those who had experience of being consulted about the Cornwall Community Care Plan which was circulated to voluntary groups and parish councils (amongst others) thought that they did not have the time or the level of expertise necessary to comment on the Plan. Our exploratory study of consultation methods found that most people's first choice was individual interviews at home (except for carers who chose the group method as equal first choice with individual interviews). This was closely followed by the group method as second choice. The groups attended appeared to enjoy the method and expressed an interest in further contact. We concluded that, if real consultation is to be possible, the mountain must go to Mohammed.

We went to the people concerned and asked for their preferences for consultation, but we were also assessing the level of information exchanged in each exercise. We felt that, overall, the method of visiting established groups was the most cost effective way to reach a large number of actual users, carers and potential users. It allowed a wide range of topics to be covered with time for explanation and discussion. Some of the groups had members who were pleased to help in further consultation by attending forums or other meetings. Those who attended disabled groups were often in a younger age bracket and most desperately wanted to be heard.

The group method could be used with the confidence that it reaches a large number of those most likely to be involved in community care at a reasonable cost. However, it needs a committed individual to do the necessary work. The persons chosen to carry out consultation exercises must have the personality and charisma to win over what are often reluctant and suspicious consumers. This aspect is of prime importance, so selection and training of involved personnel is vital if consultation is to work effectively. The need is for a community relations officer who has overall responsibility for the consultation process (Lankshear and Giarchi, 1992). This person could set up a consultation structure, possibly seeing different groups each year.

The philosophy of care underpinning consultation within the spirit of the White Paper is well summed up by the Social Services Inspectorate (1992). 'It is important for users and carers to have and to believe that they have a real voice in the planning and delivery of services'. The people of Cornwall did not have a voice and did not believe they had a voice at the time of the consultation exercise in 1992. Whatever the programme of consultation, it is necessary to stress the importance of involving existing groups of carers and users. They are in the front line where they could so easily become the prime casualties of poorly conceived community care plans.

REFERENCES

Abbott, P., (1992) *Rationalising the Skills Mix in Community Care for Disabled and Older People: A Report of Research in Cornwall*, Community Research Centre, University of Plymouth.

Carr-Hill, R., McIver, S. and Dixon, P. (1989) *The NHS and Its Customers*, Centre for Health Economics, University of York.

Cm 849 (1989) *Caring for People: Community Care in the Next Decade and Beyond*, HMSO, London.

Department of Health (1990) *Caring for People: Community Care in the Next Decade and Beyond: Policy Guidance*, HMSO, London.

Flynn, N. (1993) *Public Sector Management*, Harvester Wheatsheaf, Hemel Hempstead.

Giarchi, G. (1990) *Elderly People in the Community: Their Service Needs*, NACAB, London.

Lankshear, G. and Giarchi, G. G. (1992) *Cornish Voices: How We Would Like to Be Consulted*, Working Paper, Community Research Centre, University of Plymouth.

McIver, S. (1991) *Obtaining the Views of Users of Health Services*, King's Fund Centre, London.

Social Services Inspectorate (1992), *Caring for Quality*, HMSO, London.

Wertheimer, A. (ed.) (1991) *A Chance to Speak Out*, King's Fund Centre, London.

Wilson, G. (1993) Conflicts in case management: the use of staff time in community care. *Social Policy and Administration*, **27**(2), 109–123.

FURTHER READING

Armistead, C. G. and Clark, G. (1992) *Customer Service and Support: Implementing Effective Strategies*, Financial Times/Pitman Publishing, London.

Cambridge, P. and Thomason, C. (1987) *Some Perspectives on Participation from the Care in the Community Initiative*, Discussion Paper 546/1, Personal Social Services Research Links, University of Kent, Canterbury.

Cornwall Social Services (1992/3) *Cornwall Community Care Plan*, Cornwall Social Services.

Cornwell, J. (1989) *The Consumers' View: Elderly People and Community Health Services*, King's Fund Centre, London.

DHSS (1990) *Community Care Planning: A Review of Past Experience and Future Imperatives*, Implementation Document CC13, Department of Health Social Services Inspectorate, London.

Dixon, P. and Carr-Hill, R. (1989) *The NHS and Its Customers II Customer Feedback Surveys. An Introduction to Survey Methods*, Centre for Health Economics, University of York.

Dixon, P. and Carr-Hill, R. (1989) *The NHS and Its Customers III Customer Feedback Surveys. A Review of Current Practice*, Centre for Health Economics, University of York.

Gell, C. (1990) User group involvement, in *Power to the People*, (ed. L. Winn), King's Fund Centre, London.

Griffiths, R. (1988) *Community Care: An Agenda for Action*, HMSO, London.

McIver, S. and Carr-Hill, R. (1989) *The NHS and Its Customers I A Survey of the Current Practice of Customer Relations*, Centre for Health Economics, University of York.

National Consumer Council (1987) *Care in the Community*, National Consumer Council and Association of CHCs for England and Wales, London.

National Health Service Management Executive (1992) *Local Voices, The Views of Local People in Purchasing for Health*, Department of Health, London.

Royal College of Physicians (1986) *Physical Disability in 1986 and Beyond*, Royal College of Physicians, London.

| 16 | # Partnerships in research: working with groups |

Marian Barnes

Previous authors in this book have noted that it is difficult for the researcher to shift the balance of power away from service providers towards users or carers. In this chapter Barnes sets out some of the problems of the researcher who is committed to empowerment and to facilitating user or carer input to service monitoring and design. She discusses the nature of the relationship between researcher and participants in a project to set up carers' panels, and lists the achievements of the project in terms of inputs to the planning process and the effect on services. Her conclusion is that researchers benefit greatly from long-run involvement with panels of users but that users also benefit, individually and as members of groups. However, a range of panels will be needed to represent different groups and to make sure that interests relating to gender or ethnicity are not lost.

INTRODUCTION

Partnership and empowerment are values to which an increasing number of purchasers and providers of health and social care services profess to aspire. Implementation of these values affects workers occupying different positions within both statutory and voluntary agencies. At the level of front-line practice such values imply a redefinition of professionalism and a reassessment of the 'caring' role (Ellis, 1993; Malin and Teasdale, 1991; Marsh and Fisher, 1992). For managers a basic challenge is how to establish opportunities for dialogues with users of services from whom they have been largely separated (Barnes, 1993a). Service planners and purchasers have to explore new methods of establishing users' views of needs and priorities to add such information to the data on which service planning decisions are made (NHSME, 1992; Osborne, 1991). In each case new ways of working are implied, and new types of relationships between those who receive and those who provide services need to be developed.

A similar challenge faces researchers who commit themselves to such values. The issue is not only what is researched, but also how it is researched. There have been many critiques of the appropriateness of positivistic methods of scientific research in the context of applied social science (for example Smith, 1987; Smith and Cantley, 1988). More recently, critiques of professional researchers from within user movements have led to the identification of emancipatory research as a tactic to be employed by user groups seeking to influence the type of research undertaken as well as the type of services provided (Beeforth et al., 1990; Beresford, 1992; Oliver, 1987). Satisfaction surveys have been criticized by researchers themselves for failing to uncover honest views about services, and for not enabling the researcher to explore the way users see services and the criteria they apply to judge those services (Barnes, 1992; Wilson, 1993). Consumer research more generally has been criticized by some users of services not only for its failure to achieve results in terms of effecting service changes, but also for placing users in a passive, respondent position, equivalent to the powerless position they have experienced as clients of services. This powerlessness is seen to relate to all stages of the research process: determining what is to be researched, the process of data collection, and the interpretation and use of results (Davis, 1992).

Traditionally, researchers have been trained not to have an impact on the lives of those who are being researched. It is unusual for researchers to stop to establish whether or not their intervention has had any effect on those they have collected data from. The distance which researchers are encouraged to maintain from their subjects is something which feminist researchers in particular have questioned. Oakley (1981) established what many researchers would suspect – that simply asking people to focus on a particular issue does have some effect on them. In her study of the transition to motherhood she found that 73% of those involved in the study felt that the research had had some effect on their experience of becoming a mother. None of the women concerned felt that the effect had been negative.

Oakley noted that the conventions of scientific research hide from public view all those aspects of the research process which identify it as a form of social interaction. This appears inconsistent in a discipline which claims social interaction as its subject matter. More recently, others have sought to expose both the personal and the social aspects of all stages of the research process (Shakespeare et al., 1993), and have called for an examination of the interactive processes through which research data is obtained (Kitzinger, 1994; Stanton, 1989). In this chapter I will discuss my experiences of working with groups of carers in an attempt to develop a model of research characterized by partnership rather than subjectification. Such a model needs to be assessed in relation to the outcomes it can achieve for a research project, but also in terms of how participants, 'research subjects', themselves view both the process and the outcomes from their perspective.

DESCRIPTION

The work described below was undertaken in the context of an evaluation of the Birmingham Community Care Special Action Project (CCSAP) (for a description of CCSAP as a whole see Barnes and Wistow, 1991). Overall, CCSAP was designed to develop an inter-agency, user-oriented strategy for community care within the biggest metropolitan authority in England. It encompassed a range of developmental initiatives which sought to address services provided to all groups of users of community care services. For example, it included a service development initiative focusing on day services for people with learning disabilities, and it sought to establish a range of mechanisms through which people with mental health problems might become more influential in services. However, the initiatives which attained the highest profile of all CCSAP's activities were those that related to carers. Three rounds of public consultations were held with carers in different parts of the city. In all, approximately 600 people attended these consultations. A key purpose of the consultations was to identify an agenda for action and this gave rise to a programme of work which sought to respond to issues identified during the consultations (a description of the carers' programme is given by Barnes and Wistow, 1992a).

CCSAP largely preceded the changes which were introduced by the 1990 National Health Service and Community Care Act, and was considered by some to be influential in determining the nature of some aspects of those reforms. The carers' programme in particular was of great interest to Ministers of Health at the time, two of whom visited Birmingham to find out at first hand what was happening.

Gerald Wistow and I were funded by the Department of Health to evaluate the project as a whole and to generate lessons of value to others wanting to pursue similar approaches. We defined one purpose of the evaluation as:

'... to contribute to the empowerment of users and carers by enabling them to participate in the evaluation process.'

Barnes (1993b) describes the range of evaluative methods used. In the case of the carers' programme, we interpreted this to imply that carers should play a direct part in the process of monitoring action taken by the city following the consultation meetings. Such participation was considered to require engaging with carers on a continuing basis, rather than conducting one-off interviews.

The names and addresses of carers who attended the consultation meetings had been recorded. It would have been possible to take a random sample of attenders and to invite them to participate in this element of the evaluation.

However, we decided on a different approach. As the carers' programme developed, some of those who became involved indicated a particular interest in playing a more active part in developments. Some participated in a consultation enacted at a Social Services conference; some met with ministers; others volunteered to talk about their experiences of caring on local radio. Some had simply written to the project office asking how they could do more. Invitations to participate in the monitoring were issued to 41 carers who had demonstrated such a willingness to play a bigger part in the project. It was envisaged that such people would be more likely to respond to an invitation to join a 'Carers' Panel'. It also enabled us to respond to people's expressed desire to make a further contribution. The implications of such an approach for the representativeness of group members is considered in the detailed report of this aspect of the CCSAP evaluation (Barnes and Wistow, in press). It is a theme that I have also developed with others elsewhere (Barnes et al., 1994). Here I wish to focus on aspects of group dynamics, rather than on issues of group membership.

However, one point which is important to make in this context is that the panels were not, by and large, naturally pre-existing groups (although some participants were also members of a pre-existing carers' group). This contrasts with the Cornish approach described in Chapter 15. In Birmingham, the panels were composed of people who shared common experiences as carers. Although it was not possible initially to draw on the shared histories of members outside the group as Kitzinger (1994) has described in her focus group discussions with pre-existing groups, these shared experiences did lead to the development of friendships and action outside the panel meetings. This in turn contributed to an increasing openness in discussions, as well as to the continuation of the panels beyond the life of the research project.

Not all those who were invited to participate were able to do so. Some attended an introductory meeting, but decided at this stage not to follow this up. Eventually two panels were established comprising 24 carers in total. I acted as convenor, facilitator and note taker, and I was assisted by a woman appointed to head up a newly established Carers' Unit within the Central Executive Department of the City Council. This unit was itself one outcome of the consultation meetings. The original agreement was that the groups would meet once a month for 6 months and then review progress. At this stage the groups decided to continue meeting for another 6 months, with myself as facilitator. I then, as I had previously indicated, had to withdraw because this element of the evaluation had to be brought to a close. The groups themselves continued, and still continue to meet, albeit for a different purpose and with a different structure.

Meetings lasted for 2 hours and most took place in a committee room of the Council House. Light refreshments were provided and travel and sitting expenses were reimbursed.

The terms of reference clearly defined the panels' purpose in relation to the research evaluation. In general terms the purpose was to enable carers to determine the criteria by which action in response to consultation was to be judged;

to receive and respond to reports of action being taken; and to take a more active role in reviewing developments. Thus the agenda was broadly determined by the action points identified by CCSAP project workers from the original consultations. From time to time, and on the invitation of the group, officers of the city who had responsibility for taking action on issues such as the need for improved information services for carers and the need for services capable of responding to urgent need outside office hours met with the panels to report on progress and obtain carers' feedback on the action being taken.

NATURE OF RELATIONSHIPS BETWEEN RESEARCHER AND PARTICIPANTS

If research is to empower people who use services, then the relationship between the researcher and 'subjects' cannot leave the latter feeling exploited and powerless to influence the research process. Traditional descriptions of scientific research methods give the impression that the researcher is completely in control of her subject and subjects. Respondents are to be kept in the dark about the hypotheses to be tested, in order that too much knowledge does not 'contaminate' responses and bias results. Populations are manipulated in order to generate a random sample, and it is the researcher who determines who will and who will not be able to participate in the project. During interviews, researchers have been warned against stepping over the line which divides over-rapport from detachment (Oakley, 1981).

Much social research continues over long periods. During this time the researcher is expected to interact, but to remain uninvolved; she is expected to make people want to contribute their time, knowledge and experiences, but to hold back from contributing her views and from any action which will result in changes in those who are 'being researched'. It is no wonder that many researchers feel daunted by the demands which are made and unequal to the task.

The decision to establish the panels to enable carers to contribute to the evaluative process was based on our general (and somewhat vague) notion of the importance of contributing to the empowerment of users and carers. In my letter inviting carers to become involved I admitted to not being able to describe exactly how the process would work, because I had not done it before. I invited people to participate in something I thought was worthwhile and, effectively, to take a risk with me that it would work out. I certainly did not feel entirely in control of the process at this stage, nor as it developed. It was only through experience that it became possible to define the different roles which it was necessary for me to play in working with the panels, and to identify the different relationships which developed between us.

Group leader/facilitator

I initiated the panels and I set out the terms of reference to which I subsequently obtained agreement. The panels were established to meet a research objective which was previously determined and they were constrained by the timetable of a larger research project of which this was one element. The imperatives of achieving an outcome within the time available caused me to avoid the issue of whether a carer should act as chair of the group and not to pursue the question of responsibility for note taking when an early question indicated little interest amongst group members to take on this task.

The terms of reference also defined the agenda of group discussions and I, as group leader, usually introduced and initiated discussions around the '11 Action Points' which comprised the action agenda deriving from the consultation meetings. In particular instances I led the group through a process designed to achieve a particular outcome. A clear example of this related to the issue of respite care. In spite of the significance of this issue to carers attending the consultations, it became clear that little action was being taken by officers of the City Council or the health authorities. However, a developing preoccupation with 'quality' suggested a way forward. Thus, I suggested to the panels that they should take a proactive stance on this issue and that they should define quality criteria for a respite care service. These could then be used both to prompt officers into action, and as an inspection/review tool, to be applied to both current and future services.

The process involved encouraging carers to talk about their experiences of using respite care provision in order to identify what was good and what was bad about services. The discussion then focused on what they would look for when they went to visit a home and I used specific questions to prompt carers to think in this way. For example, the question 'When you go into a residential respite home, what would be the first thing you would look for?' prompted the response 'It's not what I'd look for, it's what I'd smell!'

Carers were encouraged to identify specific indicators of aspects of care which they saw as important. For example, all were agreed that staff attitudes were important. Through prompting it was possible to identify observable behaviours which would indicate caring or non-caring attitudes amongst staff. These included how staff would respond when an elderly person indicated that they needed help in going to the toilet; and the amount of time staff spent talking with residents in comparison with time spent on administrative and maintenance activities.

From these discussions I designed an initial draft of a Respite Care Quality Check-list which formed the basis for further discussion, refinement of the criteria already identified, and the addition of new criteria. Some panel members then tested this out during visits to local respite facilities.

I was clearly taking a lead in determining the way in which the panels responded to the purpose for which they had been established. It could be suggested that I was controlling and manipulating them, as much as I might have been if I was taking them through a predefined interview schedule. However, my role in this respect was not viewed negatively by panel members. When one of the members was invited to join me in talking about the panels at a seminar, he identified the need for groups such as this to have 'a strong lead and to address specific issues in a structured manner'. Other aspects of my role, and of the group dynamics, also served to limit the extent to which I was controlling and directing groups rather than working with them.

Co-worker/partner

Rather than interpreting my role in respect of this directive element as that of controller, it is more appropriately understood as my contributing my research skills to a joint project. Carers contributed their experiential knowledge of respite care facilities and I drew on my experience of designing research instruments to structure this knowledge in a way which would, firstly, enable quality criteria to be defined from both positive and negative personal experiences and, secondly, enable such criteria to be investigated during the course of inspection visits and in other contexts. Carers' experiences were thus captured in a way which would enable them to influence the process by which services were monitored by statutory authorities, and which would also provide a guide to carers generally who wanted to assess services they might wish to use.

The interactive process involved in such co-working stretches all participants. I was prompting carers to go beyond the expression of dissatisfaction with aspects of service, to define what a service they would have confidence in would look like. I was having to listen hard to what carers were saying to catch issues that were of concern to them and to think how they could be expressed as questions capable of gaining a response during inspection visits. For example, two issues of obvious concern were the privacy available to residents and the security of homes. Ensuring security could be seen to be in conflict with a wish to allow privacy. Making it possible for residents to lock their bedroom doors could mean it would be difficult for staff to gain access in an emergency. Together we determined that it would be important to establish whether bedroom doors were lockable, but that the locks could be overridden from the outside.

Another way in which the relationship could be characterized as one of co-working, or partnership, related to the way in which I sought to respond to issues which came up, but which were not on the original agenda. Atkinson (1993) has described the way in which she came to realize that members of a group she had established to explore the personal and common histories of people who had spent part of their lives in long-stay mental handicap hospitals were very skilled at talking about what they wanted to talk about and not what she wanted them to talk about. Her observation that:

> 'Group sessions often left me feeling out of control and powerless, as topics were sabotaged through side conversations, stage whispers, loud yawns, interruptions and the accomplished telling of extended anecdotes (on rival themes)'

has certain similarities with this experience.

I quickly came to realize that if I was to get carers to follow the agenda set by the research project, I was going to have to respond to their agenda. This could mean using my contacts to find out about matters which had come up as queries during discussion; for example, information about how to apply for money from the Independent Living Fund (which led to one member of the group not only obtaining a grant for herself and her disabled son, but also for an elderly man she visited in her work as a home care assistant). It could mean taking up issues on behalf of the group, outside the mechanisms established to respond to the consultations, or it could mean recognizing that issues raised by carers during discussion in the panels should be added to the agenda with the aim of stimulating action from service providers in response to them.

The latter point demonstrates one of the main advantages of working with groups over a period of time, in comparison with obtaining responses during a one-off contact. Issues raised by carers in the consultation meetings were unlikely to represent a complete listing of their concerns. As circumstances change new problems may emerge. But some current concerns may not be aired in a public discussion amongst previously unknown people. One topic which emerged in response to a particular difficulty being experienced by one member of the group was that of the sexual needs of disabled people. Sexual frustration was suggested by one carer as a possible explanation for the difficult behaviour of the teenage daughter of another member of the group. This led to a discussion amongst members of the group who were parents of young adults with physical or learning disabilities about the lack of recognition or response from service providers to the sexual needs and frustrations of their sons and daughters. They said it was a taboo subject. After a while, an older woman, whose husband was physically impaired following a stroke, joined in to reflect the lack of acknowledgement of the impact on sexual relationships between spouses of such impairments. Unprompted, one participant in this discussion said that this issue would not have been raised during the consultation meeting, it had only come up at this stage (7 months into the group) because members of the group had developed confidence in each other. The others agreed.

I had played no part in this discussion. However, I did feel that my role was to think how it might be used in the context of the work we were doing. At one level it constituted research data of relevance to the overall evaluation since it demonstrated the limitation of one-off public consultations as a means of obtaining views about sensitive subjects. Kitzinger (1994) has discussed the way in which groups may both censor deviations from standards, but also facilitate the discussion of taboo subjects. This was clearly what was happening in this instance, and provided a particular example of the way in which more confident members of a group may enable less confident members to disclose information or experiences which would otherwise remain hidden.

Apart from using this experience as research evidence, as a partner within the group I felt it was also important for me to take some responsive action. Whilst I could not take action directly, I could put the issue on the agenda. My knowledge of current developments within the Social Services Department enabled me to suggest a way forward for the carers. This was to contact the officer responsible for taking a lead in developing assessment procedures for disabled people, and to communicate to him the importance of including sexual needs within the full range of needs being assessed. His response was sympathetic, but I do not know how this issue was progressed.

One other aspect of this interaction does need to be noted. There was only one male member of this group and he appeared embarrassed by the discussion and played little part in it. He had previously indicated his feelings of isolation as the only male member and his attendance later tailed off. Group composition is likely to be a factor determining whether the group acts to censor or facilitate sensitive discussions.

Advocate/channel of communication

One aspect of my leadership role was that it was usually me who acted as the link between the panels and agencies which had responsibility for action. This was an aspect of my role with which I felt somewhat uncomfortable, for two reasons. First, it was a role which did not sit easily with that of an independent researcher, albeit pursuing an action research element of the project in this instance. Second, it was an important limitation on the empowerment objective of the project. Whilst I was composing letters or memos on behalf of the group, and on occasions speaking on their behalf in other forums, carers' voices were not being heard directly and carers themselves were not gaining this type of experience. That is not to say they were not speaking on their own behalf elsewhere. One member of the group reflected on her experience of representing carers' views to local authority councillors and commented that she would not have thought she would either be able to do this, or be taken seriously, prior to her involvement in the carers' programme.

The importance of effective links between the panel and decision makers was something which members referred to in their review of the panels as research involvement was coming to an end:

'I think the panel is very useful if we feel that we have a line to somebody who can help, somebody to pass things on to. It's no good just sitting around chatting amongst ourselves, but if we have a line to somebody who can do something, I think that's very valuable.'

They also recognized that the role of communicator/advocate had largely fallen to the researcher:

'... the only success we've had in doing anything at all is by virtue of [researcher] who has had access to the people who will listen ... we need someone to input at the right level.'

Carers' interests in the panels were primarily to do with action rather than research. They were prepared to participate if research could be a means to an end and thus sought to use me to help them achieve positive outcomes. At a personal level I wanted to help them pursue the achievement of service developments and I felt that a partnership model demanded some contribution from me. I used the fact that I also attended the officer group responsible for co-ordinating action in response to issues raised during the consultation to feed in specific points from the panels. I also reminded the officer group that the panels were expecting to receive progress reports informing them what action was being taken. However, I did not feel it was appropriate to pursue individual service issues, other than to pass on information about contact points or to suggest options that panel members could pursue for themselves.

PROCESS, OUTPUTS AND OUTCOMES

One clear conclusion to be drawn from this experience of working with groups of carers concerns the importance of ensuring that the process of involvement provides benefits to participants in its own right (see Barnes and Wistow, in press). This meant that a considerable amount of effort went into ensuring a relaxed, informal environment, and into recognizing and responding to immediate needs for support and information. Much of that support and information sharing took place between carers themselves, but, as I have indicated above, it also involved going beyond what might normally be regarded as the role of the researcher. It was demanding personally as well as professionally and I often left meetings feeling exhausted as well as stimulated.

Brechin (1993) asked whether the process took over from the purpose, in a collaborative research project undertaken with a group of people with learning disabilities. The purpose in this instance was to define research questions and to set an agenda for research. Brechin observed:

'In some ways looking for the bit of the process that was about identifying research questions feels, in the midst of these rather powerful concerns, like looking for a needle in a haystack.'

There were occasions in the carers' panels when I wondered whether it was right for me to be encouraging carers to focus on defining evaluative criteria when they had much more immediate priorities in their lives. Working with the groups involved recognizing and maintaining an effective balance between working towards the task which had been set and agreed, and enabling the group to operate as a support group.

The process was very important, but it did not take over from achieving key outputs and outcomes which had been intended when the panels were established. A number of specific outputs can be identified:

1. The Respite Care Quality Check-list discussed above.
2. A monitoring form was designed to records users' experiences of special

transport services. A monitoring system was also set up involving Social Services performance review section and the transport service. Initial results were obtained from completed monitoring forms from which it was possible to define user and carer criteria for evaluating the transport service.

3. The characteristics of an emergency service which would meet needs for help outside office hours were defined, and a discussion was held with the officer responsible for taking action on this issue.

4. The panels commented on the Birmingham Information File which was developed to draw together information about all aspects of community care services. Carers commented on design, content and distribution, and stressed the importance of ensuring its accessibility to those whose first language is not English, and to those with poor sight.

5. Through an analysis of discussions within the panels it was possible to identify criteria carers used to judge both particular services and services in general. Such criteria were derived from notes of discussions. In some instances it was carers themselves who effectively undertook the analysis. For example, during a discussion about benefits, the mother of a disabled son observed that benefits should not be structured so that carers are penalized for encouraging independence. In other cases the repetition of personal stories demonstrating dissatisfactions with experiences of services indicated an important criterion which was being used in judging services. Frequent stories of being passed round from one person to another indicated the importance to carers of being able to access a range of services from one contact point.

In addition to these outputs, certain outcomes of the panels' work can be identified. As is often the case, it is not possible to claim unidimensional cause and effect, but the following developments provide examples of the way in which the panels influenced developments:

1. The emergency alarm service provided by the Housing Department to elderly people living alone was extended to those living with carers. After I had withdrawn as the research was coming to an end, the panels themselves were constituted as a voluntary agency to administer money obtained from a trust to purchase more alarm equipment and to decide on its allocation.

2. One member of the panels, together with a disabled woman contacted through a panel member, joined an officer group established to address problems relating to transport and mobility within the city. As a result of their membership of the group, its strategic agenda was refocused to include more immediate, practical issues.

3. Amendments were made to the Birmingham Information File in response to carers' comments. Following the discovery by panel members that the file was not available in outlets where it should have been, action was taken to rectify this.

CONCLUSION

This description of a research method bears little similarity to traditional descriptions of 'scientific' research methods. It has strayed beyond the confines of 'research' and has addressed issues more often considered in discussions of groupwork and developmental work. Working in this way causes boundaries to become blurred and some may find this uncomfortable. But it is precisely through such blurring that this method is able to respond to criticisms which have been levelled at consumer research. The distance and unequal power relationships between researcher and research subjects are narrowed. Research 'subjects' can contribute to defining the agenda as well as responding to the researchers' predefined set of interests, and they can obtain immediate practical and emotional benefits from their participation. The link between research and action is much closer, and participants have greater influence over how research outputs are used than in traditional approaches.

The research and the researcher also benefit. Group processes act as powerful prompts which lead to the generation of rich research data. Ideas are stimulated and developed over time, and less confident participants are encouraged by their peers to contribute their views when they are ready to do so. The researcher gains a much fuller understanding not only of what carers think about services, but also why they think this way (Chapter 10 gives an example of the need to investigate why users think as they do). Their worlds are opened up to the researcher as they discuss among themselves and share common experiences using their concepts and their language.

One implication of this is that those groups who are enabled to participate in this way may be privileged in terms of the views that they express. In studies which seek to explore users' experiences of services it is important to recognize that different groups of users may have different perspectives on services which should be reflected (Barnes and Wistow, 1992b).

We need to establish whether this model of conducting research is an effective means of working with different groups. I have earlier quoted other projects in which people with learning disabilities have been enabled to participate in research projects through involvement in groups. Elsewhere, and with rather different objectives, frail older people are being encouraged to express their views about services by participating in user panels (Age Concern Scotland, 1994). Groups may be a particularly effective way of conducting research with people who share common concerns and experiences, but who may need some support in articulating their views.

Although I have not considered group membership in this chapter, further application of this model also needs to take into account issues of gender and ethnicity. The carers' panels involved few male carers, and no Asian carers. It may be necessary to work with a number of different groups in order to ensure that minority voices are not excluded.

REFERENCES

Age Concern Scotland (1994) *New Ways of Working, Fife User Panels Project,* Age Concern Scotland, Kirkcaldy.

Atkinson, D. (1993) Relating, in *Reflecting on Research Practice,* (eds P. Shakespeare D. Atkinson and S. French), Open University Press, Buckingham.

Barnes, M. (1992) Beyond satisfaction surveys. *Generations Review,* **2**(4), 15–17.

Barnes, M. (1993a) *Developing Partnerships Between Carers and Managers,* Nuffield Institute for Health, University of Leeds.

Barnes, M. (1993b) Introducing new stakeholders – user and carers interests in evaluative research: a discussion of methods used to evaluate the Birmingham Community Care Special Action Project. *Policy and Politics,* **21**(1), 47–58.

Barnes, M., Cormie, J. and Crichton, M. (1994) *Seeking Representative Views from Frail Older People,* Age Concern Scotland, Kirkcaldy.

Barnes, M. and Wistow, G. (1991) *Changing Relationships in Community Care. An Interim Account of the Birmingham Community Care Special Action Project,* Nuffield Institute for Health, University of Leeds.

Barnes, M. and Wistow, G. (1992a) *The Carers' Programme and the Role of the Performance Review Group,* A final report from the evaluation of the Birmingham Community Care Special Action Project, Nuffield Institute for Health, University of Leeds.

Barnes M. and Wistow, G. (1992b) Understanding user involvement, in *Researching User Involvement,* (eds M. Barnes and G. Wistow), Nuffield Institute for Health University of Leeds.

Barnes, M. and Wistow, G. (in press) *Gaining Influence, Gaining Support: Working with Carers in Research and Practice,* Nuffield Institute for Health, University of Leeds.

Beeforth, M., Conlan, E., Field, V., Hoser, B. and Sayce, L. (eds) (1990) *Whose Service Is It Anyway? Users' Views on Co-ordinating Community Care,* Research and Development in Psychiatry, London.

Beresford, P. (1992) Researching citizen-involvement: a collaborative or colonizing enterprise?, in *Researching User Involvement,* (eds M. Barnes and G. Wistow) Nuffield Institute for Health, University of Leeds.

Brechin, A. (1993) Sharing, in *Reflecting on Research Practice,* (eds P. Shakespeare, D Atkinson and S. French), Open University Press, Buckingham.

Davis, A. (1992) Who needs user research? Service users as research subjects or participants, in *Researching User Involvement,* (eds M. Barnes and G. Wistow), Nuffield Institute for Health, University of Leeds.

Ellis, K. (1993) *Squaring the Circle. User and Carer Participation in Needs Assessment* Joseph Rowntree Foundation, York.

Kitzinger, J. (1994) The methodology of focus groups: the importance of interaction between research participants. *Sociology of Health and Illness,* **16**(1), 103–121.

Malin, N. and Teasdale, K. (1991) Caring versus empowerment: considerations from nursing practice. *Journal of Advanced Nursing,* **16**, 657–662.

Marsh, P. and Fisher, M. (1992) *Good Intentions: Developing Partnerships in Social Services,* Joseph Rowntree Foundation, York.

NHSME (1992) *Local Voices, The Views of Local People in Purchasing for Health* National Health Service Management Executive, Department of Health, London.

Oakley, A. (1981) Interviewing women: a contradiction in terms, in *Doing Feminist Research*, (ed. H. Roberts), Routledge and Kegan Paul, London.

Oliver, M. (1987) Re-defining disability: a challenge to research. *Research, Policy and Planning*, **5**(1), 9–13.

Osborne, A. (1991) *Taking Part in Community Care Planning*, Nuffield Institute for Health/Age Concern Scotland, Leeds.

Shakespeare, P., Atkinson, D. and French, S. (eds) (1993) *Reflecting on Research Practice*, Open University Press, Buckingham.

Smith, D. (1987) The limits of positivism in social work research. *British Journal of Social Work*, **17**, 401–416.

Smith, G. and Cantley, C. (1988) Pluralistic evaluation, in *Evaluation, Research Highlights in Social Work*, **8**, Jessica Kingsley, London.

Stanton, A. (1989) *Invitation to Self Management*, Dab Hand Press, Ruislip.

Wilson, G. (1993) Users and providers: different perspectives on community care services. *Journal of Social Policy*, **22**(4), 507–526.

<table>
<tr><td>

17

</td><td>

Future developments

</td></tr>
</table>

Gail Wilson

The phrase 'asking the users' represents a clear power relationship: users are passive and are being asked to respond to an agenda fixed by others. Research on this basis, represented by most chapters in this book, will continue, but real progress with user involvement depends on users who can be active in their own interests. User-controlled research, or even user-conducted research, is urgently needed in order to redress the power imbalance between users and practitioners. It is also needed because it offers a more direct way of understanding user perspectives on services. Such developments will be difficult and are bound to be limited by the disadvantaged status of community care users. Young physically disabled people have the greatest chance of making their needs known on their own terms. Younger carers may also be able to do so. However, all users and carers could have more input into the processes of service design, delivery and planning than they do at present.

The following sections consider methodological and theoretical developments in research on user views of community care and then look in more detail at user involvement.

METHODS

As stated in Chapter 2, all research on user views of community care needs a clear statement of the aims and reasons for collecting data. The methods of analysis should be known, and nothing should be collected unless it will be used. While this may be a counsel of perfection, it offers sound guidelines in an area where there are otherwise few rules on research methods. Surveys, with or without the use of standardized instruments, may be widely accepted ways of asking users about their services, but they are not necessarily the best. When research is specific to a client group or to a service area, a variety of methods will most likely be necessary.

Data collection

Table 17.1 Methods of data collection used in this book

Method	Chapter												
	4	5	6	7	8	9	10	11	12	13	14	15	16
Structured surveys													
1 Self-completion			*				*			*		*	
1(a) Postal			*				*						
2 Interviewer			*	*	*	*			*		*	*	
3 Standardized instruments				*	*	*			*				
4 Attitude survey									*				
5 Semistructured interviews	*	*				*	*	*	*	*	*		
6 Group work												*	*
7 Observation							*	*	*			*	*

Table 17.1 lists the range of research methods used to collect data by contributors to this book and shows that multiple methods are almost universal. It also shows that the split between quantitative and qualitative data, which is often an organizing theme of methods text books, makes little sense in user surveys. Nearly all the authors collect quantitative data (1–4) in conjunction with the qualitative methods listed in the lower half of the table. The only clear division to emerge is between the service-oriented contributions in Part Two which rely more heavily, but not exclusively, on quantitative methods and the user-oriented chapters in Part Three which are consistently, but again not exclusively, more qualitative.

Each method has its advantages and limitations. Self-completion surveys can be sent by post, or handed out in a way that gives users time to reflect on their answers. They offer respondents the opportunity to refuse, but can easily result in low response rates. Interviewer-assisted questionnaires are more commonly used because they get higher response rates and allow more flexibility. For example, replies to open-ended questions can be recorded verbatim. Standardized sets of questions which have, at least in theory, been tested for consistency and reliability are often treated as more scientific. In the present stage of user research they appear to be the least satisfactory of the tools available (see below). Attitude surveys are time consuming to construct if they are based on the views of participants rather than dreamed up by the researcher, but they can be a useful way of checking user views. Semistructured interviews are the most commonly used method in this book. This is not surprising since they are most useful in exploratory research, or where there is a need to understand how individuals make sense of the subject under investigation (Chapter 3). Other more ethnographic methods, such as group work and observation, are most useful when the aim of the research is to find out as directly as possible how users feel or act.

Data analysis

Too much emphasis on collecting data can obscure the important process of analysing what has been collected. Sensitive or thoughtful analysis has the advantage that it can compensate to some extent for less than perfect data collection. At this stage, even in quantitative research, the results begin to depend on the skills of the researcher rather than the intrinsic characteristics of the method. For example, Jones and Lester in Chapter 6, faced with overwhelmingly positive responses to patients surveys, concentrated on negative responses and were able to show where services could be best improved. Reed and Gilleard (Chapter 8) met the same problem, of users who were unwilling to criticize, differently. Finding that their older service users apparently did not discriminate between the quality of service before and after a 40% cut, they used factor analysis on the quantitative data and a content analysis of verbatim comments to consider their results in more detail. They show that despite overall approval of the service, some aspects, such as not arriving on time and not giving adequate information, still show up as areas of concern.

Chapter 7 reports on a related problem. Donnelly and Hays wished to compare their results with other surveys of the effects of hospital closure on long-stay patients. Their structured questionnaire was therefore made up of several standardized instruments which had been used in related studies. However, the final questionnaire did not include a section on privacy. As they say, this omission was possibly a reflection of the fact that this part of the questionnaire had been developed and standardized on patients still in long-stay accommodation. They were able to add questions as soon as they realized the omission. Having done so they found that a high percentage (74%) of patients reported that they had adequate privacy in hospital even when living on a shared ward. Encouragingly, an even higher proportion (92%) replied positively once they were living in their own rooms in the community. Their experience shows the importance of running a pilot analysis at an early stage, even when dealing with quantitative data.

Two further aspects stand out from these accounts. In the first place, **service-oriented questionnaire design can easily miss out important aspects of user experience**, or criteria that users might think are important in evaluating a service. In the second, **users' views depend on the context or environment**. Users in hospital may expect to live in shared accommodation so their demand for privacy will be very limited. When in the community they are likely to have higher expectations.

AREAS FOR METHODOLOGICAL DEVELOPMENT

Apart from the issues mentioned above there are practical problems that need to be dealt with if user research is to progress. At present, experience of converting findings from small scale qualitative research to use in large scale surveys is limited. It may be that most user research has to be context specific and so generalizations are not to be expected. However, even if this is so, it seems certain that more could be done to move from small to larger scale surveys without losing validity and meaning, as in the process reported in Chapter 10.

User input to the design of standardized instruments

The same could be said of improvements in the design of standardized instruments (questionnaires that have been tested on different groups of people and are published as designed for a wide range of situations). They are typically made up of different components (Chapters 2 and 8 discuss components or dimensions of satisfaction). There is, as yet, no certainty that the dimensions chosen mean the same things to users as they do to the researchers. (Useful commentaries on health-related instruments are given in Bowling (1991) and Wilkin et al. (1993).) The best of these instruments do indeed measure in reliable ways, i.e. they give the same results for similar populations and can discriminate when populations differ. This does not mean, however, that they necessarily measure what they purport to measure, or that the measurements refer to dimensions which users care about. Chapter 9, for example, reports on elderly people who had very little interest in talking about their experiences as service users. They had agreed to be interviewed and willingly responded to the Philadelphia Geriatric Centre Morale scale, but few showed evidence of regarding the research as interesting to them. As things stand there are strong arguments for using standardized instruments in certain situations (such as the Northern Ireland study, Chapter 7). However, real progress will depend on designing and testing instruments which are user led in terms of concepts and dimensions – not based on professional judgements, however enlightened.

Better methodology for qualitative research

From the point of view of decision makers, an improvement in qualitative methodology which made it as respectable as quantitative would be a great advance. Even without major breakthroughs, a more rigorous approach would be useful. Much more care could be taken over **sampling**, both in the conventional sense of selecting representatives of a population and in the type of sampling needed for case studies – the decisions on who to interview, when and how often, what to observe or what to collect (this volume Chapter 3; Robson, 1993).

Qualitative analysis is always time consuming, but new developments in computer processing of unstructured data are revolutionizing what is possible. The various packages – Ethnograph, Textbase Alpha, Nud*ist and Atlas/ti, to name the most commonly used – are being improved all the time (Fielding and Lee, 1991). Each has its particular strengths and its enthusiasts, but any one allows large amounts of data to be searched and categorized in greater or lesser detail. Content analysis of interviews can be undertaken word by word, line by line or across larger blocks of text. All the packages allow multiple coding of the same piece of text and all can code selectively or can search on a range of codes. Faster and more flexible textual analysis allows greater intellectual and methodological rigour.

Values

At present much user research relies on a semiscientific paradigm and the implication that sound methods imply a lack of bias. However, as the various authors in this book have shown, **the choice of methods is always a political statement of some kind**, even though rarely a party political one. As stated above, the simple act of asking users about their services reflects an unequal power balance between researcher and researched. It may be that in the present stage of methodological development the political stance of the researcher is more important than the methods used. Users may be empowered by research using quantitative methods as discussed in Chapters 14 or 15. More usually the aim of giving users a voice leads to the use of qualitative methods.

Given the political nature of the enterprise, an understanding of the power relations involved in 'asking the users' is essential as a starting point for any research project. After that, decisions can be taken on whether to aim for emancipatory research or whether to uphold existing power relationships to a greater or lesser degree (Chapter 12). It would be helpful if all research on user views included a clear statement of values by the researchers. There might be no need to publish it, but it should be part of the conceptual framework of the project. Researcher values, overt or implicit, will influence who is interviewed, where and by whom. Some of the effects of interviewers on respondents are clearly set out in Chapter 4, in the discussion of research on ethnic minorities, but the conclusions apply to some degree across all community care users.

Theoretical and definitional problems

Theorizing links between services and users

Many key relationships in research on service users are undertheorized in terms of research methods. As shown in Chapter 2, the relationship between service satisfaction and life satisfaction is known to exist and known to influence responses to questions, but it has not so far been theorized in a way that is useful to researchers or practitioners. There are similar problems with the relation between service context and service standards demanded (consider the example of privacy from Chapter 7 above) and between experiences and service expectations. It is known that poor service induces low expectations, but the effect of this on user surveys is unknown except in general terms. As Skelcher (1993) has pointed out, a service needs to put its house in order before it can invite users to assist in quality assurance, planning or service design. A service which is poor, or perceived to be poor, is very unlikely to inspire users to become involved. Most users do not complain because they do not believe an improvement is likely, but no complaints does not mean approval. In Chapter 13 Shaw makes the same point in reverse: 'If they have been accustomed to an efficient, supportive service before they arrive, they will hardly comment on the maintenance of such standards'.

The service concept

Even the concept of a community care service is undertheorized. It is known that users, carers and practitioners have different views of services. As Mackay *et al.* (1995) say, 'Members of each occupational group have their own distinctive view of the patient. Indeed that is one of the aspects of being "professional".' Theorizing services as composed of core and peripherals (Normann (1991), as cited in Chapter 13 of this volume) is one way forward. For example, in acute hospitals patients usually see saving life or curing disease as the core service. They are often less interested in the peripherals such as staff civility, waiting times or the physical environment, which may appear in patient's charters. On the other hand in long-term care, where no cure is to be expected, it is quite possible to argue that respectful and sympathetic behaviour by staff is part of the core service. The quality of life in institutions with uncaring staff can be so poor that peripherals will matter very little to most residents.

Users and carers in the community are likely to have definitions of core services which are less clear cut than for residential care. Some community services are long-term and are similar in nature to what is provided in residential care. There is also the danger of institutionalization within the community (Gavilan, 1992). In such cases the quality of the interaction between staff and users or carers is part of the core service. Other professional activities, such as assessment, may be viewed as peripheral by users – either it results in a service package or it does not – but as core by professionals. (Chapter 9 discusses the differing perceptions of assessment by users and researchers.) The bottom line from the user's point of view is that however big or complicated the service package, most services offered in the community are peripheral to self-care or the work of family carers (Wilson, 1993b). Once again, it may be the attitude of the staff and the small ways in which they can personalize the service to suit individuals which make up the real core service. As shown in Chapter 16, respect for users, in this case for the work being done by carers, combined with flexibility and an ability to work well with other services may be the essentials for users. Often they do not know the professional background of their staff so there can be no common understanding of the service core as seen by professionals.

Each set of community care practitioners have their own definition of their core service. The core home help services used to be cleaning, shopping, collecting pensions and sometimes laundry. This has now changed and many authorities employ home helps to do personal care as well as cleaning, with cleaning a peripheral service which can only be obtained as part of a personal care package. Health professionals can also identify core services which usually relate to their training. District nurses have a core service which covers a range of conditions needing nursing care. Community psychiatric nurses (CPNs) are likewise able to identify core services which relate to their professional training. Users may take a different view. Physiotherapy may be the only community service where users and providers have a high chance of perceiving the same activities as core.

Services which are viewed by practitioners and managers as peripherals may appear in job descriptions or service aims. They include areas such as raising morale or encouraging independence. Other peripherals, which are usually not even mentioned but which are valued by users, include chatting, being cheerful, and a whole range of minor activities which vary according to the needs of individual users and their carers.

This distinction between core and peripheral services is useful when designing user surveys. It helps to structure questions and to make sense of the answers but only if the differing perceptions of users and practitioners can be taken into account. For example, the finding that users care little about the personal qualities of their therapists (Chapter 10) in the context of stroke rehabilitation but very much in a community service (Wilson, 1993a) can be easily explained by the differences in user perceptions of core services. The process of theorizing service delivery by reference to core and peripherals can therefore be related to the emerging body of knowledge on user views.

At present most research is done on core services as seen from the professional point of view. Market research may be done on the peripherals, as in patient satisfaction surveys, but from the viewpoint that they are peripherals. On the other hand, many of these peripherals are seen as core services by users. Market research designed with this in mind is likely to have different service implications.

Interprofessional relations

Meanwhile there is another issue of meaning to tackle. Community care is an interprofessional area (Soothill *et al.*, 1994; Owens *et al.*, 1995) where professionals clash in their views of each other and the service. As Mackay *et al.* (1995) say: 'Each one of us prides ourself on our own knowledge base and it often requires an act of will to recognize the skills and experience which colleagues in other occupations have to offer.' The outside researcher may ignore these differences but the research will be weaker. Practitioner researchers usually confine their inquiry to one service (Chapters 8 and 13) but they too need to acknowledge that service perspectives differ between professionals (and users and carers). All perspectives are valid and have value in certain circumstances, but the perspectives and the purposes of the research need to be clearly understood.

Individuals versus aggregates

The research methods used need to relate to the service and the purpose of the research. The popular view of good research as quantitative, and everything else as biased and unreliable, works against good research into user views. As stated in Chapter 3, qualitative research focuses on individuals rather than looking for averages. This approach is clearly appropriate for services that are meant to be offering individual care packages tailored to individual service needs. It will be helpful to professionals who want detailed information of how to develop their practice. On the other hand, averages are useful when planning services, considering how to allocate resources or checking on whether a service is generally acceptable – possibly for public relations purposes. Qualitative methods are essential for understanding the impact of services on individuals, for helping practitioners and researchers to see the service from the point of view of users and for understanding the meaning of responses to surveys and other types of research.

Service-oriented and user-oriented research

A final distinction is that between service-oriented and user-oriented research (Parts Two and Three of this book). This is a real division and not one that is easily bridged. Practitioners may want to understand the user's viewpoint for their own purposes, as reported in Chapter 10, i.e. as part of a service-oriented research exercise. On the other hand, users should have a right to be heard on their own terms – not as an addition to the professional agenda. In future it may be possible to envisage user-controlled research where users start from their own perceptions and agendas and add an investigation of the professional understanding of their attitudes.

PROGRESS TOWARDS USER INVOLVEMENT

As stated at the beginning of this chapter, asking users about their services is only a first stage of user involvement. There is a need to go further wherever possible. Charles and DeMaio (1993) have suggested a theoretical framework for user involvement in health services which identifies three dimensions for any consideration of user input: the decision-making domain; the role perspective of the person involved; and the level of participation.

In terms of involving users of community care it is helpful to modify Charles and DeMaio and to define the dimensions of involvement as set out below. Each dimension can be subdivided as follows:

- *Level of decision making*
  individual care planning/treatment
  all other policy related decisions
- *Identification of interest group*
  direct service user
  carer
  advocate/volunteer
  policy maker/expert
  taxpayer/citizen
- *Source of power*
  individual
  good will
  organizational
  political/legal

Level of decision making

The main difference in levels of decision making in community care is between input to individual care packages or care plans and all other aspects of service allocation, planning and development. Care planning and keyworking are intended to give **all** community care users an opportunity to discuss the services they are to receive. Monitoring and reassessment should make this a regular occurrence (DoH SSI, 1991). At all other levels of user involvement only selected users or carers will have an input. Away from the front line, the issues are not so much about getting the best possible care package or service for an individual as about how the service can be rationed or spread in ways that are as satisfactory as possible. Prioritizing need becomes more important than assessing individuals. User input may still take the form of pressure for more resources and a reduction in rationing, but the forum is different.

Identification with an interest group

There is no need for a person who is involved as a user or carer to confine their participation to the treatment or care planning level of decision making. As users they can present their views at all policy-making levels. Alternatively they may make their main contribution in one of the other roles suggested by Charles and DeMaio (1993) – advocate, taxpayer, fund raiser, volunteer or policy maker. Users may choose the interest group(s) which they represent. It is possible to represent a range of interests and most users do once they have become involved (Chapters 15 and 16). Even at individual assessment level they may sometimes see themselves as taxpayers or as citizens, rather than simply as service users. As citizens they may agree that other groups of people, such as the young, have a greater right to resources than they have. Alternatively, training in rights awareness can enable users or carers who start off from an individual perspective to represent a much wider group of interests.

Carers, a diverse group comprising young and old and some men as well as a majority of women, have interests which may be in harmony with those they look after, but will sometimes be opposed. Some voluntary groups are made up of users and carers but many are composed of advocates for a client group rather than the group itself. Any or all of these can become involved in decision making as policy makers, taxpayers or altruistic citizens.

Sources of power

In the final reckoning it is the amount of power or influence which individuals or groups can bring to bear on decision making which will determine how effective user involvement is. Early transatlantic authors (Arnstein, 1969; Feingold, 1977) agreed on citizen control as the highest point in the ladder of citizen involvement. Charles and DeMaio (1993) call this level lay control. Skelcher (1993), writing in the British context, defines the top level of consumer or citizen power as 'decisions devolved to citizens/consumers'. This is perhaps more realistic for community care services in the UK. Ultimate power, either in terms of political or administrative responsibility, or of financial control, is likely to remain with central or local government. Even if user co-operatives were set up to deliver services – a possible development in some areas – the chances are high that they would depend on state funding, either through contracts or via government payments to users who cannot fund themselves. Even such relatively limited devolution of power seems far away in the British context.

As has been stated many times in this book, users have little personal power. They are frequently socially disadvantaged and may have communication difficulties. The more energetic and determined can be helped by training, formal or informal, to increase the personal resources they bring to user involvement at all levels. Experience will also help (Chapters 13, 15 and 16); Hunter et al. (1988) provide a discussion of user power in influencing GP care decisions in Scotland.

Professionals who wish to deliver good services that actually enhance the quality of life of users can see that consultation will help them get it right. Here front-line practitioners have the advantage. They can, if they wish, work with users and carers within the bounds of the resources that are available. Partnership is entirely feasible. Individual power can therefore be supplemented by the goodwill of practitioners who have a philosophy of user involvement.

This can be an important ingredient in user empowerment, but it is not a reliable source of power because it is likely to be withdrawn if a conflict of interests between practitioners and users develops.

It is more useful if organizational structures are modified to include defined roles for users – places on committees (in sufficient numbers to give them the confidence to speak up), training, user forums with specific powers, reporting to relevant officers, etc. All these roles and organizational arrangements need to be funded in some way – a point that is often overlooked. At the very least respite care (Chapter 16), and transport have to be provided. Officer time also needs to be taken into account. Real consultation is not cheap. Each, or any, of these developments could improve user involvement but more than one will be needed if users are to have any real power within the organization (Winkler, 1990). Political and legal sources of power will always be essential in times of conflict between user and service interests. Local authorities now have a statutory duty to **consult** users but they are under no compulsion to act on the results of the consultation. The legal change has furthered user involvement but it need not involve any real transfer of power.

At present it is difficult to identify other sources of power for community care service users (as opposed to their advocates in voluntary sector pressure groups). They are rarely well enough organized or present in adequate numbers to influence politicians, either central or local. Health services at present allow very little political control except from the centre. Local authority services are theoretically responsive to local political demands but, with notable exceptions, users have little political clout and do not band together easily. Voluntary agencies may have user representatives on their governing bodies and private services are, in theory, responsive to paying customers, but user empowerment is limited. When funds are tight, very little can, in reality, be changed and users are aware of this and make few demands.

Few users will stay involved, even in their own care planning, unless they see some concrete results of their input (Chapters 15 and 16). Chapter 15 reports on many instances of consultation fatigue and a disillusionment with official processes. Individual practitioners, providers and purchasers will all have to offer users some degree of power sharing if they wish them to participate. Research which validates user views or gives a voice to disadvantaged groups will help but action will be better.

CONCLUSION

Whatever the progress in advancing research methods or developing theory, there are two major problems with research into user views of community care. The first is that it is only tokenistic unless the effort is made to understand the point of view of users. The second is that research can never be as useful as involvement in decision making. User research should ideally encourage user empowerment rather than simply recording aspects of the status quo. There is a need for much more overtly political action on behalf of all groups of community care users – and for legislation. If users are only to be asked for their views, rather than enabled to give them as participants in real decision making, there should be the possibility of user-controlled research on standards of service and delivery. Financial resources will be essential (Chapter 14 illustrates the effects of underfunding on user-oriented research).

The main effort of researchers should therefore be to develop initiatives in partnership with users and carers as outlined in Chapter 16. Where this is still not fundable, stake holders need to be clearly identified, along with their roles in facilitating or blocking user involvement. At present purchasers and providers stand to get more out of research on user views than the users themselves. This may be inevitable but it is still worth fighting against.

Users who become involved in policy and planning risk being coopted by the organizations they assist (Charles and DeMaio, 1993). When this happens their contribution will be weakened but their presence should still have some effect. In any case it is a hazard worth taking because there is a need for users to be part of the structure of service planning and delivery, as well as a presence in outside pressure groups. Only if users are accommodated at all levels in care agencies will front-line preferences have a chance of informing macro planning and resource allocation decisions. Such developments depend on finance (for transport, training and respite care) and the acceptance of a critical mass of users onto key committees or in key decision-making positions.

As a final point, groups which are not represented in this book, such as people with dementia and members of ethnic minorities, demand special attention. As shown in Chapter 4, developments in methods of research using interpreters are urgently needed. Unpublished work by Hall (1994) shows how much more could be done to represent the views of people with dementia. The authors who present research on people with learning difficulties (Chapters 11 and 12) show that here, too, much more work is needed. Ethnic minorities, including white minorities such as Cypriots and widely scattered minorities like the Chinese, are still almost invisible.

In community care users and carers do most of the work themselves. It is in the interests of efficient and effective service delivery to give them more say in how the services which supplement their input to self-care and informal care are planned and allocated. Involvement which leads to more power for users need not mean less power for service providers. Better services will benefit all who are involved. In other words power sharing is not a zero sum game, but it may look like one when conflicts arise. Researchers can help to combat the negative stereotypes which disadvantage all community care user groups, but legislation and a more positive attitude to citizenship for all will be more important in the long run.

ACKNOWLEDGEMENT

I am indebted to Julie Dockrell for helpful comments on this chapter and to Veronica James for drawing my attention to the work of Charles and DeMaio (1993).

REFERENCES

Arnstein, S. R. (1969) A ladder of citizen participation. *Journal of the American Institute of Planners*, **35**, 216–223.

Bowling, A. (1991) *Measuring Health*, Open University Press, Buckingham.

Charles, C. and DeMaio, S. (1993) Lay participation in health care decision making: a conceptual framework. *Journal of Health Politics, Policy and Law*, **18**(4), 881–904.

DoH SSI (1991) *Care Management and Assessment Care Manager's Guide*, Department of Health Social Services Inspectorate, HMSO, London.

Fielding, N. G. and Lee, R. M. (eds) (1991) *Using Computers in Qualitative Research*, Sage, London.

Feingold, E. (1977) Citizen participation: a review of the issues, in *The Consumer and the Health Care System*, (eds H. M. Rosen, J. M. Metch and S. Levey), Spektrum, New York.

Gavilan, H. (1992) Care in the community: issues of dependency and control – the similarities between institution and home. *Generations Review Journal of the British Society of Gerontology*, **2**(4), 9–11.

Hall, S. (1994) *Quality Issues in a Mental Health Service for the Elderly*, unpublished MSc thesis, London School of Economics.

Hunter, D., McKeganey, N. P. and MacPherson, I. (1988) *Care of the Elderly Policy and Practice*, Aberdeen University Press, Aberdeen.

Mackay, L., Soothill, K. and Webb, C. (1995) Troubled times: the context for interprofessional collaboration, in *Interprofessional Relations in Health Care*, (eds K. Soothill, L. Mackay and C. Webb), Edward Arnold, London.

Normann, R. (1991) *Service Management*, Wiley, Chichester.

Owens, P., Carrier, J. and Horder, J. (eds) (1995) *Interprofessional Issues in Community and Primary Health Care*, Macmillan, Basingstoke.

Robson, C. (1993) *Real World Research*, Blackwells, Oxford.

Skelcher, C. (1993) Involvement and empowerment in local public services. *Public Money and Management*, **13**(3), 13–20.

Soothill, K., Mackay, L. and Webb, C. (eds) (1994) *Interprofessional Relations in Health Care*, Edward Arnold, London.

Wilkin, D., Hallam, M-A. and Doggett, M-A. (1993) *Measures of Need and Outcome for Primary Health Care*, Oxford University Press, Oxford.

Wilson, G. (1993a) Users and providers: perspectives on community care services. *Journal of Social Policy*, **22**(4), 507–526.

Wilson, G. (1993b) Conflicts in case management: the use of staff time in community care. *Social Policy and Administration*, **27**(2), 109–123.

Winkler, F. (1990) *Who Protects the Consumer in Community Care?*, Greater London Association of Community Health Councils, London.

Index